TALES OF THE AFRICAN FRONTIER

TALES OF THE AFRICAN FRONTIER

J. A. HUNTER

ASSISTED BY

DANIEL P. MANNIX

Safari Press Inc.
P. O. Box 3095, Long Beach, CA 90803

Hunter, J. A.

Safari Press, Inc.

1999, Long Beach, California

ISBN 1-57157-123-X

Library of Congress Catalog Card Number: 54-9215

10 9 8 7 6 5 4 3 2 1

Readers wishing to receive the Safari Press catalog, featuring many fine books on big-game hunting, wingshooting, and sporting firearms, should write to Safari Press Inc., P.O. Box 3095, Long Beach, CA 90803, USA. Tel: (714) 894-9080 or visit our Web site at www.safaripress.com.

CONTENTS

A Note by Daniel P. Mannix

It was the summer of 1951, and I was sitting with John Hunter on the porch of his home in Makindu, listening to native drums beating hopefully for rain and watching the snow-topped slopes of Kilimanjaro swimming in the blue sky like a distant cloud formation. Hunter had written the story of his life as a professional hunter and I had been his guest for several weeks, working with him on the manuscript, cutting it and getting it in shape for publication. Now I was about to return to the States with the manuscript.

We sat smoking our pipes and enjoying the cool evening breeze after the heavy heat of the day. Occasionally a cloud of red dust showed where a car was speeding along the highway from Nairobi to Mombasa—a highway that follows almost exactly the old slave trail along which, in the memory of living men, the Arab slavers drove their slave gangs, yoked together with forked sticks, from the central lakes to the coast. Far away came the distant whistle of a train—a train running on a line whose construction had been delayed for three months because man-eating lions kept carrying off the construction crews. I had seen the man who shot those lions a few weeks before when he dropped into the bar of the de luxe Stanley Hotel in Nairobi. Some Wakamba natives strolled past on their way home after working the afternoon shift at the new sisal plant a few miles away. Hunter called one of them over; an old man who could remember when the Wakamba attacked the fort at Machakos, some eighty miles away, and came within an ace of wiping out the little garrison. "Bwana, we weren't really interested in killing the soldiers," the old fellow assured us. "All we wanted was to get their empty cartridge cases. We used them for making snuff containers."

After the old native had left, I said to Hunter, "Africa must be the only place in the world that has changed from savagery to civilization within the span of a man's lifetime."

"Aye, within my lifetime," said Hunter thoughtfully. He laid down his red-hot pipe, selected another from the rack beside him, and stuffed it full of a particularly villainous pitchlike tobacco. "When I came out here as a lad, I was mad with enthusiasm for Africa. There was nothing I didn't dream of for the place and every man and woman I met was the same. Yet if you had told us how the country would develop in fifty years' time, we'd have thought you daft. Nairobi a great city. Mombasa another one. Thousands of farms. Buildings springing up so fast it makes a man's head swim. From the coast to the lakes was once a three months' safari and you did it on your flat feet. What is it now? Two hours in a plane."

"I don't know much about the opening of the country," I remarked. "I've heard of Stanley and Livingstone and that's about all. But you lived through it."

Hunter pressed down the tobacco in his pipe with a hard finger. "Stanley and Livingstone were a bit before my time, yet only the other day I read in the paper that the old native porter who carried Livingstone's body back to the coast died in Mombasa. It was no great while ago when Africa was truly the dark continent."

"What kind of men opened this country?" I asked.

"There were many kinds, good and bad, but they were all strong men," Hunter said quietly. "There was Colonel Grogan who walked from the Cape to Cairo, the first man in history to perform that feat. He's still with us. There was my old friend, Johnny Boyes, who arrived here on an Arab dhow with hardly a shilling in his pocket and made himself king of the Kikuyu tribe. There were James and Mary McQueen, the first settlers in these parts. James delivered their six children himself as there was no doctor within three hundred miles. There was Fritz Schindelar, who is said to have been a member of the Hungarian royal house and hunted lions from horseback. There were missionaries, slavers, ivory hunters, traders and police officers who went out against wild tribes with a score of native askaris armed with condemned rifles that only fired once out of three tries. There were remittance men who came here because there was no other place for them to go and doctors who walked fifty miles over elephant trails to help a sick native child. Many of them I knew. Others, I have only heard people speak of. But this I say—they were a race of giants."

"You've just finished a book about the animals in Kenya. How about a book about the people?"

Hunter looked doubtful. "There are still men about who can remember the opening of the country, but they're old now—very old. In Kenya, we hear their tales and marvel at them, but we never take the time to write them down. Soon the last of the old-timers will be gone and their stories with them."

"Let's see if we can't do something about it," I said.

That was the beginning of this book. Though it was nearly two years before I could return to Africa myself, Hunter began to dig into his amazing memory of things seen and heard. Meanwhile, he and I read several dozen books on the early days. In 1953 I returned and, during the next six months, I traveled from Lake Victoria to the island of Zanzibar, talking to men and women who remembered the opening of Kenya. Although we have tried hard for accuracy, already many stories of the early pioneers are beginning to take on the patina of legend. We heard five versions of Fritz Schindelar's tragic death, several conflicting accounts of the early native wars, and many anecdotes which may or may not be true concerning men who have now passed away. Some day a formal history of Kenya and the people who made the colony will be written. In the meanwhile, we have done our best to give a feeling of the times and the people.

When the first settlers came to Africa, the country was virtually unexplored, and as remote from the rest of the world as though it were another planet. It was inhabited by thousands of native tribes, differing as much in language and customs as a Scottish highlander differs from a Greek fisherman. Many of these tribes had incredibly complex religious and social organizations, yet materially they were living under conditions nearly as primitive as the great animals that roamed the veldt and jungles. The settlers had to combat strange diseases, completely unknown to medical science. They had to protect themselves and their herds from wild beasts of enormous strength and, often, gifted with astonishing cunning. They had to depend completely on themselves, for the home government was a remote and, at times, almost a hostile force. Now a second and even a third generation is springing up in the country that they won. When these youngsters speak of "home" they do not mean Great Britain as their parents did but Kenya.

This is the story of the opening of one of the last great frontiers as seen through the eyes of the people that did the job. It is a story that is already being forgotten. The authors are glad that they have had the opportunity to record some of the tales while the last survivors of that incredible era are still with us.

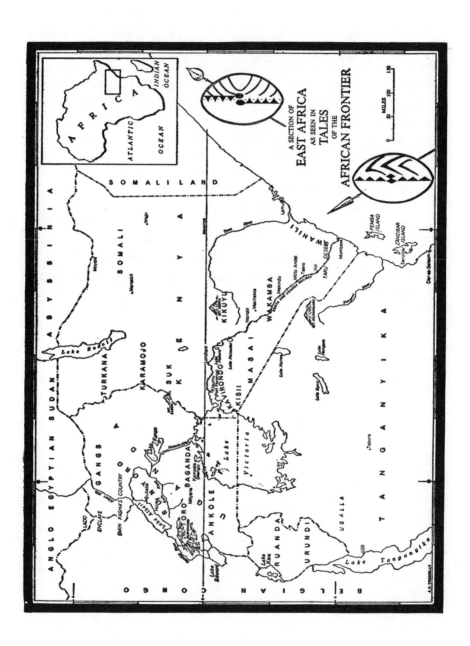

A SECTION OF
EAST AFRICA
AS SEEN IN
TALES
OF THE
AFRICAN FRONTIER

Daniel P. Mannix

I

Tippu Tib—"A Sound of Guns"

In the 1870's, visitors to the exotic island of Zanzibar, which lies a few miles off the coast of East Africa, often commented on the great numbers of white shells that covered the bottom of the bay. These objects were not shells. They were bones of dead slaves, who had been dumped over the sides of the Arab vessels that brought twenty thousands of these wretches every year to the great Zanzibar slave market, the largest institution of its kind in the world. The man who was responsible for a goodly number of these bones was Hamed bin Muhammed, called by the natives Tippu Tib, an onomatopoetic term meant to imitate the sound of his rapidly firing guns. Tippu Tib was probably the greatest slaver in history. He was also an outstanding explorer, an excellent administrator, an ardent patriot, and the man who, by his generous assistance, made possible the work of Livingstone, Stanley, and the explorers, Speke, Cameron and Wissmann. When Zanzibar abolished slavery in 1897, Tippu's slaves refused to leave their beloved master. His house in Zanzibar still stands, a memento to this remarkable man.

Through the kindness of some Arab friends, I had the privilege of meeting Tippu Tib's daughter-in-law in Zanzibar. She was an old lady of great character, rather thickset, with a firm jaw and alert black eyes who set cross-legged on the couch of our friend's house as modern custom prevented her from taking her usual seat on the Persian carpet. With our friends as interpreters, she answered my questions with decision and authority—not unnatural in a

1

woman who had once had complete control over several hundred slaves.

"Tippu was the man who really opened East Africa, not these foreign explorers who are given the credit," she said firmly. "Livingstone, Stanley, Burton—all of them simply followed along the trails he had opened. None of them would ever have gotten through if he hadn't broken the power of the native chiefs first. He civilized the country and was ruling there when the Belgians, Germans and English intimidated our sultan and then divided the country among themselves. And now look at the mess they're all in! It's the result of their racial prejudice. We had slaves, but no racial prejudice. An Arab would marry a Negro slave girl, or take her as his legal concubine, and her children had just as much rights as any by his Arab wife—if he had one. Tippu Tib himself had Negro blood. It meant nothing to him or anyone else. The Europeans have tried to force this 'white supremacy' nonsense on the natives and as a result they're hated far worse than we ever were."

"Tell me something about your father-in-law," I asked.

"He was the kindest man who ever lived," said the old lady. "His slaves regarded him as their father. When he went on one of his trips to the mainland, even if he were gone for five years the household would move about as though in a trance, waiting for him to come back."

"But he was a slaver, reported to have killed thousands of helpless people," I said.

The old lady sniffed. "You foreigners can't understand a man like my father-in-law," she said disdainfully.

Hamed bin Muhammed, later to be known as Tippu Tib, was born in a little village on the island of Zanzibar called Kwarara, about fifty miles from the capital city. The date of his birth is not known, but it was probably about 1850. His father was a moderately successful trader and took his son with him on trips up and down the coast and occasionally on short safaris into East Africa. On these trips, little Hamed would listen to the old traders, sipping their thick brown coffee in a native hut or warming their bones around a brazier on the deck of a dhow, tell of the fabulous villages that lay in the interior. These villages used elephant tusks for stockades, built their chiefs' thrones of ivory, and lined the sides of their huts with the precious stuff as though the tusks were logs of wood. There a man could buy a beautiful girl for a handful of beads and the streams were yellow with gold. Listening to these stories, young Hamed swore that he would someday find these villages and be a great explorer like Ebn Haukal, the famous Arab geographer who discovered Lake Victoria in the tenth century, or Jabl-ul-Qumar who traveled to Uganda and described the Mountains of the Moon.

In 1867, when Hamed was about seventeen years old, he determined to lead an expedition to the central lake district and return rich in ivory and slaves. This was merely a trading-exploration trip, not a punitive expedition. The Arabs at this time did not use force in obtaining slaves. Slavery was common among the African tribes and the Arab traders bought slaves in the villages just as they bought ivory and other merchandise. The relations between the Arabs and the natives were so peaceful that the Arabs proudly boasted, "An Arab can walk across Africa with no weapon except a cane."

To raise money for his trip, Hamed borrowed heavily from the Indian moneylenders in Zanzibar who charged interest running up to 700 per cent. His relations were so proud and confident of the youngster that they put up their property as security. Hamed sailed for Dar-es-Salaam, the port of modern Tanganyika, with a few Arab followers and as soon as he landed, set about hiring porters.

Recognizing that Hamed was an inexperienced boy, the porters demanded the outrageous wage of ten dollars for the trip, which, as it was only to last five years, was ridiculous. The innocent Hamed agreed, and then issued each porter half of the sum to support his family during his absence. The first night out, the porters all quietly deserted, leaving Hamed with his bales of trading goods and his followers alone in the jungle.

When Hamed woke in the morning and found what had happened, his senses nearly deserted him. In his despair, the boy realized that not only he was ruined, but also his trusting family who had mortgaged their homes to the moneylenders. Now Hamed showed the determination that was to make him Tippu Tib. He and his men went back to the village and seized every man they could find. As the Zanzibarians had guns and the natives did not, no resistance was made. Hamed marched his captives to a black-smith and had them fastened together with chains. Then he set out on his trip, confident that this time his porters wouldn't desert.

Hamed and his caravan reached Tabora, an Arab frontier post near Lake Tanganyika. Tabora was "the end of the line" as far as caravans were concerned. But here were no stockades made of ivory or lovely girls being sold for a few beads. The traders chuckled as they listened to the boy. Yes, thirty years ago that might have been the case but now both ivory and slaves were scarce and expensive.

Unless, of course, Hamed wanted to trade with King Nsama. Nsama, whom Livingstone later described as the "Napoleon of Africa," was a local ruler who had successfully conquered and enslaved all the tribes near his kingdom. He was reputed to have a vast store of ivory. A short time before, an Arab caravan had gone into his kingdom to trade with him. None of them were ever seen again.

Hamed decided to trade with King Nsama. First, he used up the last of his money to buy all the guns he could in Tabora. The guns were old "Brown Bess" muskets, even then regarded as obsolete, but in Tabora, they were worth their weight in gold and gunpowder its weight in silver. Hamed had a handful of Arab followers, all with more or less Negro blood. In addition, he had some fifty Manyemas, a particularly warlike tribe which the Arabs used as mercenaries. Thus equipped, Hamed and his men went off to inter-view King Nsama.

Nsama lived in a fortified village, surrounded by a high stockade and a deep ditch, the bottom of which was studded with dagger-sharp bamboo stakes. The sides of the stockade were covered with thorn branches that served the same purpose as barbed wire. How-ever, the king received the young Arab most graciously. He had the

drawbridge lowered over the moat and asked Hamed and his followers to come in, merely stipulating that they leave their guns
behind.

The Zanzibarians obeyed, except that they concealed their guns
under their long, white robes. However, there was clearly no cause
for alarm. King Nsama received them politely and accepted the
gifts Hamed had brought him. Then as his guests turned away, the
king shouted an order. Instantly, the drawbridge was raised, armed
warriors appeared on all sides and a murderous hail of arrows came
from archers concealed in the watchtowers on the stockade.

Two of Hamed's men were killed instantly. Hamed himself
received three arrow wounds. In spite of his injuries, Hamed rallied
his men. They pulled out their concealed guns and opened fire. The
astounded warriors fell back and Hamed and his men fought their
way to a hut. Meanwhile, the rest of his party opened fire on the
village from across the moat. Under this crossfire, the natives could
not hold out. They lowered the drawbridge and fled, the king leading the rout. Hamed and his men were left in possession of the
village.

This victory was achieved with twenty guns. That a small body of
men, armed only with muskets, could defeat a powerful ruler and
his warriors seems incredible but allowance must be made for the
psychological effects of the almost unknown firearms. Also, these
Central African tribes were simply not the fighting men that the
Zulu or the Kenya Masai were.

In the king's storehouse, Hamed found 1,950 frasilahs of ivory (a
frasilah was about 35 pounds), worth approximately $50,000. This
Hamed appropriated. He returned to Tabora with his spoils, to the
astonishment of the Arab traders. The natives gave him the name of
Tippu Tib, so impressed were they by his musketry. "I learned that
day in Nsama's village that the gun is king of Africa," said Tippu Tib
grimly. Certainly, he developed a passion for firearms that lasted all
his life.

Tippu Tib invested part of his ivory in more guns and struck out
for unopened country. Near Lake Tanganyika, he met Dr. Livingstone. The young Arab was greatly impressed by the missionary's

courage and sincerity. "Although he was not of my faith, he was unquestionably a man of God," said Tippu Tib. He gave Livingstone some much-needed supplies and then went on. In his books, Livingstone speaks of Tippu Tib with marked respect although naturally he vehemently condemns the Arab's methods.

In Ugalla, to the northeast of Lake Tanganyika, Tippu Tib took the next step that was to make him king of Central Africa and of the Arab slavers. He and a few of his men entered one of the fortified villages to trade while the rest of his force remained outside in the Arab camp. While Tippu Tib was negotiating with the chief for some ivory, one of his followers purchased a bowl of corn from a woman and started to carry it away. An aggressive young warrior knocked the bowl out of his hands and started scolding the woman. A general altercation followed, in which both Arabs and natives joined. Tippu Tib tried to stop the dispute, but the angry voices had run throughout the village and a number of young warriors rushed up, flourishing their spears and giving their war cries. Spears and arrows began to fly and the chief turned to run. One of the Arabs shouted to him to stop and when the chief kept on, shot him. Instantly the battle was joined.

The Arabs were driven from the town and fell back on their camp. They found it deserted. The war drums of the village were thundering out the alarm and already scores of warriors were pouring in from the outlying areas to avenge the death of their chief. Tippu Tib and his few supporters were in a desperate position. Tippu decided that their only chance was to return to the village, capture it, and entrench themselves behind the stockade. But as they approached the gate, an overwhelming force rushed out to meet them. At the same moment, they were attacked from the rear by the hostile tribesmen.

Tippu Tib knew it was all over. He called on his men to kill as many of the pagans as possible before they died. Then the force pouring out of the village began to fire, not at Tippu and his men, but at the oncoming tribesmen. For a moment, Tippu could not believe his senses. Then he saw the blood-red flag of Zanzibar floating over the group and recognized the faces of the men he had left in the camp. When the fighting started, these men had attacked the village from the rear and had occupied it while Tippu Tib and his party were being driven out the main gate.

For the next two days, the Arabs looted the surrounding villages and enslaved the inhabitants. After a victory, the Manyema mercenaries took for granted that all prisoners were to be used as slaves and Tippu Tib made no attempt to interfere with this custom. It would have been worth his life if he had, as the Manyemas got a percentage on all slaves taken. The captive villagers were loaded with ivory from the chief's store and sent to the coast where both were sold. The resulting profits were tremendous. Under the old system of hiring porters to carry the ivory, only a small profit could be made on each shipment, but this device opened a whole new era in Africa.

Tippu Tib had stumbled, partly by accident and partly by force of circumstances, on the first half of the formula that was to make him famous: capture a village, enslave the people, have them carry their ivory to the coast, and then sell both slaves and ivory. The second half of the formula fell into place a few months later.

While trading near Lake Kissale, part of the chain of Central African lakes, Tippu Tib was invited by a certain tribe to purchase ivory in their villages. This tribe was constantly at war with a rival tribe, and over the years a curious understanding had sprung up between them. After a war, the winning tribe settled on the lake shore while the losers retired to the jungle until they felt themselves strong enough for a return match. If they won, they took the lake area while the defeated group in turn hid in the jungle.

It was the tribe then living in the jungle who had asked Tippu Tib to trade. Tippu set out with his caravan but on the way was attacked by the lake tribe, who refused to allow the Arabs to trade with their enemies. Tippu and his men were driven back. In a rage, the Arabs joined forces with the jungle group and marched against the lake people. The guns of the Arabs naturally decided the already delicate balance between the groups. But this time the defeated lake people were not allowed to escape into the jungle. The victorious tribe, because of the Arab support, was able for the first time to inflict a complete defeat on their enemies. Those who were not killed and eaten by the conquerors were sent to the Zanzibar slave market by the Arabs, so that the beaten tribe was completely exterminated.

Tippu Tib moved on to new regions, but the victorious tribe, no longer afraid of attack by their ancient enemies, now started a series of raids on other neighboring people. Soon they became so arrogant that they demanded Tippu Tib pay tribute on all ivory caravans sent back through their country. Tippu Tib promptly organized the neighboring tribes against them and soon the erstwhile conquerors were themselves headed for Zanzibar with yokes around their necks and laden with their treasury of ivory.

The formula was now complete. From then on, Tippu Tib applied it with almost monotonous regularity. The Arabs would move into a village and offer to buy ivory. As all the native tribes were hostile to each other, jealous neighbors would sooner or later attack the village. Then the Arabs would support their friends. The Arab guns always decided the issue and the winning tribe, confident that the victory was due solely to their own tribal courage and ability, would start on a career of conquest. Eventually they would turn on the Arabs. Then the Arabs would form a confederation against them and soon they would go the same path as their victims. In this way, the power of Tippu Tib continued to grow and a constant stream of ivory and slaves flowed out of Central Africa to Zanzibar.

Tippu Tib always claimed that he was really a man of peace and would have much preferred to conduct business without the constant series of wars caused by the mutual suspicion among the tribes. This may have been more or less true. Certainly whenever possible Tippu Tib used peaceful methods to obtain his ends rather than expend valuable gunpowder. On several occasions, he cemented friendly relations with a tribe by marrying one of the chief's daughters, although from the Arab point of view, he was merely taking her into legal concubinage. He and his men were outnumbered more than a thousand to one and could count on no support from Zanzibar in case of trouble, so he could not rely simply on force. The Arab spent endless weeks and months chatting with the natives, learning to understand their point of view, their prejudices and their traditions. Often the information he received was worth more than all the guns in Africa.

In one village, Tippu talked to a slave girl who had been captured from a country far in the interior. The girl told him that years before the daughter of the chief had been carried off by raiders. The chief was now old and wanted to retire but the only rightful heir to the throne would be the son of the missing "princess." From the girl, Tippu learned the tribe's language, customs, religion and the genealogy of the royal family. Then he traveled to the country and presented himself as the heir to the throne. The Arab's strong admixture of Negro blood made this possible and the simple villagers could not imagine how a complete stranger would know their language and customs unless he was indeed of their people. The old chief joyfully retired and Tippu Tib took over.

Tippu Tib's conquest of Central Africa was not always so simple. The Arabs were constantly being attacked and repeatedly caravans were ambushed and wiped out. On several occasions, things grew so hot that even Tippu's hardened followers begged him to abandon his ivory and escape while he could. Tippu merely retorted, "My ivory is worth more than my life," and time after time led his men to victory over the disorganized tribesmen.

Like any other successful businessman, Tippu Tib soon had many imitators. These men had learned only too well his grim motto, "The gun is the king of Africa," but they did not possess Tippu's knowledge of the natives and his ability to administer a district after he had conquered it. These men deliberately provoked native wars and then reaped a harvest in slaves. "Kill the men and rope the women" was their slogan and they lived up to it. The names given these Arab slavers by the natives are descriptive. There was "The Clean-Sweeper," "The Destroyer," "Bitter as Bile" and many more. The slave trade, always a grisly business, now became a screaming horror. The caravan routes were marked by the lines of white bones scattered on either side of the path. Livingstone believed that only about one slave in five survived to reach Zanzibar but many well-informed men considered the doctor's estimate too conservative. The area around the shipping ports resembled a huge abattoir and worse, for the slaves considered too weak to survive the voyage to Zanzibar were thrown out to die among the corpses of their friends. The stench of the rotting bodies, the moans of the dying and the constant screaming of babies, disregarded after their mothers had died, made the ports hideous. Among the other ghastly sights were scores of little boys with their intestines protruding through wounds caused by the Arab's crude attempts to castrate them for eunuchs. These miserable children crawled about the streets until they died. It is thought that only one in twenty survived the operation.

Many of the early missionaries and explorers urged the Arabs to take better care of their slaves if only for motives of self-interest. The historic answer to this plea was given by a British official who remarked, "The Arabs regard it like transporting ice. You know most of it will melt away, but there'll be enough left to show a profit." With an unlimited source of supply in the interior, there was really no reason to worry about the high mortality rate.

But the supply was not unlimited. The Arab slavers were actually beginning to depopulate Central Africa. As soon as the numbers of any species are reduced below a certain point, there is not enough "breeding stock" left to maintain the race. The native wars, savage as they were, had seldom resulted in the complete extermination of a tribe. This now became common. The suffering of the slaves was a comparatively minor matter compared to the fact that whole villages were being wiped out to obtain a handful of women and children. The villagers left behind were so few that they couldn't rebuild their homes, clear their fields or protect themselves from wild animals. Great areas were so desolated that the caravans had trouble getting through them, for there was no food of any kind to be obtained.

What was the man like who had caused this holocaust? Stanley gives the following description:

"He was a tall, black-bearded man of negroid complexion in the prime of life, straight and quick in his movements, a picture of energy and strength. He had a fine, intelligent face with a nervous twitching of the eyes and gleaming white, perfectly formed teeth. He had the air of a well-bred Arab and was courtier-like in his manner. I came to the conclusion that he was a remarkable man, the most remarkable that I had met among the Arabs. He was neat in his person; his clothes were of spotless white, his fez-cap brand new, his waist encircled by a rich dagger-belt, his dagger was splendid with silver filigree and his whole appearance that of an Arab gentleman in very comfortable circumstances."

Tippu Tib was a very devout man. He belonged to a puritanical Mohammedan sect that severely condemns any form of laxness and forbids even the use of tobacco to its adherents. Tippu Tib was deeply shocked and disgusted when he found one of his best lieutenants drunk on native beer in a village and refused to have anything more to do with the man. Although some of the slavers were apt to be free in their relations with native women, Tippu scrupulously observed his religious principles. Although he had a harem of several dozen women who traveled with him, these were all legal concubines and their children were, according to Moslem law, legitimate and entitled to a share in their father's estate. A concubine was not a slave and could not be sold, although she did not have the position of a true wife. Tippu Tib always refused to allow himself to be carried in a litter by slaves or even ride a donkey. "I am a poor Arab whom Allah has raised to greatness," he said. "I walk so that I will not forget my humble origin."

Tippu Tib made many trips back to Zanzibar during this period with a fabulous amount of slaves and ivory. As a young man, he had planned to make only a few trips to Central Africa, collect a huge profit, and then retire to live the life of an Arab gentleman. His first trip had brought him in even greater profits than he had dreamed of, but the sultan levied a heavy tax on both slaves and ivory. By the time Tippu Tib had paid off the moneylenders and the sultan's tax, given his followers a percentage of the loot and settled his other expenses, he had barely enough money left to equip another expedition. Then as his empire grew, his overhead also increased. There is no doubt that Tippu Tib did become enormously rich, but by then his sights were set higher, and what would have seemed like fantastic riches to most Arabs merely provided for the upkeep of his Zanzibar estates. So, in order to increase his fortune, he continued to open fresh country, always counting on the big haul that would enable him to retire in comfort.

The explorers and missionaries whom Tippu Tib helped reads like a roll call of all the great names in early East Africa. Although the Arab perfectly understood that these men had come to destroy the slave trade which was the source of his wealth, he never turned down a request for help. He gave food and guides to Cameron, the first man to cross the continent, and Cameron later said that without Tippu Tib's help he would have died. He helped Speke, who discovered the sources of the Nile; Wissmann, who made the first west-to-east crossing of the country, and many others. When these men tried to draw him into a discussion on the ethics of the slave trade, Tippu Tib would gently reply that Abraham and Jacob had slaves and God favored them. He also pointed out that once the slaves reached their various destinations, they were well treated and most of them far better off than under the cruel rule of the native kings. "Belgium, France, Brazil and Portugal are buying the slaves I supply," he remarked. "Are not these all civilized, Christian countries? Let them stop demanding slaves and I will stop supplying them." If the conversation grew acrimonious, the Arab would say courteously, "On these matters we do not agree, but do not let us quarrel."

In 1870, some of Tippu Tib's lieutenants brought him word that a strange white man was wandering about the country at the head of an enormous safari of armed porters, saying he was looking for the lost Dr. Livingstone. The Arabs had politely assured this curious individual that Dr. Livingstone was not lost at all but living quite comfortably at the prosperous Arab village of Ujiji on Lake Tanganyika. Tippu Tib instructed his men to give this stranger food and take him to Dr. Livingstone.

Tippu Tib was interested in this foreigner, as he was in all Europeans, and arranged a meeting with him after he had found Dr. Livingstone. Thus Tippu Tib met Stanley, a momentous meeting for both of them as events turned out. At first, Tippu was amused by the self-confidence and boastfulness of the American, so unlike the quiet restraint typical of the upper-class Arabs. Stanley exhibited a repeating rifle which he claimed could shoot many times in succession. Tippu, with his great passion for firearms, begged for a demonstration. "No," said Stanley, "the bullets cost too much." "Ah, indeed," said Tippu politely, who was now convinced that this bombastic stranger was a fraud. "By a curious coincidence, I know of a native tribe that has a bow which will shoot twenty arrows at one time and every arrow kills a man. Unfortunately, the arrows are so expensive they never shoot it." Stanley grabbed up his rifle and fired a series of shots into a tree in quick succession. Tippu Tib was greatly impressed. He decided that this stranger, in spite of his loud talk, was able to live up to his claims.

Stanley wanted Tippu Tib's help, as did all the early explorers. Stanley had heard of a great river running westward from the central lakes which he thought might eventually flow into the Atlantic Ocean. This river was the Congo, but neither Tippu Tib nor Stanley knew that at the time. Stanley planned to follow the course of the river and thus cross the continent.

Tippu Tib agreed to help Stanley reach this river. The Arab was always greatly interested in Europeans, who he knew had technical knowledge and power greatly exceeding that of his own people. He also admired Stanley personally. The natives called Stanley "The Stone Breaker" because of his ability to smash his way through all obstacles, and this was a quality Tippu could understand and respect.

After a long and exhausting journey, the river was reached. When the time came for Tippu Tib and his men to return, Stanley gave them a farewell party. One of the events was a foot race. Tippu Tib took this contest very seriously, spending hours trotting up and down the river bank to get into condition. He won the race, beating Pocock, one of Stanley's assistants, by a few yards, to the Arab's great satisfaction. He and Stanley parted with many expressions of mutual friendship and Stanley promised to send Tippu Tib a handsome present when he got back to the United States.

When Tippu Tib returned to his own district, he found a letter awaiting him from the sultan of Zanzibar, ordering him to return immediately. Tippu got together a great caravan of slaves and ivory and started for the coast "at all speed," as he put it. Some impression of an Arab's idea of speed may be gained from the fact that the trip took three years. As he passed through Tanganyika, he was astonished at the changes that had taken place in the last few years. Mission stations dotted the hills, ships were sailing on Lake Tanganyika, European trading posts and forts had sprung up along the old caravan routes. The country was growing.

Tippu Tib had been so long in the interior that for three years little ivory had reached the markets of the world. Ivory cutters in the factories of London, India and Connecticut were starving. When swift clippers brought the news that a big shipment of ivory was headed for the coast, the church bells were rung and people fell on their knees in the streets to give thanks that Tippu Tib had once again won through.

Tippu Tib arrived in Zanzibar a hero. There he found the present Stanley had promised. It was an autographed photograph of the explorer. Instead of being indignant, Tippu Tib considered this most amusing. He told the story as a great joke on himself for many years.

Tippu's meeting with the sultan was less amusing. Years later, Tippu reported his conversation with the sultan to Dr. Heinrich Brode, a German resident of Zanzibar. The sultan, Tippu explained, desperately needed his advice. The German government had laid claim to Tanganyika and enforced their demands by anchoring the German fleet in Zanzibar Harbor. The British government, goaded by the Anti-Slavery Society, was blockading the coast in an effort to stop the slave trade. The Belgians had already announced that the Congo was their property. Tippu was furious. "East Africa belongs to your majesty," he protested. "I took it for you. I was the first man there and these foreigners simply followed in the paths I made. Give me guns and powder, and I'll raise the natives and drive them out." "Do you think I'm worried about the mainland?" cried the sultan. "My only problem is whether it's better to have Germany or Great Britain take over Zanzibar as a protectorate. What do you think?"

"When I heard that, I knew all was lost," said Tippu Tib to Dr. Brode.

Tippu Tib was a patriot, but he was also a man of hard common sense. In the next few weeks, he was convinced beyond all question that the European powers were too strong for the Arabs to resist. Nothing was left except to make the best terms possible. Yet he could not help mourning the loss of East Africa, that great area he had opened with sweat and blood.

While Tippu Tib was still in this despairing mood, Stanley arrived in Zanzibar with a fresh scheme.

Stanley's rescue of Livingstone had been the great journalistic sensation of the day. But now that was all over and some new sensation had to be found that could top it. At first, this seemed impossible, although the newspapers had worked frantically to find someone, somewhere, who had to be rescued. At last, they hit on Emin Pasha.

Emin Pasha, born Edmund Schnitzer, was a scholarly, serious, conscientious German Jew who had accepted a position as governor of the southernmost provinces of Egypt. He had done a magnificent job. Emin Pasha, to give him his Egyptian title, was not only an excellent governor with a deep sympathy for the natives, but also a zoologist, botanist and anthropologist whose papers on these subjects had aroused great interest throughout the world. In 1883, the Mahdi —a half-mad dervish or a great national leader, depending on your point of view—had led an uprising against the pasha of Egypt and the British who had put the pasha in power. Emin had been cut off from Egypt by the Mahdi's forces. Then Kabarega, the great warrior king of Bunyoro in northern Uganda, had also gone on the warpath and cut Emin off from the south. "Who will save Emin Pasha?" cried the newspapers. The anxious people of Europe and America, many of whom had never heard of Emin Pasha a few weeks before, gladly raised $100,000, then a huge sum, to outfit an expedition to rescue him. Stanley was elected to head it.

Stanley was no fool and he knew that he could not possibly get through to Emin without the help of Tippu Tib. He also knew that Tippu would not exactly fall over himself in his efforts to help Stanley a second time. But Stanley held a trump card. After explaining the situation to Tippu Tib, Stanley produced a letter from the king of Belgium, telling Tippu that if he helped Stanley his majesty would make him governor and virtual king of the Congo, which the Belgians had recently seized. How Stanley ever talked the Belgian king into this arrangement is a mystery. It was certainly one of the greatest pieces of salesmanship on record.

The Arab's hands must have shaken as he read the letter. The Congo was his country. He had discovered it, subdued the tribes, built the first trading stations there, knew the people intimately. Now he was being given the chance to return once again as a king. True, he would be theoretically under the Belgians but Tippu Tib knew what that meant. As long as he paid the Belgians a certain amount of ivory and provided "free labor" for the rubber plantations, he would be a complete ruler. He accepted Stanley's terms.

Rescuing Emin would be simple. Tippu Tib knew the trails and exactly how they should go. But Stanley had other ideas. The rescue of Emin had to be so thrilling that it would even surpass the rescue of Livingstone. He couldn't just walk in and rescue the man. Stanley's idea was to sail south from Zanzibar completely around the continent of Africa by way of the Cape of Good Hope. Then he would outfit an expedition at the mouth of the Congo, sail up the river, and finally go up along Lake Victoria to Emin's rescue. It would be an amazing and highly dramatic feat.

Tippu Tib thought this idea was madness. But Tippu Tib wasn't paying for this trip and the newspapers and the public were. Stanley won.

The first part of the trip went smoothly enough, although it was just as well that Emin Pasha didn't have to hold his breath while the rescue party sailed four thousand miles and then traveled up the Congo against the current. When the expedition reached a point some two hundred miles north of Leopoldville, their boats were in such bad condition that Stanley decided to go on by foot. The trip up the river had taken much longer than expected, so Stanley resolved to press on with a small group and have the rest of the supplies brought up by a rear guard. It was agreed that Tippu Tib was to remain in the Congo as governor but he was to send off the rear guard with five hundred porters as soon as possible.

Stanley went on with his small force as rapidly as possible. He had to pass through districts laid bare by "The Destroyer," "The Clean-Sweeper" and "Bitter as Bile." There was no food to be had by threats or trade goods. His men lived on roots. The porters began to die. Wild tribes attacked them. Stanley sent back desperate messages, imploring the rear guard to hurry but the rear guard did not come. The men finally abandoned their loads and staggered on as best they could. Emin Pasha heard of their coming and sent out a force to meet them. Finally, Stanley and what was left of his force staggered into Emin's camp and collapsed on the ground.

At least, Stanley had finally reached Emin. Now a completely unforeseen problem occurred. Emin positively refused to be rescued. He would not abandon the native tribes who had trusted him, for he knew only too well what would happen to them at the hands of Kabarega, the king of Bunyoro.

This put Stanley in a horrible position. The newspapers of the world were eagerly awaiting the news of how he had rescued Emin Pasha. He argued, pleaded and even threatened the stubborn governor. Fortunately for him, Emin's troops mutinied and Emin was forced to start back for the Congo with Stanley, although the now almost hysterical governor resisted every step of the way.

The trip north through Uganda to reach Emin had been a living death, but the trip back was far worse. Stanley not only had his own men to feed but also Emin's forces. Time after time he sent messages for the rear guard to bring up supplies but the rear guard still failed to appear. At last, the exhausted group reached the Congo. Stanley considered the failure of the rear guard to come was due solely to Tippu Tib, who had betrayed him. The furious explorer got rid of Emin as soon as possible and left for Zanzibar. There he started a lawsuit against Tippu Tib for not supplying the porters. This lawsuit was one of the *causes célèbres* of its day.

Why hadn't Tippu Tib sent the rear guard? Although I had read many accounts of the unfortunate Emin Pasha mission, I had never found a satisfactory explanation of Tippu Tib's strange conduct. Then while I was in Zanzibar, I was able through the kindness of the curator of the Peace Memorial Museum to see a letter Tippu Tib sent to Zanzibar by runner while Stanley was trying to reach Emin. In the letter, Tippu Tib points out that Stanley had promised to supply him with gunpowder, then a very precious commodity in the Congo, so he could arm the men who were to protect the rear guard. He had reminded Stanley of this promise, but the explorer, who was eagerly rushing off after Emin, told him to get the powder as best he could. "But there is no powder to be had," wrote Tippu Tib to his friend in Zanzibar.

Much against my better judgment, I did send off 500 porters with a few Arab guards. They were attacked by natives, just as Stanley had been. They managed to beat off the natives but by that time had used up their small supply of powder and had to return. Send me powder by the quickest caravan route as Stanley is in a serious situation.

The British had now taken over Zanzibar as a protectorate, partly in an attempt to satisfy the Anti-Slavery Society and partly in response to a plea from the sultan, who feared the growing power of Germany. Tippu Tib received a notice from the British judge in Zanzibar that unless he appeared in court within six months to answer Stanley's charges, all his possessions in Zanzibar would be confiscated. The Arab's traditional calm was not easily disturbed, but this summons threw him into a white-hot fury. His friends urged him not to return to Zanzibar, arguing that he could expect no justice at the hands of the Europeans and would probably find himself thrown in prison. The once invariably courteous Tippu Tib snapped at them, "Mind your own business! I'll have my name cleared if I lose my life doing it."

Tippu Tib sped back toward the coast by a series of forced marches—no leisurely three-year jaunt this time. He was no longer a young man and on the way he collapsed. A mission station of the White Fathers nursed him back to health. As soon as he could raise his head, he ordered his men to put him in a litter and take him on. While crossing Tanganyika, word was brought him that a group of Arabs planned to murder an English missionary named Alfred J. Swann who had been particularly outspoken in his condemnation of the slave trade. "The fools!" snapped Tippu Tib. "What do they hope to accomplish by that? It will only bring the English down on us." He sent some of his men ahead to bring the missionary to Tippu's camp for protection.

Swann gives an almost stenographic account of his meeting with the old slaver in his book *Fighting the Slave-Hunters in Central Africa.* Tippu Tib received him with the usual formal politeness, but the Arab was so seething with his wrongs that soon he burst out into bitter denunciations of Stanley and the European nations that had taken his kingdom. Throwing the judge's summons on the floor of the tent, he exclaimed:

"Look at that! I am ordered to be at the coast two months from now. Stanley says I deliberately tried to hinder him from reaching Emin Pasha. If I had wanted to stop Stanley, I would have had him killed years ago. I do not merely hinder, I destroy! And if I help, I help at all costs."

Counting on his fingers, he went on, "Who helped Cameron, Speke, Livingstone and Gleerup? Who has just saved your life? Haven't I always helped even the missionaries who are trying to destroy my business? I am mad with anger when I think of what I did for Stanley. In order to make a big work out of nothing, he went up the Congo to find Emin Pasha. Why didn't he go straight across from the coast? I didn't want to go that long way around, preferring to take the familiar caravan routes, but he would not be denied, so out of courtesy I went with him. I help foreigners and then they turn on me and seize the country I discovered. You Europeans are very unjust!"

Swann replied, in effect, that the cruelty of the Arabs had caused them to forfeit any rights they had in Africa.

"Is that so?" exclaimed Tippu Tib. "How did you get India?"

"We fought for it."

"Then what you fight for and win belongs to you by right of conquest?"

"Yes, that is European law."

"So it is with us Arabs. I came here as a young man, fought these natives and subdued them, losing both friends and treasure in the struggle. Is it not therefore mine by both your law and ours?"

"It is only yours as long as you govern and use it properly."

"Who is to be my judge?"

"Europe!"

"Ah!" said the Arab, smiling grimly. "Now you speak the truth. Do not let us talk of justice. People are only just when it pays. The white man is stronger than I am. They will eat up my possessions as I ate those of the pagans, and . . ."

He paused and then went on fiercely: "Finally someone will eat up yours! The day is not as far off as you think. I see the clouds gathering in the sky. I hear the thunder!"

These last, terrible words sounded like a curse. Swann never forgot them.

When Tippu Tib arrived in Zanzibar, Stanley had already gone. The explorer had left a bill of indictment against Tippu Tib in the name of "Emin Pasha and his people." Emin indignantly repudiated the use of his name and so the judge dismissed the case. But Tippu Tib was so embittered that he never returned to the mainland. He retired from the slave trade and spent the rest of his life in Zanzibar.

In 1890, the Arab slavers in the Congo rose against the Europeans, calling on Tippu Tib to join them. Tippu Tib refused. He knew that resistance was hopeless. He was right. After a few minor victories, the Arabs were completely crushed. "The Destroyer" was killed and eaten by the Belgians' cannibal native troops. "The Locust" was taken prisoner. "Bitter as Bile" was captured and shot. Only "The Clean-Sweeper" managed to escape. What happened to him, no one knows. Among the others to die were one of Tippu Tib's sons who had joined the uprising and his nephew who was drowned while trying to escape the Belgian troops by swimming a river.

There were also minor revolts against the Germans in Tanganyika and the British in Mombasa. These were both put down. The British fleet shelled Zanzibar and established their own sultan in power. By the end of the century, the Arab empire which Tippu Tib had established was gone. From his home in Zanzibar, the old Arab watched the collapse sadly but philosophically. There was nothing he could do. It was the will of Allah.

Sitting in our Arab friends' comfortable living room and listening to Tippu Tib's daughter-in-law tell of these wild and terrible days, it seemed incredible that within the memory of this old lady the Arabs had once owned East Africa and parceled out areas as big as European countries as their private man-hunting grounds.

"I married into the family of Tippu Tib when I was a young girl of thirteen," the old lady explained in answer to one of my questions. "My home was in Lamu, an island about five hundred miles north of Zanzibar. The old Arab families in Lamu were rich and dignified and had the reputation of bringing up their daughters very strictly. Tippu's son—this wasn't the boy who was killed in the war against the Belgians, but another of his children—was a wild young man. He kept getting married and divorced until finally his father decided to get him a Lamu girl to steady him down. So he and my parents arranged the marriage. I came to Zanzibar in a special dhow with painted sails and the stern covered with brightly colored, hand-carved woodwork. The gunnels of the ship were inlaid with silver and we sat on thick Persian carpets spread over the deck. We sailed into the harbor with drums beating and conch shells blowing. Tippu Tib's son came out to meet us in a barge rowed by slaves in brilliant uniforms, also with drummers and trumpeters. It was the great moment of my life. Girls today can never know what it was like.

"My husband was all right, although he was a typical rich man's son. I got his household straightened out and then as I grew older, men being what they are, I picked out his concubines for him. I made sure that they were good, steady girls with no nonsense about them. But the boy was never the man his father was. Everyone worshiped his father. All the Arabs were generous, but none as generous as he. Every day, forty or fifty poor people would come to our house for food and they were never turned away empty. At a certain hour, the slaves would blow a horn as a signal and within ten minutes the courtyard would be full of people. At the end of Ramadan, our great religious celebration, Tippu provided all the poor in Zanzibar with new clothes. He had hundreds of acres of land, worked by slaves. The slaves worked in the morning for him and then in the afternoon did whatever they pleased. They could till their own fields which he had given them or, if they wanted to work on his estates, they were paid for it. The lucky ones were the household slaves. We had hundreds of them, mostly just for show, and their main duty was to wear lovely clothes and look impressive. Of course, they waited on us. We women never lifted a hand. Anything we wanted was instantly brought to us by the slaves. When I think of how my daughters are living today, in fact how I am living, well . . . let's continue to talk of the past.

"In the autumn [which in Zanzibar corresponds to our spring, as the island is south of the Equator] we would leave the town house and go out to our country estate where it was cooler. That was the big event of the year and there was always great excitement. On the day of departure, everyone was up before dawn. We women rode snow-white mules, with saddles studded with gold and silver. A slave would kneel and you stepped on his back to mount. Of course, we were all veiled in those days and wore our long robes. A slave walked by each of us holding a parasol over our heads and other slaves, on Arabian horses and armed with muskets inlaid with silver, rode on either side as a guard—just for show, of course. Everything was carried on the heads of slaves and we had a line of two or three hundred of them. There was an old slave who acted as major-domo and sometimes we girls would race each other on our donkeys and get ahead of the main party, which always made the old fellow furious with us.

"A party under another old slave had gone on to the country estate several days before, so when we arrived everything was ready for us. We amused ourselves walking under the big mango and fig trees— they've been cut down now to make room for the clove plantations —or playing with our pet animals or using the baths [a system of Turkish baths regarded as a necessity in all big Arab homes]. Mostly we just sat around and gossiped, exactly as we're doing now.

"Tippu Tib was always very courteous to the women but he didn't talk to us very much. In those days, when an Arab went to see a woman, it was for a purpose and there wasn't much conversation involved. He was always most correct in his behavior. He only had one wife, although our religion allows us four, and he made a point of spending the morning with her. The afternoon he spent with the favorite concubines. Then in the evening, he saw the other concubines too."

My wife, who was busily taking notes, asked, "Were those the only women he saw?"

The old lady looked at her in amazement. "Good heavens, for an elderly gentleman, wasn't that enough?

"When the English freed the slaves, there was a terrible period of disorder on the island," she went on. "The slaves were like children with no sense of responsibility. Bands of them wandered around the island, robbing and killing. Finally the English had to send troops here to control them. I remember how disgusted we were when we first saw the English women—utterly indecent and with no sense of hygiene. They went around with naked faces and carrying little dogs. As everyone knows, a dog is an unclean animal. They'd even kiss the creatures on the nose and you know into what sort of things a dog sticks his nose. Of course, we're used to them now.

"They threw us out of Africa and now the natives are going to throw them out, exactly as Tippu Tib said would happen."

After the old lady had left, our friends explained that she was living under very simple circumstances in a small apartment in the town, but even so she was far better off than most of the old Arab aristocracy who had been completely ruined when the slaves were emancipated. She had been shrewd enough to exchange most of her possessions for jewelry and was living on the proceeds from the sale of the ornaments.

Tippu Tib died in Zanzibar on June 13, 1905. All his heirs, both by his wife and his concubines, shared in the distribution of his estate according to Arab law, so his great fortune was quickly dissipated. His house is still standing in Zanzibar, although it has now been cut up into apartments.

It is said that on his deathbed, Tippu Tib became delirious and thought he was once again in the Congo, leading his wild hordes against the stockaded villages and shouting his war cry, "Allah conquers! Kill, kill, kill!" while his guns went "Tip-tip-tib." Thus died this great and terrible man, and modern East Africa began.

John A. Hunter

I I

Colonel Ewart S. Grogan, Gentleman Adventurer

In the winter of 1899, Captain Dunn, a British officer stationed in Egypt, took a small native craft and went on a shooting and fishing trip along the Sobat River in the lower Sudan. He stopped to camp one night on the shore. South of him lay thousands of miles of jungle, swamps and desert, unmapped and unexplored. Captain Dunn's astonishment may well be imagined when, the next morning, he saw coming out of this wilderness a small group of porters, clearly at their last gasp, led by a young Englishman with an unlit pipe in his mouth and a sporting rifle slung over his shoulder. The young man's face was swollen by mosquito bites, he was flushed with fever, and he was clearly unable to use one arm. The porters collapsed on the ground, but the stranger removed his pipe and bowed politely.

Their conversation has been recorded. It went like this:

Captain Dunn: "How do you do?"

The stranger: "Oh, very fit, thanks. How are you? Had any sport?"

Captain Dunn: "Pretty fair. Have a drink? You must be hungry. I'll hurry on lunch. Had any shooting?"

But at lunch, the captain's English reserve gave way and he could not help blurting out, "Excuse me, but do you mind telling me where the devil you came from?"

"From the Cape," replied the stranger.

The Cape of Good Hope lay four thousand miles to the south—four thousand miles of country full of cannibal tribes, wild beasts

and mountain ranges. It was generally considered well-nigh impassable. Captain Dunn may well have thought the young man delirious.
Yet this was not the case. He had indeed made this amazing trek
on foot, the first man in history to accomplish the feat.

The young man was Ewart S. Grogan, now Colonel Grogan, and I
am proud to say he is a friend of mine. After his famous walk, he
settled in Kenya and now has a magnificent farm near Taveta in
the southern part of the colony. Although now in his eightieth year,
the colonel is still as slim and straight as he was when he walked
from the Cape to Cairo. A prominent figure in the government, he is
equally famous for his great knowledge of African affairs and his
biting wit. Although many stories could be told of him, I will confine this narrative to an account of his notable walk, which I consider one of the great feats of all time. I have based this story on the
colonel's writings and he has been kind enough to fill in a number
of details not mentioned in his diary of the trip.

The flip of a ha'penny started Ewart Grogan on his adventuresome
career. His father, a prosperous land agent, sent the boy to Cambridge and after graduation, young Ewart decided to become an
artist. His father, nothing loath, sent the boy to one of the best art
schools in the country. But as Grogan now admits, "After being at
the school awhile, I didn't particularly like the look of the kind of
people who were artists." One day his bearded teacher held up a
sketch the young man was working on and after examining it said
impressively, "If you work for many years, living, dreaming, thinking
nothing but art, art, art, then you may someday be a great artist."
He waited for the young man to faint with joy.

"But I'm not sure that I want to be an artist," remarked Grogan.
"I think that I'd rather be a policeman."

His teacher nearly exploded with rage. "I suggest you make up
your mind," he snapped.

"Right you are," agreed Grogan. He pulled a ha'penny out of his
pocket. "Heads, I become an artist. Tails, I become a policeman."
He flipped the coin. It came down tails. "Sorry!" said Grogan politely.
Getting his hat and coat, he left the studio never to return.

Grogan did indeed become a policeman but it was a policeman of a somewhat special sort. The Matabele Uprising had broken out in South Africa, one of the numerous native wars with which the British Empire was constantly plagued during the Victorian era, and Grogan enlisted as a trooper. He joined a gun crew and served as Number Four man on a muzzle-loading seven-pounder. After the war, Grogan returned to England so wasted by fever that the doctors thought he might never completely recover.

This was a sore blow to young Grogan, for during his tour of service in South Africa, he had met Cecil Rhodes and caught that remarkable man's dream of a British Africa, extending from Capetown to the shores of the Mediterranean. Rhodes believed that the first requirement for linking the vast continent together was a railroad running down the spine of Africa, to open the interior to commerce. But was such a railroad possible? What mountain ranges would it have to cross, how many rivers, how many stretches of jungle and desert? Even more important, would it have to cut across areas already parceled out among nations hostile to Great Britain? It was Grogan's dream to make the long trek from the Cape to Cairo and map a possible route for the proposed railway.

However, the doctors told the young man that he must take a rest before even considering such an adventure. A long sea voyage was advised, and Grogan decided to go to New Zealand and stay with an old Cambridge chum who had settled there. During the voyage, he studied books on engineering and surveying and by the time he arrived in New Zealand, he had a rough knowledge of the subject.

His friend had an extremely pretty sister named Gertrude Watt. She and Ewart Grogan fell in love. They planned marriage but Miss Watt had a guardian who did not approve of Ewart.

"Young man, you appear to be drifting down the river of life without a rudder," the pompous old gentleman told Grogan. "A girl in the position of my ward can expect to marry an outstanding man."

Grogan reflected, "If I were to walk from the Cape to Cairo, would you consider me sufficiently outstanding?"

The older man was not amused. "I can only suppose that you are either a fool or have decided to play one. The jungles of Central Africa are impassable. Stanley was able to get about only on rivers and he had to take an armed guard of six hundred men to fight off the native tribes. To traverse the continent you would need a small army."

"Oh, hardly that," remarked Grogan. "If you have a large group, you arouse suspicion. I believe a small party could get through without too much trouble." This, then, might be said to be the start of the famous walk. Grogan returned to England and a few months later sailed for South Africa in company with another young man named Arthur Henry Sharp, who had decided to come along part of the way.

I should like here to say a few words about the typical upper-middle-class young Englishman of the Victorian era, of which these two young men were fine examples. According to our modern standards, they were in many ways a pampered lot. It was taken for granted that they would attend the best schools and afterward go to a famous university. The problem of making a living was a minor one, for their parents were usually well-off. They were a class born to command and to possessions. Yet there was another side to the lives of these young men which is now largely forgotten.

They were brought up under a code so strict that many today would regard it as just short of brutality. When still children, they were sent off to schools where the slightest infringement of the rules was punished by a cane in the hands of a master or a prefect. For a boy to shirk the roughest games or complain of the most savage bullying promptly condemned him as an effeminate sniveler. They were generally introduced to blood sports as soon as they could sit a horse or hold a gun and for many of them the seasons of the year were divided up according to what animal it was appropriate to hunt or shoot. To many people, this would seem a faulty upbringing but most of the young men grew up from childhood knowing how to handle a gun, how to endure hardship and how to put their horses at the most difficult hedge without flinching.

When Grogan and Sharp left on their memorable trip, they were already first-class shots. The habit of command was strong in them, and in dealing with savage and unruly porters this ability was worth more than all the beads and trinkets in Africa. There was still another side to their nature, also typical of the time. Although they could take only the barest essentials on such a trip, they included several volumes of poetry as naturally as they included ammunition for their guns.

The two young explorers differed strikingly in appearance. The pictures of Grogan show him as a slender, clean-shaven youth who always seemed to have a pipe stuck nonchalantly in the corner of his mouth. Sharp wore the mustache and carefully trimmed whiskers so fashionable among the young men of the period. He was a quieter, more matter-of-fact individual than Grogan but with an almost equal love of adventure. For equipment, they had a battery that consisted principally of two sporting magazine .303 rifles—weapons I would consider somewhat light for even the larger antelopes, but which in their hands served admirably for everything from ducks to elephants. Each man had a small tent, a camp cot, mosquito netting and a few changes of clothing. Their medical equipment was a bottle of quinine and another of potassium permanganate for wounds. The bulk of their outfit consisted of boxes of beads and rolls of the brightly colored cloth called "Americani," manufactured in the United States and used as a standard form of currency among African tribes. They also took along cameras and surveying instruments. Although they had some supplies, they intended to rely mainly on their rifles to provide food for the expedition.

In February, 1898, the two young men arrived in South Africa and began their memorable trek. The beginning of the trip across the great, open plains of the veldt proved reasonably easy yet it was here that they first encountered African big game. One afternoon while Grogan and Sharp were fishing, they were attacked by a buffalo. Grogan promptly dove into the stream in reckless disregard of the crocodile-infested waters. Sharp, who had no idea of the power of a buffalo, stood his ground. As coolly as though firing at a target on a rifle range, he put bullet after bullet into the oncoming bull. As he was using soft-nosed .303's, the odds were a hundred to one on the buffalo. But one of his shots broke the bull's jaw. The buffalo staggered and Sharp fired again, breaking the animal's fetlock. The buffalo rolled to within three yards of the young man who was then able to finish him off. As Grogan emerged dripping from the stream, Sharp said to him in tones of mild surprise, "I had no idea these animals could take so much punishment. Next time one charges me, I'll follow your example and get out of his way."

So far, the young men had been able to travel by ox wagon and mule-drawn carts. But when they reached Salisbury in southern Rhodesia, there was no other means of transportation north except their own feet, and equipment had to be carried by porters. Generally, native porters refused to travel more than a few miles from their village. In each new district, it was necessary to pay off the old group and hire a new batch. However, a few miles north of Salisbury, the young men were fortunate enough to hire some Watonga porters who had a taste for adventure. Four of these porters stayed with Grogan all the way to Cairo. He assured the porters that he would show them great mountains that spit fire and passes so high that water turned to stone. Grogan always claimed that the Watonga went with him mainly because they didn't want to miss the chance of being with such a talented liar.

The safari pressed northward until by April they reached Ujiji on Lake Tanganyika where Stanley had found Livingstone thirty years before. Tanganyika was now a German protectorate, but there were still a number of old Arabs in the town who had settled there in the days of Tippu Tib. Slavery had been abolished, but these elderly men were still being cared for by their old slaves who had refused freedom. Ahead of the young men lay a series of mountain ranges which the old Arabs assured them were impassable. But Grogan and Sharp determined to make the attempt. As there would be no game in the mountains, all food for the expedition would have to be carried by porters. They hired 130 rough-looking local natives who said they were willing to go. Grogan and Sharp organized ten of their Watonga porters into a sort of tiny standing army to handle this wild crew and started across the range.

Trouble began almost immediately. The nights were so cold that the porters, used to the heavy heat of the lowlands, sat shivering around their campfires unable to get warm. The Watonga felt the change even more than the new porters. The expedition crossed a ridge seven thousand feet high, and the next morning two of the Watonga deserted. This was a particularly serious blow as Grogan and Sharp had looked on the Watonga as the noncommissioned officers of their little force.

The weather constantly grew worse. Every morning dawned with the mountains covered by a cold, dank mist. The men had to force their way through masses of mimosa bushes heavy with dew. Within a few minutes, every man was as completely soaked as though he'd been under a shower. As the mist usually did not lift until afternoon, no one ever had a chance to get properly dried out. Sharp was bitten so badly by mosquitoes that his hands became infected and he could scarcely use them. Both he and Grogan began to have constant attacks of fever which they could not throw off because of the chill and constant wetting.

Then the ten Watonga who had served as guards deserted in a body. Sharp came down with blackwater fever. Grogan was semidelirious with malaria and running a temperature of 106.9. The two boys nursed each other and struggled on until they finally crossed the range and dropped down into a little valley on the other side. Ahead of them a new range of mountains stretched on, apparently endlessly, but in the valley was a small native village. Here they stopped—collapsed would be a better term—while their porters returned to Ujiji, leaving Grogan and Sharp with the last four of the Watonga.

They stayed in the village for several weeks. Grogan was in a "pitiable condition," as he wrote in his journal, and Sharp, although very little better, acted as nurse. Ahead of them lay unknown country, the first completely unexplored territory they had reached. "Our expedition was really only just beginning and yet there I was, dying before the trip had actually started," Grogan told me. For days, the boy lay on his cot looking at that great sea of mountains ahead of him, some of the most magnificent scenery in all Africa. Somewhere beyond those ridges lay the great Kivu Lake and the volcanoes reported by earlier explorers who had come in from the East Coast. Whether or not it was possible to reach Kivu from the south still remained to be seen.

Grogan did not recover as rapidly as they had hoped. The intense, mucky heat of the valley seemed to augment his fever. At last, it was decided to push on and see if he would not, do better in the cool highlands. As he was too weak to walk, Sharp arranged to have him carried in a litter. A new group of porters was hired and the boys headed out across the valley toward the distant ridges.

I doubt if any other country in the world shows such sharp variations in climate as Africa. Central Africa is tropical but in the highlands a man can walk for days through great forests and swear that he is in Canada or Norway. Then, within a space of a few hours, he drops down into a valley full of palm trees and grass huts where elephants roam and the streams are full of crocodiles. By the next morning, he may be crossing a desert where the only sign of life is an occasional lizard. That night he may reach a plateau region that closely resembles the English countryside—pleasant grasslands cut up by little streams flowing gently between green banks. In another day or two he may be floundering through papyrus swamps, being eaten alive by mosquitoes and listening to the bellow of hippos in the reeds around him.

In the next few weeks, Grogan and Sharp passed through all these types of country and many more. They saw their first elephant. Grogan left his litter to stalk one big bull—he was still so weak that his porters following him with the litter in case he fainted—but the elephant escaped. Then the expedition entered a well-inhabited, prosperous district. Great herds of cattle with enormous horns grazed on the mountain slopes, guarded by naked children who hardly came up to the beasts' bellies. In the lowlands were forests of banana trees, carefully cultivated. Women, nude to the waist, worked in the fields of peas and beans. As they approached the shores of Lake Kivu, Ngenzi, the king of the district, came out to greet them. He even accompanied them for several miles with his retinue as a gesture of friendship.

When the king had left, the young men proceeded to check their stores and discovered to their horror that the king had not departed empty-handed. Much of their precious clothing had been stolen, but this was a minor matter. A tin box had been taken, containing their sextants, artificial horizon, thermometers and many of their records and photographs. In a few minutes, much of the hard work of the last months had been lost and the value of the rest of the trip seriously curtailed.

The old chief foolishly hung about the outskirts of the safari, hoping for another windfall. The young man explained to him how important the missing articles were, but the chief professed complete ignorance of the whole affair. "There are many bad men in this country," he explained blandly. "I can't keep track of them."

Grogan and Sharp may have had many shortcomings, but indecision was not one of them. The astonished chief suddenly found himself looking down the muzzles of two rifles. Before he could protest, he was grabbed by the scruff of the neck and flung into the boys' tent. When his bodyguard moved in to rescue him, they were also confronted by the two steady guns. After thinking the matter over, the bodyguard decided to let the chief stay where he was.

After bitterly protesting his innocence, the chief finally asked to speak to some of his officials. He gave them a few orders and the men left, returning shortly with the boys' missing clothes. Grogan and Sharp demanded their records and instruments, but the chief denied all knowledge of them.

Then the explorers had an inspiration. The natives obviously cared little about the chief, but they were vitally interested in the welfare of their cattle. Leaving Sharp to guard the camp, Grogan took a small force of the porters and set out for the nearest village. There he and his men seized a herd of 190 cattle and started driving them back to camp. Within a few minutes, the alarm drums sounded and hundreds of armed warriors began to assemble on the hills. Through the guide-interpreter, the young men shouted to the warriors that they would return the cattle as soon as the contents of the tin box was returned.

The next morning, the tribesmen sent in a deputation. "We have already returned your clothes and those were the only valuable things we took from you," they explained. "The other articles were worthless—you couldn't wear them, you couldn't eat them, you couldn't cook your food with them. So we threw them down a crevice in the hills. They are gone for good, and even if you shoot the chief and take all the cattle in the country you can never get them back. Now please go away and leave us alone."

Brokenhearted and miserable, the boys could do nothing else. They could only make a resolve never to allow the instruments and records still remaining to get out of their sight even for a moment.

The expedition passed through the country of the Watusi, the giant men who average over seven feet in height and have for their slaves the Wahutu, the original inhabitants of the district. Although the Wahutu outnumbered their giant masters a hundred to one, they regarded them with almost superstitious awe and never questioned their authority. A few marches farther on, the young men saw their first pygmies, little men scarcely four feet tall who live on the borders of the giants' country.

So far, Grogan and Sharp had been concerned about the natives' stealing from their porters. Now they ran into the problem of how to keep the porters from stealing from the natives. They passed through districts so poor that the porters could hire the local inhabitants to carry their loads for them. The average wage for a native at that time was three shillings a month (about seventy-five cents). For a few pennies, the porters were able to employ helpers. Then as the safari passed through still more poverty-stricken areas, the substitutes hired substitutes, who in turn hired other substitutes until the load was finally carried by a small boy or a starving old man while the original porter and two or three "middlemen" walked alongside like gentlemen of leisure. The young Englishmen did not feel it was their responsibility to interfere with this system as long as everyone was satisfied, but soon they received complaints from local chiefs that the idle porters were raiding villages, molesting girls and looting houses. It must be remembered that one of the old foot safaris often stretched out for miles. The men were constantly stopping to rest, take snuff, chat or readjust their loads. The safari seldom averaged more than ten miles a day and latecomers were usually dribbling into camp three or four hours after the main body. The two young Englishmen could not possibly patrol the entire safari.

Several of the looters, caught red-handed, were punished on the spot, the instrument of punishment being the terrible rhino hide whip known as the kiboko. But the looting and rape continued. The reputation of the expedition began to precede it. Instead of welcoming the travelers, the local inhabitants fled to the hills, taking their families and livestock with them as though before an invading army. Unable to buy food, Grogan and Sharp were once forced to cut enough bananas from a native plantation to feed the porters and themselves. "That was the only time in my life I ever commandeered food from natives," Grogan told me.

The young men decided that their half-wild porters would have to be put under some sort of discipline. The next day, they forced the long, straggling line to close up, and that night kept the porters in camp instead of allowing them to bivouac in a village. The result was soon forthcoming. The whole body of porters deserted the next morning leaving their loads scattered on the ground.

Grogan and Sharp started after them. They came on a small group and these Sharp stopped at the point of his revolver. Grogan kept on after the main body. Topping a little rise, he saw the deserting porters walking along below him. Grogan called to them to come back and one of the headmen, who had been a ringleader in the troublemaking, shouted an insult. Grogan fired, knocking off the man's head covering. The other porters found the bewildered expression on the headman's face so amusing that they burst into howls of laughter and returned willingly to camp. They gave no more trouble for several weeks.

On the other side of Lake Kivu, the expedition passed a number of great volcanoes, some of them still active. Grogan, who remembered how the Watonga natives had considered him a brilliant liar when he told them of the volcanoes, pointed out the smoking cones to the four who were still with him. "What do you think now?" he asked them.

"We still think you're a great liar, Bwana," said one of the boys cheerfully.

"But there are the burning mountains in front of you," protested Grogan.

"Bwana, there is no such thing as a burning mountain," said the boy confidently. "You put those there by magic in order to fool us."

Grogan gave up.

Many of the conelike peaks had never before been seen by white men. Grogan and Sharp mapped the district and named several of the unknown mountains. One of them was named Mount Watt by Grogan, in honor, needless to say, of the pretty young girl in New Zealand who had played so prominent a part in launching the expedition.

The natives here were very friendly. There was only one case of theft. The man had greased himself, thinking that even if he were caught, no one could hold him. But Grogan tackled him around the legs and turned him over to the local chief. The next day, the safari passed the thief's head impaled on a sharp stake planted beside the trail as a warning to others. In that district, thieves were not encouraged.

Each tribe the expedition encountered had its own customs and the dietary taboos were constantly changing. In one district, the natives were astonished when the white strangers refused to eat snakes. In another, the tribesmen were surprised and disgusted when Grogan and Sharp tried to buy eggs to eat. Although this tribe had plenty of chickens, they never ate the eggs. Finally one old man brought them a basket of eggs but the eggs contained live baby chickens. When the young Englishmen refused to eat them, the angry native said, "I knew you people didn't really eat eggs. You were just trying to make a fool of me." In another area, the people refused to eat fish, considering them a kind of reptile. In still another, the natives, although desperate for meat, were revolted when Grogan suggested that they eat an elephant he had shot. "Couldn't you shoot us hippo?" they asked. "No one eats elephant meat."

In spite of illness, porter troubles and geographical obstacles, the safari continued to push on, making fairly good time. Then the party reached the borders of Mushari, between Lake Kivu and Lake Albert Edward. Here they came to a halt.

Between them and the Mushari district lay several miles of old lava beds—black, rocky, sharp-pointed rivers of stone that formed a serious barrier to the barefooted porters. But the lava beds were little more than a detail. The local natives assured the young men that a nomadic, cannibal tribe had swept into Mushari from the Congo and was laying the whole country waste. Grogan and Sharp were not fools. They had no desire to walk into the center of a district torn by native wars. So they spent several weeks trying to find some way to go around the area. On their first attempt, their native guide deserted them in a forest of impenetrable bamboo. They were miles from water and had a hard time making their way back to camp. They made a second attempt with another guide. He also deserted them, having first taken them to the top of a particularly unpleasant mountain. At this point, Grogan lost his temper.

He decided to go directly over the lava beds and so through Mushari. "I didn't believe that there were any cannibals there and if there were, I no longer cared," he admits. "I was sick of listening to native lies and native deceits. I was told that it was impossible to cross the beds. I was told there was no water there and we would all die of thirst. I was told that the country was full of savage lions. Then all our porters claimed that they were sick. They hobbled around with sticks, swearing they were too weak to walk. Fortunately, they had made themselves so unpopular with the local natives that they didn't dare be left behind and as soon as they saw we were determined to push on, they started making sandals for the trip over the lava and collecting water skins."

It was decided that Grogan would go on with a small force and Sharp would follow later with the heavier equipment and a small flock of goats which were needed as food, there being no game in the district and no way of preserving meat in the intense heat.

So at dawn one morning Grogan started out with his little force across the supposedly impassable lava beds. "It was very much like crossing the Aiguille-du-Dru glacier in Europe, with blocks of stone instead of blocks of ice," he told me. By late afternoon, they had crossed the beds and reached the fertile country on the other side. They camped that night by a little pool of clear water, delighted at having so easily surmounted the barrier.

The next morning, Grogan was astonished to see men and women who had been living in holes among the lava rocks like wild animals, come crawling out to beg for food. These wretched people told him that a few weeks before the Bareka, a cannibal tribe, had invaded the country and were killing and eating everyone they could catch. "At night, we steal down to our grain fields and try to grab a few armfuls of the unripened grain," a shivering woman told him. "But the Bareka are watching the fields and each time they catch some of us."

Grogan fed the poor creatures, but he privately thought they were probably the victims of one of the innumerable tribal wars which were so common as hardly to cause comment. Like most Europeans, he regarded cannibalism as something of a myth. He managed to persuade one of the men to act as a guide across the district and started on.

The little party now passed through some of the most beautiful country of the entire journey. On the horizon, a line of great volcanoes stood out against the sky like a Japanese painting. They walked along a well-defined path leading through green, rolling country, dotted here and there with groups of little grass huts squatting under stately trees. The emerald green of the banana plantations contrasted with the gold of the ripening grain fields, and in the distance lay vast rolls of purple hills.

As they neared the first of the grain fields, Grogan could hardly believe his eyes. Along the edges were scattered the remains of the natives who had been caught the night before by the cannibals. Cooking fires were still smoldering beside congealing pools of fresh blood. In a daze, the little party kept on. Every few yards they passed a spot where trampled grass, a few torn bits of clothing, white bones and the black ashes of a fire showed where one of the unhappy villagers had been captured. It was like walking through a huge abattoir set in the Garden of Eden.

As Grogan and his men topped a little rise, they were silhouetted against the sky for a few, brief moments. Instantly they were seen by a group of the Bareka who were camped in one of the captured villages. The cannibals had not expected anyone to walk into the area in broad daylight and so had kept no watch. But after one astonished look, they leaped to their feet, grabbing up their spears and shields, and charged Grogan's party howling like wolves.

"What are they saying?" Grogan asked his guide.

"They say that they're going to kill and eat us," said the anxious guide.

"Indeed?" said Grogan. He unslung his sporting rifle from his shoulder and kneeling beside a clump of grass took steady aim. When the oncoming Bareka were within comfortable range, Grogan dropped the leader. The cannibals simply shouted the louder and came on. They knew about firearms and had expected to lose one man. But the firearms they had encountered hitherto were the muzzle-loading muskets of Arab traders. Grogan fired again and another Bareka fell. Now the yells grew less confident but still the raiders did not stop. Grogan dropped four more men in rapid succession. At last the Bareka broke and ran for cover, terrified by this strange new weapon that apparently never ran out of ammunition.

Reloading, Grogan led his party toward the now deserted village. A cloud of vultures rose from the place as he approached. The Bareka and their families had been interrupted at breakfast. Their fires were burning and their cooking utensils still in place. Grogan and his men walked through the street of the empty village. They passed a string of human entrails drying on a stick, a pot of soup stewing over a fire covered with human fat, a partly gnawed thighbone with shreds of half-cooked meat attached, and a head with the top of the skull removed as though for a trepanning operation sitting on some hot coals. A spoon was still sticking in the sizzling brains. Nearby was a partly roasted hand, still impaled on the end of a long stick which had been used as a sort of toasting fork. By the next fire was a child's head, partly skinned, with one cheek and one eye eaten, the other eye still in place and staring. The stench was incredible. Over the whole village floated a black blizzard of scraggly necked vultures and carrion crows.

"I can only say that although my porters were hardly delicately minded, they went without food for forty-eight hours rather than touch so much as a yam growing in that accursed ground," Grogan recalls.

Grogan sent a runner back to warn Sharp not to attempt to cross the district but to find another route north no matter what the difficulties. Grogan and his party were by no means out of danger. He describes the next two days as the worst of his life. He and his men traveled fast, hoping to escape from the area before the Bareka could recover from their alarm. Every village through which he passed had been sacked and burnt. "Skeletons, skeletons everywhere!" he wrote in his diary to describe this dreadful place. The next district had also been destroyed by the cannibals and even the next. The Bareka lived on human beings much as some other tribes lived on game animals and, when they had exhausted one area, moved on to the next.

Grogan and his men traveled from dawn to dark. They were afraid to stay on the trails and had to force their way through the jungles. Food became a major problem. Even drinking water was scarce as the streams were polluted with corpses.

While the party was skirting the edges of a papyrus swamp, they suddenly came on a small group of the Bareka. The raiders instantly charged, yelling with delight. Grogan dodged a spear and fired into them. One man dropped. The rest ran, leaving behind them two women and two small children. Grogan examined his captives. They were miserably thin. "Things are very hard with us," explained one of the women pathetically. "There are fifty people in our party and in the last week, our men have only been able to catch two people." Grogan took the women and children along with him, partly as guides and partly as hostages. Later, Grogan shot some game and the starving cannibals fell on it like hyenas, though Grogan is convinced that they missed what was to them a "normal" flavor in their meat.

Grogan's party finally managed to win clear of the cannibal area and camped for several days until Sharp, who had come by a different route, managed to catch up to them with the main safari. Reunited, the two young men worked their way north along the shores of Lake Albert Edward to Uganda. Here they separated permanently. Sharp decided to go east, crossing what is today Kenya, and take ship at Mombasa for England. Grogan continued northward, following the course of the Nile toward Egypt.

Grogan was now completely on his own and it is hard to understand how he ever managed to get through those terrible miles of swamp and desert. He lived with fever. He was almost never free from the weakening effects of dysentery. In one place, the only additional porters he could find were an old dervish prisoner with a broken leg, a small boy and a criminal lunatic in chains. A few days later, while Grogan was away trying to shoot some food, the lunatic called in the local natives and carefully distributed all Grogan's equipment among them. Then he deserted. The honest natives waited until Grogan got back and returned his belongings to him. Grogan hired canoes and tried to go north by water, but the Nile was so blocked by masses of floating water plants called "sudd" that he had to abandon this plan. He spent one night with the Baris, a people who had been driven out of their country by the warlike Dinkas and lived on islands in the river made of the compressed sudd. The mosquitoes were so bad here that at night the Baris covered themselves with dung, leaving only a small opening for breathing, and slept as though encased in plaster casts. All through this district, the mosquitoes were a constant nightmare. One of his porters who fell sick and could not drive them off was literally killed by them during the night. Once Grogan was driven to firing the dry reeds and he and his porters sat in the smoke to obtain a few hours of relief from the insects.

During this part of the trip, Grogan had serious trouble with the natives only once. While passing through the Dinka territory, his group was surrounded by over a hundred of these giant people. The Dinkas averaged over six and a half feet and were stark naked. They wore their hair in a tuft, somewhat like the crest on a dragoon's helmet, which added to their height. At first these strange people seemed friendly. They crowded around the terrified porters, fingering their loads and trying to talk to them. All might have gone well if the porters had not lost their heads and bolted. Instantly the

Dinkas attacked them, much as a dog will snap at anything running from it. One of the porters was speared. Two more went down under the Dinkas' clubs. Grogan was carrying a double-barreled rifle. He shot the Dinka chief and another man. At the same instant, he was attacked by a giant Dinka swinging a club. Grogan took the blow on his arm and jammed the empty gun into the man's belly. The Dinka staggered back, giving Grogan a chance to reload. He shot the man and then fired into the thick of the yelling crowd. They sullenly drew back, leaving one of the porters dying and three more insensible from club wounds.

"I never expected to see England again," Grogan admits. However, he managed to get his hysterical porters together and went on, the Dinkas following. Once, Grogan stopped and shot two more of them. The rest withdrew to a safer distance but still continued to follow.

"Camp that night was hardly a cheerful place," Grogan said. "Exhausted as we were, we still had to post sentries. I had a bad cold and my arm was so stiff from the club blow that I could hardly use it. My cook was crippled with dysentery, one of my porters had an infected foot which almost prevented him from walking, and two of the porters who had been clubbed were delirious. We could not make a fire as there was no fuel in the area. I found that my last two tins of tobacco had gone moldy so I could not even enjoy a smoke. The mosquitoes were so thick that they took turns sitting on my empty pipe, waiting for a chance to bite me."

The next morning, they went on. One of the porters who lagged behind vanished and was never seen again. Day after day the little party struggled north, sometimes through swamps where they waded in mud up to their chests and sometimes across stretches of waterless desert. All the porters were sick. They had to be prodded along at the point of a spear to keep them from lying down and dying. There was no sign of game and the last of the grain that the porters were carrying had given out. Grogan computed that in another four days' travel, he should reach the Sobat River where there should be hippo and possibly waterbirds. But could they last four more days? Grogan seriously doubted it.

Then, while plodding across the desert, Grogan saw ahead of him a long, thin stick swaying in the wind. It did not look like a tree. It was too tall for a reed. Hardly daring to believe the truth, Grogan realized it was the mast of a small boat. He had reached the Sobat. A few minutes later he met Captain Dunn, the owner of the boat.

From the Sobat, Grogan and his men went on by boat to Cairo. The news of his amazing feat had preceded him and in Cairo the young man went from dinner to dinner and from reception to reception. The four Watonga porters, who had stayed with Grogan all through the long trip from Nyasaland, were interested but not unduly impressed by the wonders of civilization. One day Grogan was out with his gunbearer when they saw a train speeding across the desert toward them. The gunbearer tapped Grogan on the shoulder, pointed to the oncoming train, and then casually handed him his elephant gun.

Grogan returned to New Zealand where he and Miss Watt were married. They traveled extensively in Europe and the United States, but like many another man, Grogan could not get Africa out of his blood. When the Boer War came, he promptly enlisted as a captain in the Fourth Royal Munster Fusiliers. An attack of malaria laid him low, and he was hospitalized next to another young man who was planning to go to Kenya after the war and start a timber concern. The two men formed a partnership and at the end of hostilities, traveled to Nairobi, then a city of tents. Here Mrs. Grogan joined her husband.

The young colony was racked by many troubles, not the least of them being the problem of administering an area three times the size of the British Isles with a force of a few hundred white men. Grogan threw himself enthusiastically into politics. His methods hardly endeared him to the government, but they were effective. At one period, a defect in the mining laws allowed a man to stake out a claim anywhere in the colony. Irresponsible men were laying out mining claims across the intended routes of main highways and valuable farming lands. After vainly pleading with the government to have the law altered, Grogan went out one evening and gravely pegged out a claim all around Nairobi. A special meeting of the alarmed council had to be called in the middle of the night to change the law as Grogan was threatening to start tearing up the main street with a pickax.

Grogan left Kenya to take part in the First World War during which he received his colonelcy and a D.S.O. In World War II, he acted as the West Coast liaison officer for the British forces. In his later years, the colonel decided to take up farming. He and Mrs. Grogan settled at Taveta, not far from the Tanganyika border. By an ingenious system of irrigation canals, he tapped the melting snows of Kilimanjaro and turned what was once one of the most barren and desolate stretches of bush country in all Kenya into one of the most prosperous farms.

There were many young men like Colonel Grogan in the England of fifty years ago. Today, I fear that they are a vanishing breed. The world is the poorer for their passing.

I I I

Joseph Thomson, Explorer

The El Dorado of East Africa was Uganda—the great area lying to the north and west of Lake Victoria. In this fertile region, first discovered by Tippu Tib and the Arab slavers, lived the great elephant herds. Ivory was the gold of East Africa and every effort was made to reach this remote country.

There were two possible routes to Uganda. One was the route used by the slavers: across Tanganyika to the central lakes and then north to Lake Victoria. This was a long way around and led through swamps so fever-ridden that often two-thirds of a party died before reaching the promised land. The other route was by far the shorter: a straight line northwest from Mombasa direct to Uganda across what is now Kenya. The southern route was impractical for large caravans. If the country was to be opened, it must be along the northern one. But no one had ever explored this northern route and nothing was known of it. The reader may well ask, why not? The answer lies in one word, Masai.

What the Zulus were to South Africa, the Masai were to Kenya. They were a tribe of professional fighting men, living on the other tribes around them much as the lions and leopards lived on the antelope. Their diet was a mixture of blood and milk, the blood drawn from the veins of their cattle. They ate no vegetables of any sort and no wild game. The whole life of the tribe revolved around the warriors called the "moran." When a boy reached the age of fourteen or thereabouts, he was taken into the warrior band. A subject tribe clever in metal-working made the young moran his long, slender spear which he always carried with him from that day forth. This servant tribe also made his great buffalo-hide shield, inscribed with heraldic designs showing his clan, age group and rank. The moran did no work of any kind. Their only function was to raid other tribes and loot them of their cattle and women. For sport, the moran amused themselves spearing lions. They were given the free run of all the young girls of the tribe. If a girl refused a moran, he was entitled to flog her until she consented. Masai war parties made raids throughout Kenya right down to Mombasa, a distance of some five hundred miles. A moran never ran away from a battle, he never left survivors if it were possible to catch them, and he never avoided a contest no matter what the odds might be.

To give some idea of the results of a Masai raid, I quote the report of Commander Dundas, who, in 1893, passed through an area in the wake of a Masai war party.

On our return journey through the Mbe country, a most harrowing sight presented itself. What only a few days before had been prosperous villages standing amid fields of grain were now smoking ruins. Bodies of old men, women and children, half burnt, lay in all directions. Here and there might be seen a few solitary individuals sitting with their heads buried in their hands, hardly noticing the passing caravan and apparently in the lowest depth of misery and despair. On questioning several of these unhappy beings, I was informed that the Masai had unexpectedly arrived one morning at dawn, spearing and burning all before them and carrying off some 250 women and large herds of cattle. Only a few of the unfortunate people had escaped by flying to the mountains.

The Masai's country lay across the northwestern part of Kenya, between Uganda and the coast. This, then, was the reason why the so-called northern route was closed and Kenya considered impassable.

In 1883, the Royal Geographic Society decided to send an expedition to explore the possibilities of the northern route. The man selected to head this expedition was Joseph Thomson. Thomson was twenty-six years old at the time. Although many of the men who opened East Africa were strange types, I think it can be said that Joseph Thomson was the strangest of them all. A precocious young

man, with an uncanny insight into the native temperament, he succeeded where many others had failed. Knowing full well that he
could not force his way through Masailand, he threw himself on the
natives' mercy and, by a series of parlor tricks and taking desperate
chances, won through to Lake Victoria.

Joseph Thomson was born February 14, 1858, in Dumfriesshire,
Scotland, my own home. His father was a stone mason, a man in
most humble circumstances. His brother, who later became a minister, wrote a biography of the explorer in which, according to the
fashion of the times, he described the youthful Joseph as being a
paragon of all possible virtues. However, among the mass of Victorian platitudes some facts about the lad clearly emerge. Young
Joseph was a great dreamer who devoured the novels of Walter
Scott and was known to weep because the days of high adventure
were no more. He was a keen naturalist and when little more than a
child wrote several papers on plants, bird observation and geological
notes which were published in scientific journals. He also possessed
to an amazing degree what might be called "controlled recklessness."
Once his agonized mother saw the boy climbing down the face of a
great cliff after birds' eggs, chanting to himself the while cantos from
The Lady of the Lake, and yet remembering to test every handhold
before trusting his weight to it.

When Joseph was still a boy, Stanley set out on his immortal
search for Livingstone. The newspapers gave an almost day-by-day
account of the search and Joseph followed each installment with
feverish interest. One day while his father was working in the
quarry, he saw the boy running toward him in a state of such wild
excitement that the mason, thinking some disaster had occurred,
dropped his tools and ran to him.

"Father!" screamed Joseph as soon as he was within earshot.
"Stanley has found Livingstone!"

When Joseph was twenty, he read that the Royal Geographic
Society was planning an expedition to the chain of lakes that run
up the center of Africa. Joseph, by then a graduate of Edinburgh
University, applied for a position as field naturalist with the group.
The society happened to need such a man and, as the boy came

cheap, decided to take him. During the trip, the leader of the expedition died and Joseph, in spite of his extreme youth, had shown so much ability that he was made head of the party. Later, when the rest of the group returned to Great Britain, Joseph stayed on and led two more expeditions into Central Africa. So, by the time he was twenty-five, he had achieved a reputation as an outstanding African explorer.

At this time, Thomson was a tall, slender young man, quiet and somewhat bashful in company, but so sure of his own opinions that at times he must have been a bit hard to bear. He wore a small mustache and the long sideburns of the period and, when in England, he took great pride in being perfectly turned out. James M. Barrie, who knew him well, wrote that Thomson took a boyish delight in being lionized by London society yet when a compliment was paid him, he would blush like a girl. As long as the dinner table talk dealt with Africa, Thomson would both listen and talk with great eagerness, but when the conversation turned to other fields, he would soon grow restless. On several occasions, he wandered away from parties given in his honor like a bored child. As his writing shows, Thomson was subject to fits of the blackest depression, alternating with bursts of almost mad self-confidence. His most outstanding characteristic was his amazing knowledge of the native mind and his ability to get along with savage tribes under conditions few other men of his time would have tolerated. Most explorers relied on force to smash their way through hostile tribes. Thomson, on the limited budget allowed him by the Royal Geographic Society, could not take a large expedition and so learned to trust to his wits rather than to his gun.

When Thomson heard that the society was contemplating an expedition to map the northern route to Lake Victoria and Uganda, he eagerly offered to head it. As no older and more experienced man would consider such a trip without a powerful safari and several hundred armed men, Thomson was told to go ahead and do his best.

Like all safaris of the period, the expedition was organized in Zanzibar. Thomson's first problem was to obtain porters. Unfortunately for him, he arrived on the island at a time when several other safaris had just left for the mainland and taken the pick of the porters with them. Those who were left refused to go when they heard that the expedition was headed for Masai country. The success of an expedition depended on its porters, as Thomson well knew. Traditionally a porter received half his wages before leaving, to support his wife and children while he was gone. Many men specialized in joining expeditions and then deserting a few days out. As a lone explorer was hopelessly outnumbered by his porters, he was more or less at their mercy, and the men knew it. A man could be murdered by his porters, who would then steal his equipment. Many men who volunteered as porters had only the vaguest idea of the hardships and perils of safari life and as soon as the going got rough, would desert. At times of crisis with wild tribes, there was always the chance that the porters would join the tribesmen in hope of saving their own lives. Such an expedition as this could only be made successfully with the best of such men.

While Thomson was in Zanzibar, he heard that a German named Dr. Fischer had already set out to reach Uganda by the northern route. Thomson went nearly mad at the news. He collected a group whom he described as the "very refuse of Zanzibar rascaldom." They were criminals trying to escape the island, runaway slaves, well-known wage-jumpers, men so crippled by disease that they were unable to find any other work, and robbers obviously waiting until they had the young man alone in the bush before cutting his throat. With this conglomeration, Thomson intended to penetrate the country of the all-powerful Masai.

He had two powerful assets in his favor. He had secured as his right-hand man a Maltese sailor by the name of James Martin. Martin could neither read nor write but he was a man of great ability who later became a district commissioner in Kenya. Martin was a good bushcraftsman and absolutely trustworthy. Thomson's other asset was a Negro named Ali the Bull. Ali had been on one of Thomson's previous trips where he had been the ringleader of all trouble. A man of great strength, a bully, and possessing both a savage ferocity and a hail-fellow-well-met jollity, he was a natural leader among the men. Here Thomson showed both his insight into human nature and his willingness to take great chances, for he made Ali headman in charge of the porters. As headman, Ali carried no loads but strolled about with his kiboko, a whip made of rhino hide, and enforced discipline. Ali turned out to be invaluable. The men both liked and feared him.

The expedition left Zanzibar on March 6, 1883, for Mombasa, the gateway of Kenya. During the brief voyage and throughout preparations for departure, the porters did everything in their power to cause trouble: stealing articles from their loads, trying to desert, threatening Thomson and Martin with knives, and announcing that they were too sick to move. Thomson babied them along as best he could, only remarking grimly to Martin, "Wait until we get these men well out in the bush. We'll bring them back to Zanzibar a changed lot."

Finally the expedition set out. There were 143 men in all. Seventy-seven were carrying the beads, brass and iron wire, and calico goods that were used as currency in the interior. Five carried boxes of ammunition. Forty carried supplies such as scientific instruments, clothes, tents, etc. Martin and Thomson had gunbearers. The rest of the porters carried food, except for ten armed askaris, native soldiers.

Some mention should be made here of the native askari, for modern East Africa has been built on him. "Askari" is an Arabic word and might be translated as meaning "fighting man." The reader must remember that Africa was cut up among a large number of native tribes with completely different customs, languages and physical appearance. The Arabs quickly learned to use certain of these tribes as semitrained troops and referred to them as askaris. When the explorers came, they found it necessary to select natives who were outstanding mentally and physically as a tiny standing army on safari, both to control the wild porters and to protect the expedition from wild beasts and hostile tribes. Adopting the Arab term, they called these men "askaris." Later, when the British government came, they organized the askaris into military organizations, such as the King's African Rifles, and as policemen in such groups as the British East African Police.

Although the askaris did not come from any one tribe, it was only natural that the bulk of them were drawn from the more war-like tribes. In Kenya today, two-thirds of the modern askaris come from the Wakamba tribe, who are by tradition a fighting people. Somewhat strangely, the Masai, Kenya's most warlike nation, cannot be used as askaris. They refuse to accept any kind of discipline. The askaris have always been volunteers, for it is considered a great honor to join their ranks. Generally speaking, the askaris have been outstanding men, showing great loyalty and pluck under the most trying circumstances. Just as a Frenchman will, in wartime, readily fight a German (although both are Europeans), so the askaris show no hesitation in fighting other tribes. If required to fight against their own comrades, the matter naturally becomes more complicated.

I remember a young British officer who was sent to the northern part of Kenya with a company of southern askaris to fight some of the wild tribes in that region. After the campaign, half the company decided to desert with their rifles, cross the border into Abyssinia, and become bandits. The other half decided to remain in the British service. As they all belonged to the same tribe, neither group sought to impose their will on the other. One afternoon, the whole company tied up their officer and then half of them departed for the border while the rest sat around the bound man, taking snuff and chatting until they were sure their comrades were safe. They then untied the officer, saluted smartly, and asked whom they were to fight next. As this company were all first-class fighting men and the government badly needed their services, they were not punished in any way but merely assigned to duty farther from the border. But such incidents were indeed exceptional and everyone in East Africa, no matter what the color of his skin, has always depended on the native askari in times of need.

Thomson's camp arose at five o'clock, ate breakfast, and started at dawn. There was a long rest in the middle of day and then, as soon as the sun dropped, the march was resumed until nightfall.

Thomson knew well that the porters would desert at the first opportunity. He warned his askaris that if they allowed a man to get away, they would have to carry his load themselves. The askaris were told to shoot down a deserting porter instantly. At night, the porters were collected in a great boma or circular fence made of thorn bushes and guards put over them. Martin and Thomson took turns at sentry go to make sure no one got away.

When the safari reached the Taru Desert, the first great obstacle, the porters threw down their loads and refused to go forward. The kiboko and the rifles of the askaris forced them on. The next few days had considerable effect in taming the porters. Water was almost nonexistent and the porters refused to husband the supply in their canteens, gulping it down in the first few hours of the march. As a result, they were nearly dead by the time they reached the next waterhole. The water was so putrid that Thomson, although he was forced to drink it, refused to wash even his feet in the loathsome stuff. A mouthful of water a day became the allowance for each man.

It is of interest to note that Thomson was famous in the early days for his benevolent treatment of porters. Two other expeditions which had preceded him had collapsed because the porters had mutinied, seized the explorers' guns, and set off on a campaign of looting and terrorizing the native villages. In dealing with such men, the explorers used a heavy hand and the fact that Thomson did not promptly hang any porter who revolted was regarded at the time as dangerous tolerance.

The expedition crossed the Taru Desert and reached the Tsavo River, a cool, pleasantly wooded spot. Here an amusing incident occurred which, I think, shows the strange difference between Victorian codes of behavior and those of today. The exhausted porters, thoroughly dehydrated by the terrible desert, stripped off their clothes and fell into the stream. Thomson and Martin were about to follow suit when they saw some virtually nude native women watching them curiously. The two white men, although in as bad a state as the porters, refused to undress in the presence of ladies. They sat on the banks of the stream until nightfall and then, protected by the darkness, stripped and took a swim.

After a brief rest at Tsavo, the expedition pushed on. Soon they passed signs of the Masai raiding parties. They went through an area littered with the debris of a recent battle between the Masai and the Wakamba, the tribe that inhabited the area. The Wakamba are magnificent bowmen, using poisoned arrows with great effect. It was to this that they owed their lives, for in the twisting game trails of the bush the Masai spearmen were at a disadvantage.

The Wakamba told them that the Masai war parties were roaming the district, the safari having avoided a meeting with the fierce warriors by sheer luck. "We were very glad to hear that the Masai were both in front and behind us," Thomson records, "as we knew that we need have no more fear of the porters deserting." Most of the early explorers were more afraid of their porters than they were of the wild tribes. Reassured by the comforting fact that the porters had to stay with him now for their own sake, Thomson went on.

The Wakamba were far from friendly and several times made semiserious attacks on the caravan. This was to be expected, as natives loved spearing a loitering porter or taking pot shots with poisoned arrows at strangers. Explorers generally resorted to their guns to beat off such an attack, which often resulted in turning what was nothing but good-natured fun into a serious uprising. It was typical of Thomson that he understood the native attitude in such matters and used other means to distract them. He had brought with him a galvanic battery, capable of giving a man a serious shock. In times of trouble, he would unload this battery and persuade some of the hostile natives to come in and try it. Once a man took hold of the electrodes, the current contracted his muscles so that he could not let go. The spectacle of one of their friends screaming in agony while the current went through his body so delighted the natives that they would roll on the ground in delight. Once the man was released, naturally his first idea was to find some new victim so he could enjoy watching him suffer. By use of this battery, Thomson was able to establish friendly relations with the villages and avoid bloodshed. Unfortunately for Thomson, one local ruler was so intrigued with the battery that he insisted Thomson give it to him before he would allow the party to proceed through his country. Thomson had no choice and so he lost a device which he had been counting upon to help him with the Masai.

The expedition went on past the great white cone of Kilimanjaro and entered the outskirts of Masailand. Here Thomson learned from some natives that Dr. Fischer, the German explorer, had been attacked by the Masai and forced to turn back. Thomson was greatly relieved that he now had a clear field, but if the German, who had a heavily armed safari of three hundred askaris, had been unable to reach the lake, what chance had he? Still, he determined to keep on.

The safari met its first Masai about a hundred miles north of Kilimanjaro. While going through a forest, some of the local natives who were accompanying them came screaming in with the news that a war party of Masai were ahead. Thomson hastily snatched up a handful of grass, the traditional sign of friendship among the tribes, and hurried forward with Martin.

Through the boles of the great trees, they saw the war party approaching at a trot. The tall, lean warriors (the average Masai is over six feet tall and their blood-and-milk diet keeps them very thin) were painted with red and white clay and naked except for the single hide garment thrown over their shoulders. Each man carried his great shield with its vivid, heraldic markings as easily as though it were a toy, although it weighed some fifty pounds. Their long spears, knitting needle thin, and so sharp that a man could shave the hairs on his arm with the blade, were in their hands. They wore headdresses of ostrich plumes which made them seem even taller than they were. They were chanting as they came, for the Masai feared no one and never bothered to conceal their presence unless stalking some victim.

In spite of the peril of the moment, Thomson's first emotion on seeing the approaching warriors was, "What splendid fellows!"

The war party showed no surprise on seeing the white man. They surrounded the three men and stood leaning on their spears. The moran leader approached and began to talk, emphasizing his points by motions of his short club, not unlike the ancient Irish shillelagh, which the Masai used for close work. The leader explained that they knew all about the movements of Thomson and his caravan. But the Masai, he went on, were not nearly so bad as they had been reputed. One of the Masai clans had indeed attacked Dr. Fischer and driven him back but that was because the doctor had tried to coerce them with his armed askaris. No one could threaten the Masai and escape punishment. However, Thomson seemed like a good sort and they had decided to let him through. This decision, the leader remarked casually, had been reached only after a considerable talk and some bloodshed, as several of the Masai had wanted to attack him. The leaders of the opposition were now dead, so Thomson had no need to worry.

This news seemed too good to be true. Thomson thanked the warriors. The moran trotted on, chanting their marching song, raising and lowering their spears in time to the music. In a few minutes, they had disappeared.

Thomson was enormously impressed by these moran. "How unlike they were to the other natives I had met!" he later wrote. "No pushing, no demands for hongo [tribute], no wild threats followed by cowardly panic. Only dignity, self-possession and a brief talk, much to the point."

Still feeling as though he were in a dream, Thomson led his safari into Masailand. He passed the huts made of dried cow dung and saw the herds of cattle, each beast covered by a maze of intricate brands that told the animal's whole history. From each corral he passed, the people would come out to see the strange safari, walking in dignified silence and trying not to stare but still obviously eaten up with curiosity. The young moran, each with his "dato" or girl-mistress, would stand watching the caravan pass by, the girls obviously fascinated, the young warriors watching with good-natured contempt as they leaned on their long spears. The romantic Thomson became more and more delighted by the noble bearing of these people. They were, he thought, the finest race he had ever seen.

Unfortunately, there was another side to the Masai that Thomson was soon to discover. As the porters passed one of the Masai corrals, a haughty young warrior shouted, "Look at those creatures carrying loads. They aren't men, they're donkeys." This sally produced a roar of laughter from the morans and delighted titters from the girls. The warrior, pleased with his success, began to goad one of the porters

with his spear, yelling, "Hurry up, donkey!" The terrified man
staggered on, the sharp point of the spear entering his flesh at every
thrust. Then another of the watching moran barely gave a flick of his
club and crushed the porter's skull as indifferently as a man would
kill a fly.

The askaris raised their rifles and Thomson and Martin ran to the
scene of the murder. Always before, the sight of rifles had provoked
a panic among the natives. The moran looked at the guns contemptuously, although they perfectly understood their power. Not
even bothering to lift his shield, one of the warriors asked in deri-
sion, "What are you going to do? Fight? Very well. You'll kill some
of us but then we will kill you." Thomson knew these men were
not bluffing. He went on amid a chorus of laughter and insults.

As the march went on, the party was subject to constant insults by
the swaggering young moran. They ripped open the flap of Thomson's tent in the evening, made him get out of bed and tore off his
clothes so they could examine him. The girls were almost equally
aggressive. Without any trace of the fear usually felt by native
women of strange men, they surrounded Thomson, handled him in
the most intimate manner, and giggled among themselves at his
strange hair and color. When Thomson tried to buy off some of the
moran with strings of beads, the warriors examined the trinkets
contemptuously, tossed them to the squealing datos, and demanded
more. From time to time, a moran would saunter up to a porter and
try to snatch his load. When the man resisted and the askaris came
to his help, the moran would look them over as much as to say, "Just
try laying a finger on me, you scum!" and then swagger away, making humorous remarks to his amused friends.

Thomson was a long-suffering man, but at last he reached the end
of his patience. One evening, after a long march, the young man
had collapsed on his cot, when a group of moran and their girls
arrived in camp and ignoring the protesting askaris, forced their way
into Thomson's tent. Thomson was not only exhausted but suffering
from malaria. When one of the warriors began to pull up his trouser
legs, the better to examine him, Thomson angrily kicked the man.
Instantly the warrior drew his "simi," the long Masai knife, and

rushed at the explorer. Thomson's life was saved by his askaris who intervened, but the warrior left vowing vengeance and Thomson knew that he was in for it.

The next day, his fears proved only too true. Armed bands of moran came trooping down from the low hills on all sides to gather around the safari. Thomson called a halt and had his men build a boma around the camp. But he well knew this was at best a temporary measure. He could hear the Masai war horns calling the warriors to battle, and by evening Thomson knew he must retreat.

Fortunately for the safari, there was no moon that night and a thunderstorm was brewing. As soon as it was dark, Thomson gave the word for the porters quietly to assemble their loads. The explorer anxiously watched the pitch-black clouds sweeping over the sky and, when the first splatter of rain fell, he gave the order to march.

The night was as black as the bottom of an inkwell. Thomson had a bull's-eye lantern and, by shielding the lantern with his coat and slipping back the dark shade, he was able to take occasional readings of his compass. With this as a guide, the safari threaded its way back among the camps of the sleeping moran and through the thorn bushes. The porters moved noiselessly, for their lives depended on it. "The first half mile was the worst," Thomson records. The only sound was an occasional grunt when one of the barefooted porters stepped on a sharp rock or thorn. By dawn, they were out of the most dangerous area but Thomson did not dare to stop. In five marches, the safari covered 230 miles. One day they went 70 miles. When they were finally well out of the Masai country, the whole group collapsed.

During the next few days, Thomson passed through one of the periods of black despair which were typical of the man. After seeing all his hopes and dreams dashed to the ground, it is hardly surprising that he should be discouraged, and most men would have abandoned the project then and there. But such was Thomson's nature that during this time he succumbed to a fit of such complete hopelessness that it is amazing his reason did not give way. "What am I striving after?" he cried in agony. "Wealth? Fame? I know I shall never find either. I am condemned to be a failure." During this period, Martin very wisely kept out of his leader's way and did what he could to reorganize the beaten and discouraged safari.

The mood passed and Thomson became his usual confident, intelligent self. He determined to return to Masailand and this time, "either reach the lake or leave my bones there for I will not be beaten a second time." A return trip was impossible with the present group of porters. They were demoralized, exhausted and most of them hopelessly crippled by malaria and dysentery. Leaving Martin in charge of the few capable men, Thomson took a handful of followers and returned to Mombasa. While crossing the Taru Desert, he hit a period of drought when even the few waterholes were dried up and came within an ace of dying there. The hot sands blistered his feet through his boots and at one time he had to crawl on his hands and knees. At last he reached Mombasa and returned with a fresh group of porters, determined this time to keep his temper at all costs.

Once again the expedition started out for Masailand, this time following a different route through the country. As before, the safari was repeatedly stopped by wandering groups of warriors and Thomson was subjected to constant humiliations. One may well ask why, if the Masai were opposed to allowing caravans through their country, they did not simply fall on Thomson's little party and kill them. The Masai had no fixed set of policies. Like children they could be unbelievably cruel but also like children they could be easily diverted. A curious example of this was shown during one of Thomson's first meetings with the warriors on this second trip.

The safari had been stopped and was virtually held captive by a group of moran who exhibited Thomson to their sweethearts and friends as though he were a wild animal. Infuriating as this treatment was, the moran were curious rather than threatening. However, they soon tired of this sport and to amuse themselves began stabbing at the porters to make the men scream and jump. Then they turned on Thomson. As he put it, "They played with me like a cat with a mouse." The warriors swept their simis within a hair-

breadth of his face and ordered him to strip for the amusement of
the datos. Thomson had already learned the futility of resistance and
was at his wit's end. Then he had a sudden inspiration.

Thomson had two false teeth. Holding up his hands with an impressive gesture, he muttered a few words and then, reaching in his
mouth, pulled out the teeth. The warriors yelped in astonishment
and then crowded around, motioning him to repeat the performance.
This Thomson did, time and again. From his account, it is not quite
clear whether the Masai regarded him as a magician or a clown.
They would go into bursts of laughter, and then move away from
him nervously. At least, this trick served to divert their minds and
finally they went away, leaving the safari in peace.

During the next weeks, Thomson had need to perform the trick
with his teeth countless times. When the warriors grew tired of this
feat, he tried to think of other ways to amuse them. A mirror fascinated them for hours. He put effervescent fruit salts in water and
the Masai were delighted by the way they foamed and bubbled.
At times, Thomson's tricks put him in an awkward position. Once
he showed the Masai a photograph of some friends in England.
The Masai were greatly interested, so much so that they demanded
Thomson make the people come out of the picture. When Thomson
tried to explain that this was impossible, the warriors promptly
grew threatening. Thomson at last managed to convince them that
the people in the photograph were asleep and should not be disturbed.

One of Thomson's most serious predicaments came about in a
curious way. A Masai elder, a most influential man, appeared at the
explorer's tent with his coy, young wife. The elder explained that
he was interested in Thomson and wanted his wife to have a child
by him. He had sounded his wife out on this matter and the girl,
after a careful study of Thomson, was keen to oblige. The young
Victorian Englishman was now in a frightful quandary. He tried to
pass the matter off as a joke, but the elder was so insulted and the
jilted girl so furious that Thomson quickly realized that the matter
was serious. After some rapid thinking, he filled a mug with water,
added some fruit salts which made the water fizzle, and told the

girl to drink it, explaining that this was the way white people conceived.

The old Masai regarded the mug dubiously. "That's certainly a strange way to make a baby," he remarked through the interpreter. "Here we have a different system." Thomson told him gravely, "If you could only read the maker's claims on the label, you'd know that according to him these fruit salts can do anything." The girl drank the potion and went away well content. Thomson breathed a sigh of relief, knowing that before the requisite time was up, he would be out of the country.

Throughout this terrible journey, Thomson was in constant peril. He was much in the position of a man dealing with a group of lunatics who might at one moment attack with murderous intent and yet be diverted by a passing butterfly. Once, while in the Abardare Mountains, one of the porters died from the cold. Thomson was confronted by a serious problem. The Masai believed that to bury anyone put a curse on the land. On the other hand, they were fearful of disease and if they knew one of the safari had died, they would turn the whole group back, thinking they were infected with some ailment. At the time of the man's death, there was a Masai war party in the camp. Thomson had purchased some donkeys from the Masai and he had the body covered with cloth and strapped on a donkey's back like a bale of goods. That night, the body was buried with great secrecy.

Throughout all these dangers Thomson continued to map the route to Uganda. Although he might be surrounded by warriors, he would stop at each convenient hill, set up his theodolite, and take readings. He patiently allowed the warriors to peer through his sextant and continued his observations even though the Masai several times protested that he was putting some sort of curse on the land. Then Thomson would distract them by some trick or a gift of beads for the girls. He regularly took recordings of the morning and evening temperatures, measured the height of Mount Kenya, and took long detours to see unknown lakes and geological formations. He discovered Thomson's Falls, which still bear his name, and made careful notes and accurate measurements of the mountain lakes. In addition, he kept constant records of every new bird, animal, bush and flower he saw. Once when the safari was starving and Thomson was lucky enough to shoot a gazelle, he took the time to study the animal before it was cut up and suggested that it might be a new species. So indeed it turned out to be and is now called the Thomson gazelle.

In December, the natives told Thomson that he was nearing his destination, Lake Victoria. The safari had to beat off one attack by the Kavirondo, a stark-naked tribe who believed that the white man was coming with some potent magic that would cause the lake to disappear. This was the last time the safari's war cry of "*Bunduki! Bunduki!* (Guns! Guns!)" had to be raised. A few days later, some of the scouts forging ahead topped a low range of hills. In a moment the men were dashing back, screaming "*Nyanza!* (the lake!)"

The march broke into a run. The range was crossed and the men staggered through a mud and reed stretch of swamp to the lake. The askaris fired their guns into the air, the porters waded knee-deep into the cool water, splashing it over each other and crying with joy. Afterward, everyone came to Thomson and shook his hand, congratulating him on at last reaching his goal.

I would like to report that the trip back to the coast was simple. On the contrary, Thomson nearly died during this return trek. He was gored by a buffalo and had to be carried on a litter almost the entire distance from the lake to Mombasa. His wound infected, he was racked by disease and so weakened by the endless dysentery that even the optimistic Martin gave up all hope. The Masai were more aggressive than ever. On one occasion, they not only killed a porter but afterward demanded that Martin pay them for the trouble they'd gone to in spearing the man. At last in May, 1884, the caravan reached Mombasa—a little over a year from the time they had originally set out.

Joseph Thomson returned to England where he was hailed as a hero—as indeed he was. But after a few months in London, he became restless for Africa again. "I am doomed to be a wanderer," he wrote his brother in one of his black moods. "I am not an empire builder, I am not a missionary, I am not truly a scientist. I merely want to return to Africa and continue my wanderings."

And so he did, although he was now riddled by tropical diseases. He went up the Niger River to the Sudan, explored the Zambezia, and traveled across the Atlas Mountains in Morocco. This last trip was undertaken mainly because Thomson believed that the Arabs, in spite of their great cruelty, were frequently better able to get along with the natives than the British. He hoped by living in an Arab community to discover their secret but the customs of the desert tribes revolted him and his only conclusion was that the Arabs owed their success largely to the fact that they were tee-totalers. As Thomson was also an abstainer, this may well have influenced his belief.

In 1895 he returned to England. His clergyman brother carried the great explorer in his arms like a child from the railroad station to a waiting carriage. No great feat this, for Thomson was by now little more than a skeleton. A few days later, he lay on his bed and the doctor, after taking his flickering pulse, looked up meaningly at the waiting relatives. Thomson caught the look and smiled. "If I were strong enough to put on my clothes and walk a hundred yards, I would go to Africa yet!" he said. A short time later, he died.

Already missionaries and traders were following the northern route he had opened to Uganda. Already forts and trading posts were springing up in the sites of his old camps. Although Joseph Thomson had died before he could see the results of his trek, he had made possible the opening of Uganda and the settling of Kenya.

IV

Reverend Arthur Fisher, Missionary

"If you want to know about the early days in East Africa, the man for you to see is the Reverend Arthur Fisher," I was told in London. "He's the last man alive who saw the hoisting of the British flag on the shores of Lake Victoria." So I went to Eastbourne, a seaside town on the southeast coast of England, where Mr. Fisher and his wife live.

The Fishers' home was one of a line of neat, white cottages in a side street and Mr. and Mrs. Fisher met me at the door. Although Mr. Fisher is now eighty-six years old, he is still very active, with signs of the amazing physique that enabled him to endure twenty-two years under the most primitive conditions possible. Ruth Fisher, his wife, was a slender, alert woman who still does all the housekeeping although she is only a few years younger than her husband. They took me into their tiny living room, ornamented with African spears and containing a cabinet full of magnificent native ivory carvings. The exotic collection contrasted strangely with the simple English cottage and the quiet couple.

"Everything here has a history to us," said Mrs. Fisher, seeing me look at the unusual objects. She took down a cow's horn, ornamented with cowrie shells. "This is a witch doctor's medicine horn. The black, pitchlike substance around the tip is dried human blood. If a witch doctor thought a man was possessed of evil spirits, he would make a hole through his ear and drain off the blood into one of these horns."

"Sometimes the patient didn't survive the treatment," added her husband. Mr. Fisher had recently been unwell and he took the horn with somewhat trembling fingers. "We saw a man killed with one of these. The witch doctor cut too deeply. I remember the man scratched the ground for some time and then went into convulsions. Ruth and I worked over him that evening, but we couldn't save him."

"Of course, the witch doctor thought he was helping the man," said Mrs. Fisher. "The witch doctors were usually very intelligent men, but not educated, you know. Many of our best native teachers were ex-witch doctors. Now I'll leave you to talk to the Padre while I make some tea."

Mrs. Fisher usually referred to her husband by this affectionate name. She left the room with brisk, efficient strides while her husband lowered himself into a big armchair and I unrolled a huge map of Uganda, showing the area where the Fishers had spent so much of their lives.

"Now let me see," said Mr. Fisher, running a broad thumb over the map. "Yes, there's Lake Victoria and here we were to the north and northwest of it. But, dear me, this is a very small map. Why, it hardly shows anything. From the lake to the Ruwenzori Mountains seems only a step, but it was well over 150 miles through swamps and jungles. It took two weeks of hard trekking to make the trip. And the rivers are hardly shown at all. Now about here," he drew a shaking line with a pencil, "there was a very bad river, very bad. Full of crocodiles. One had to keep shooting in the water to scare them so the porters could get across. That was near the border of Toro, King Kasagama's country. Now here's the Kafue River where Kabarega defeated the Baganda. What, you never heard of Kabarega? Or Kasagama? And you're writing a book on Uganda? Well, well, I think I'd better start at the beginning."

Arthur Fisher was born in King's County, Ireland, in 1868. His father was an excise man and farmer. While Arthur Fisher was in his early twenties, he attended a meeting of two American evangelists called Moody and Sankey, who were traveling through the British Isles giving revivalist meetings somewhat like Billy Graham. Young Fisher had never been particularly devout, but at this meeting he received a deep and heartwarming sense of salvation which changed his entire life. He determined to become a minister.

While studying for the ministry at the University of Dublin, Fisher went to a meeting addressed by Bishop Tucker, one of the great figures in the African mission field. The bishop explained that a few years before, a small group of missionaries had gone to Baganda, a native kingdom in what is today southern Uganda, bordering on the northern shore of Lake Victoria. Mwanga, the king of Baganda, watched the growth of this new religion with suspicion, regarding it as a threat to his power. Finally, he decided to stamp it out. He put the handful of missionaries in a boat and sent them out into the lake with orders never to return. Then he turned on the native converts. In one year, he killed two hundred men and women. Some of the men he tied to crosses and, when they refused to recant, had his torturers cut off parts of their bodies and cook them in front of their eyes. The men died singing the hymns that the missionaries had taught them. Others were tied to stakes along the shores of the lake for the crocodiles. By the end of that terrible year, Mwanga felt confident that he had obliterated Christianity for all time in Baganda.

But the missionaries felt differently. Bishop Tucker intended to lead a new group to Uganda and re-establish the church. He made an appeal for fifteen thousand pounds and seven young men willing to risk their lives. When the bishop shouted, "Who's for Baganda?" the audience leaped to their feet cheering.

Contributions poured in. Those who had no money wrote pledges on slips of paper and dropped them in the collection plate. One old lady pledged the income from the best three acres of her farm. Young Arthur Fisher had no money but he had himself. He volunteered to go as one of the seven missionaries.

In the spring of 1892, Bishop Tucker and his little group arrived in Zanzibar, then the starting point for all expeditions into East Africa. Their reception was discouraging. Sir Gerald Portal, the

British Consul-General, grimly warned Bishop Tucker that the government could not take any responsibility for the missionaries or give them any protection. "We have asked for no protection nor do we expect it," replied Tucker. "We take our lives in our hands."

Bishop Tucker had decided to take the northern route through Kenya, following Joseph Thomson's old way, but the Masai war parties were still attacking caravans and porters refused to go with the missionaries. After months of effort, the party was at last able to proceed with a scratch group of porters. On their way across Kenya, the missionaries passed slave gangs being driven to the coast, the Arab slavers riding ahead on their magnificently caparisoned mules and behind them the long line of natives, yoked together. A month out, two natives staggered into camp and collapsed after gasping out, "Masai!" They were part of a group traveling north and the rest had been wiped out by a Masai war party. The missionaries left the main caravan route and continued north along little-known trails that their guide showed them. They passed the great swamp where Nairobi now stands, crossed the Rift Valley, and pressed on toward Uganda. In December, they reached the edge of Lake Victoria and on Christmas day arrived at Mengo (now Kampala), Mwanga's capital, built on five hills that overlooked the lake.

Mwanga's palace was on the most prominent of the hills. The palace was surrounded by ten stockades built in a series of concentric circles like a maze with armed warriors guarding the entrance to each stockade. All night fires were kept burning in front of each gateway to make sure that no assassin crept past the guards. Mwanga spent most of his time in his great hut in the center of these fortifications together with his wives, his grand vizier, and chief executioner.

"You may wonder why the king didn't have us killed as soon as we arrived," remarked Mr. Fisher. "But as the whole country was in a state of chaos, he thought we might be of some help to him."

Mr. Fisher explained that Uganda was broken up into a number of small kingdoms and semi-independent villages all more or less at perpetual war with each other. Each of these kingdoms had its own royal family and Mr. Fisher would casually rattle off the complicated genealogies of these various petty rulers in a way that made my head swim. Kabarega, the king of Bunyoro in northern Uganda, was threatening Mwanga's country and Mwanga was trying desperately to find allies. "He hoped that by treating us well, he could get the British to take his side against Kabarega," Mr. Fisher explained.

A short time after his arrival in Mengo, Mr. Fisher was given an audience by Mwanga. The missionary was led through the stockades and passed the armed guards into a great building made of mud and wattle with a thatched roof that was the king's palace. Mwanga received him sitting on a velvet-upholstered chair given him by some traders and flanked by his courtiers and principal wives. The king was a weak, nervous man who had a habit of seizing one of his courtier's hands and clinging to it hysterically when something was said that disturbed him. Mwanga was in the curious position of being an absolute despot and at the same time terrified of every stranger and even of his own people. As a result, he might cringe before someone in the morning and have him put to death with the most horrible tortures in the afternoon.

Fisher asked the young king, "Why do you hate the missionaries so? Have they ever tried to harm you?"

"No," admitted the king, shifting his feet uncertainly. Then he added savagely, "But if you foreigners grow in power here, we kings can no longer do as we want."

As Mwanga's father had once had the inhabitants of an entire village thrown into Lake Victoria because a witch doctor said it would cure the queen's toothache, Mr. Fisher knew the king was quite right.

Mr. Fisher spent the next few weeks learning something of the language and customs of the people. He also met some of the earlier missionaries who had been driven out by Mwanga but had returned when the king's fury abated. Remarkable men they were. There was Pilkington, a double blue from Cambridge, who was busy translating the Bible into the language of the country. There was Mackay who had carried a small, hand printing press up from the coast and was now whittling out the type for it from bits of wood. There was Walker who had repaired the boat when a hippopotamus attacked it on the night when the missionaries had been exiled by Mwanga. These men would have laughed had anyone referred to them as heroes, but few of the famous African explorers had ever run such dangers with such little support.

"When I started out for Uganda, I'd thought that all a missionary had to do was preach the gospel," said Mr. Fisher, chuckling. "My own conversion at the Moody and Sankey revival had been a great experience to me, and I wanted to 'publish the glad tidings' that had given me so much happiness. I suppose it was a little like a man who has read a book which has been a great inspiration to him and eagerly recommends it to his friends so that they can share his pleasure. My book was the Bible. I wanted the whole world to join in the comfort that I'd known when I left that meeting. Well, well, I soon found that a missionary has more to do than stand under a fig tree and read the Scriptures to a group of natives. In Uganda, he had to be a combination explorer, doctor, carpenter, linguist, big game hunter and with a bit of the politician thrown in too. You had to know the different chiefs, their rivalries, the boundaries of their countries, and be careful not to offend anyone. Quite a problem."

"Did the natives object to having you interfere with their own religion?" I asked.

"No, I can't say they did," said Mr. Fisher thoughtfully. "You see, they really didn't have a proper religion of their own. It was mainly what might be called devil worship. A man would pay the priests to give him a fetish to keep off evil spirits or, if he or his family were sick, he'd pay the priest to drive off the evil spirit that was troubling them. The priest usually did that by mutilation. If a child cried, the mother thought he was possessed by a demon and the priest would brand the child with a hot iron or cut off the poor little mite's ears to drive out the spirit. You never saw a child who didn't carry the marks of the branding iron or the knife. In fact, natives would stop and stare at the children of our native converts because they weren't mutilated. They called them 'Jesus children.' The native priests also laid such a heavy tax on the people that it impoverished them. Now 'the destruction of the poor is their poverty' and one can't expect people ground down in that manner to have a high standard. The natives had no idea of sin. They couldn't understand why we thought it was wrong for a man to beat his wife to death or for a strong community to conquer their neighbors and sell them to the Arab slavers. Today we hear a great deal of how good the original native religions were for the people, but only 'fools make a mock of sin' and I can't agree with it."

Mr. Fisher went on to say that the ancient religion of the Baganda had, indeed, been a very fine one, resembling to an amazing extent the Old Testament. "But it was only by talking to the native priests themselves that we learned anything about it," he explained. "The common people had no knowledge of their religion. Through the ages, the priests had found it more profitable to concentrate on the sale of fetishes and stress the threat of demons, so the religion had degenerated completely."

Mr. Fisher's first task was to learn the language. "I was very slow at it," he told me, smiling. "Pilkington, who was a very brilliant man, learned the language from a porter on the way up from the coast. When he arrived in Uganda and spoke to the people in their own tongue, they thought he was a god. I was never able to do that. Yet I learned in time. Then I was sent out to found mission stations in different parts of the country. For that work, the only qualification a man needed was to be a good talker and a good fighter. Being Irish, both came naturally to me."

Mr. Fisher's first station was near Mityana, a community some fifty miles west of Mengo. The local chief hated missionaries and had persecuted several sent out to his locality. But considerably to Mr. Fisher's surprise, the simple eloquence of the young Irishman soon won him over. Weeping, the chief begged to be baptized. "I want to be called Saul because I too persecuted the Christians," the old man explained with tears running down his cheeks. Glad at so easy a victory, Fisher promised to accept him into the fold and retired to sleep in a straw hut the chief had built for him. That night the chief got roaring drunk on native beer and shot the hut full of burning arrows.

"I had a good deal of trouble with that old man," Mr. Fisher admitted regretfully. "He would get converted every day and at night get drunk and set fire to whatever hut I was sleeping in. After the third time, I lost patience. I took off my coat, rolled up my sleeves and went and had a long heart-to-heart talk with him. After that, we got along very well."

The natives were deeply interested in this new religion, although they had some doubts. "Is this gentle God of yours strong enough to fight evil spirits?" one man asked Mr. Fisher doubtfully. "There was no question of talking down to the natives," Mr. Fisher assured me. "They were very intelligent and asked many searching questions."

Most questions dealt with the apparent conflict between the various Christian sects. The French were pushing into Uganda from the Congo just as the British were pushing in from Kenya. The French were Roman Catholics and the British were Protestant. This should not have led to any conflict, but unfortunately it did, especially as the religious distinctions were drawn along political lines. The natives often took the position that as long as the white men couldn't agree among themselves what was true, all Christianity was nonsense.

Mr. Fisher was once talking to a native king who said restlessly, "How am I to know what is true? You tell me one thing and the French another." Mr. Fisher gave him a copy of the Gospels which Pilkington had translated into Uganda and Mackay had printed on his tiny press. "No one can tell you what to believe, your majesty," he told him. "Here is all we know. You must decide for yourself."

The natives were fascinated by the idea of "paper that can talk" and were desperately eager to learn to read. At first, the mission group gave away the translations, but the demand was so great this proved impossible. They began to charge for them, five hundred cowrie shells (the standard currency of the country) for a copy of the four Gospels. "It often took a man three months of hard work to earn enough shells, but Mackay could hardly turn out the books fast enough," said Mr. Fisher proudly. Pilkington's translation became so revered in Uganda that, when some minor errors of translation were discovered later, the natives refused to allow the book to be changed and it is still in use today. "Porters in caravans would carry their copies of the Gospels with them, although on long trips every additional ounce counts," said Mr. Fisher. "In the evenings around the fire, a man who possessed a copy would read to the others. Often half a dozen men would have to share one copy sitting in a circle, so a number of the men would learn to read upside down and couldn't read in any other way."

We who have grown up accepting Christianity as part of our lives can hardly appreciate the tremendous impact that the gentle doctrines of Our Lord and the force of His personality can have on people raised to regard religion merely as an oppressive force in the hands of witch doctors. "Of course, all was not smooth sailing," Mr. Fisher assured me. "One doesn't transform a savage into a Christian overnight. I remember in particular one old chief who expressed great interest in the new religion and I made a long journey to expound the Gospels to him. He was converted—the conversion seemed a sincere one—and I left some of my native converts to carry on the good work. A short time later, the local witch doctor got hold of the old man by a few magic tricks and persuaded him to fall back into his pagan ways. He started a persecution of the converts and they had to go into hiding. Then the chief sent for the witch doctor and demanded that he find where the converts were. When the witch doctor said he couldn't, the chief was furious. 'I thought you were a magician, and you can't even do a simple thing like that. I'm going to be a Christian again.' And so he did."

The missionaries did everything possible to encourage the natives to read so they could study the Gospels for themselves and also so they could read other books which would enable them to lift their standard of living. While he was at Mityana, Mr. Fisher started a native school which has now grown into Makerere College, one of the finest educational institutions in all Africa. Here he also hit on a plan which, Mr. Fisher believes, was his most important contribution to mission work. At that time, it was taken for granted that all teaching and converting would have to be done by Euro-

pean missionaries, the natives acting merely in the role of a congregation. "I didn't see any reason why native converts couldn't
go out as missionaries themselves," Mr. Fisher told me. "They spoke
the language, knew the people, and could travel far more easily
through the country than we could. So I began to organize groups
called 'sunagogi,' composed of enthusiastic young men who wanted
to help us in spreading the Gospel. These groups were small at first,
but 'how great a matter a little fire kindleth.' These young men
spread out through the country and each one started his own
sunagogi. So the movement spread like ripples in a pool."

There were so many demands being constantly made on the
missionaries it is not surprising that after a time these various duties
took up more and more of their time. "The witch doctors had always
acted as medicine men so the natives couldn't believe that we
weren't doctors too," Mr. Fisher remarked. "We did have some
slight medical knowledge and with so much suffering about, one
couldn't refuse to help." Soon many of the missionaries found that
virtually all their time was taken up with treating the sick. There
were constant political questions. "A village would say to me, 'Our
neighbors have raided us and stolen many young girls. As Christians, we are forbidden to fight, but we must now invade their
country and rescue our families,'" Mr. Fisher explained. "Then I
had to see the enemy chief and try to arrange for a peaceful settle-
ment." Many communities were threatened by dangerous big game
and the natives expected Mr. Fisher to shoot the beasts. There was
also the problem of fugitive slaves. "Slaves would run away from
their masters and take refuge with our converts. Their masters
would demand their return and our converts would refuse to give
them up. As slavery was the law of the land, I could only reluctantly say it must be done, but it was a terrible decision."

So many of these problems arose that the missionaries gradually
became what we would call "trouble-shooters," called in to arbitrate
quarrels, keep down dangerous game, advise on crops, and treat the
sick. All these were good works, but the basic task of teaching religion
was gradually pushed into the background. "There was so much
to do, so much to do," said Mr. Fisher sadly. Then, a year after he

arrived in the country, a native convert named Musa Yubauanda came to the missionaries and announced he was returning to his old faith. "You people aren't teachers of religion, you're white administrators," said Musa angrily. "I'm going to seek God elsewhere."

Several other native converts followed Musa's lead. This news came like a blow in the face to the mission group. "I'm afraid that we were sometimes impatient with the natives," Mr. Fisher told me regretfully. "Once I was explaining to a woman about the treatment for her sick child. I'd come a long way to see her and brought some drugs which had to be carried up from the coast by porter and were very precious as a result. When I finished, I asked, 'Do you understand exactly what to do?' 'Oh, I wasn't listening to you, I was watching those people out there,' she said casually. When you're tired, running a fever, and have so many obligations, it's hard to keep your temper. Yes, we were doing good works but 'though I speak with the tongues of men and of angels and have not charity, I am become as sounding brass or a tinkling cymbal.' Good works aren't enough. What use does it do to sew up a spear wound in a man's chest if the next week he's going out to raid another village and get a fresh one? It's his soul that must be helped as well as his body."

Pilkington, who had been putting in sixteen hours of cruel hard work a day, suddenly dropped everything and retired to an island in Lake Victoria to ponder the question and pray. "When he returned to us, God had answered his prayers and the Holy Ghost had descended on him as truly as it ever did on the apostles," Mr. Fisher told me, with tears in his eyes.

Unfortunately, I am not writer enough to record in print what must have been a deeply moving experience for this small band of men, cut off by a thousand miles of jungle from the coast. But briefly, Pilkington felt that the missionaries had been devoting too much time to temporal matters. "A man must walk by faith, not by sight," Mr. Fisher expressed it. Material benefits, no matter how important they might be, were meaningless if the natives had no ethical code and no religious faith to help them. "Suppose a man's cattle and even his family are menaced by a lion," Mr. Fisher explained. "You say, 'I am a civilized, educated man so I will give this savage a gun to shoot the lion and protect himself.' This is not enough. If the man is still a savage, he will promptly use the gun to shoot his neighbors and seize their property. He must have the gun to help him to live, but even more important he must have religious scruples which will enable him to use the gun wisely."

As the missionaries listened to Pilkington, the religious inspiration which had originally sent the group to Uganda returned to them more strongly than ever. "Iron sharpeneth iron; so a man sharpeneth the countenance of his friend," said Mr. Fisher. "Without that additional inspiration, we could have never gone on."

Shortly after this revival of faith, Mr. Fisher was sent to Toro, a native kingdom in the foothills of the Ruwenzori Mountains. The young king, Kasagama, had asked that a missionary be sent to his kingdom and Mr. Fisher was selected. He stayed in Toro several years and in the mission field, his name is largely identified with this nation.

"Yes, that was my country," said Mr. Fisher. He affectionately stroked the section of the map that had been the place of so many of his youthful hopes and dreams. "King Kasagama was a wonderful young man. He stood six feet two, splendidly built, and was most intelligent. He was very interested in European customs. I taught the young men how to play football, thinking it a better exercise than spearing their neighbors, and the king played too. I remember he had one servant run after him holding the imperial umbrella over his head all the time and another servant follow him with a stool in case he wanted to sit down. Sounds a bit ridiculous, yet remember that the kings of Toro had been taking themselves so seriously that a few years before they would kill anyone who didn't prostrate himself on the ground as they passed. A great change in so short a time. He had seen a flower garden at one of the mission stations, so he started one too. The flowers did very well, but the young king seemed unhappy about them. Finally he said to me anxiously, 'They look very pretty, but what do you do with them?' He was quite puzzled when I explained they were only for show. To a native, anything planted is for food."

My friend John Hunter is recognized as one of the greatest of Africa's big game authorities, and he considers the leopard as the most dangerous of African big game. I think it was typical of these early missionaries that Mr. Fisher should mention shooting these savage cats quite casually and simply as one of his many duties. "I never saw such a country for leopards as Toro," he remarked. "The natives kept great fires going around their villages all night long to keep them away, but the leopards would still come in. They'd tear their way through the roofs of the huts to get at the people inside. When the natives went out to hunt them, they'd beat the war drums as though going to war. They hunted with spears and I'd go along with my gun. I was never much of a hunter, but I got quite handy at shooting leopards. The natives would track one down and then form a circle around him. They'd leave an opening in the circle and I'd stand there with my gun. Then they'd drive him toward me. You'd be surprised at how fast those creatures can move. Come at you with a great rush. I must have killed dozens while I was in Toro."

The people of Toro were in a desperate condition, due to the long native wars and an epidemic of rinderpest that had wiped out most of their cattle. "The poor little children had absolutely no clothing and at night they used to coat themselves with mud in an effort to keep warm," Mr. Fisher told me. "I know people laugh at the missionaries for trying to put clothes on the natives. Well, I certainly wished I had some of that clothing there. I believe the infant mortality must have been nearly 90 per cent." The women were only a little better off than the children. "One afternoon while I was sitting in the semidarkness of a hut talking to a local chief, I saw some creatures crawling about in the shadows searching for stray bits of food. Then, as my eyes grew more accustomed to the dim light, I saw that they were the chief's wives. The women seemed incapable of any thoughts except food and competition for their husbands' favors. How are any people to improve if the women are so degenerate? It's the woman who must build the home and train the children. Now here was a good example of what I mean by the importance of Christian ethics. As long as the men felt that there is nothing morally wrong in treating women like dogs, teaching crop rotation and healing the sick wouldn't do a mite of good."

Unfortunately, Mr. Fisher found that he was unable to reach the women. They were suspicious of a strange man and avoided him. "Yet the whole key to the situation was the low status of the women," Mr. Fisher assured me. Then King Kasagama suggested that an appeal be sent to England, asking for women missionaries to come to Toro. The letter, composed by the earnest young king, read:

To my dear friends of the Church in Europe. I greet you very much in Our Lord Jesus Christ who died for us on the cross to make us children of God and how are you sirs? Please send us English ladies to teach our women. I want very much that they come.

"Several young ladies answered the call," Mr. Fisher told me proudly. "Among them was a Miss Ruth Hurditch. I liked her so well that I married her."

"I'm afraid the poor man didn't have much choice," said Mrs. Fisher, who had come in with a tray laden with a teapot, cups, saucers, sandwiches and cakes. "I was the only white woman in Toro. Now that I think of it, I didn't have much choice myself. It was either Arthur or a cannibal."

The Fishers smiled at each other.

"How did you get up from the coast?" I asked Mrs. Fisher.

"Rode on my bicycle," said Mrs. Fisher promptly. "We followed the elephant trails up from Mombasa and they're quite smooth, you know. There were seven of us, six were 'freshers' [newcomers]. Then there was a married couple and of course our guide and the porters."

To me, there was something very appealing in the idea of seven young Victorian ladies, dressed in the costumes of the times, riding bicycles eight hundred miles through jungles, deserts and mountain passes. I asked for details.

"Victorian girls weren't nearly as delicate as people think," Mrs. Fisher explained. "When I was young, my friends and I used to take long walking tours through Scotland and England. I think we took more exercise than most girls do now. When I read King Kasagama's letter in the newspaper. I was wild to go to Toro, although to tell the truth I had only a vague idea where Toro was. My parents were opposed to the idea at first, but after all there were a number of children in our family and each of the others was living in a different continent. The Empire was a big place in those days, you know. So they decided to let me go."

When the party arrived in Mengo, Ruth and another young girl went on to Toro under the chaperonage of a missionary and his wife. The missionary came down with fever and he and his wife had to return to Mengo. So the two girls went on with their porters.

"King Kasagama had huts built for us with rooms divided by bark cloth and reed shutters in the windows," Mrs. Fisher explained. "We used our packing cases as wardrobes and made ourselves quite at home. The trip from Mengo to Toro had been harder than we'd expected and we'd had to abandon everything except absolute necessities—even our hairbrushes, combs and toilet articles. I'm afraid we felt the loss of those things quite keenly. We were young girls, you know, and liked to keep ourselves looking neat."

The first efforts of the two English girls to make friends with the native women were not outstandingly successful. "King Kasagama sent us four women to train," Mrs. Fisher explained. "But the poor things remained huddled in one corner of our hut like prisoners and wouldn't make any attempt to talk to us. During the night, they all ran away." So the girls decided to appeal to the women through the children.

There was unlimited work to be done with the children. "Many of them had been orphaned by the wars and other causes," Mrs. Fisher pointed out. "And the natives believed that the birth of twins was unlucky. So if a woman had twins, the babies were left out in the forest to die. Then the witch doctor would say to the mother, 'Two dogs were born to you,' and that was the end of the affair." As there was no way of feeding very young infants, the girls improvised a nursing bottle out of an old ink bottle. "Everything took months to come up from the coast," Mrs. Fisher explained.

"And, as they had to be carried all the way by porters, even the simplest things were prohibitively expensive. However, once I ordered two dolls for the little girls in my care. I know the money could have been spent on far more necessary things—medicines or food—but the children had never seen a toy before and I wanted to surprise them. The dolls made a great sensation. All the children in the village wanted to play with them so finally I had to have them queue up and each child was allowed to play with a doll for fifteen minutes. Then I discovered that the little boys were trying to disguise themselves as girls so they could play with the dolls too. I didn't mind that, but I was annoyed when the native men tried to steal the dolls. They thought they were powerful fetishes and wanted to keep them as idols."

"How did you and Mr. Fisher meet?" I asked.

"On a leopard hunt," said Mr. Fisher smiling.

"To tell the truth, there wasn't any great need to shoot that leopard," said Mr. Fisher smiling. "I'd seen Ruth and wanted to show her what a chap I was."

"Oh, but there was a need," said Mrs. Fisher earnestly. "That leopard was a menace to the whole community. The Padre was called to the village where my friend and I were living to kill the animal. The Padre went off with some warriors. When they got back after the hunt, I had to dress the wounds of the men who'd been mauled in the fight. Luckily, I'd had the forethought to take a course in first aid while I was in England but I'm afraid I was hardly prepared for such injuries as those men had. One man was in such awful condition that for some time I couldn't even find his face. Both cheeks were gone and his scalp had been torn off and was hanging down over his chin. I sewed the scalp back in place and did a very crude job of plastic surgery on his cheeks. There's a rather nice sequel to the story. Two years later, when I was desperately ill and had to be taken to the mission hospital at Mengo, this man reappeared and offered himself as one of the litter porters. Carrying a woman on a litter over jungle trails was such hard work that the other porters had to be changed every few miles, but this man would never relinquish his post and carried me the whole way."

A year after Ruth arrived, she and Mr. Fisher were married. Bishop Tucker officiated and King Kasagama gave the bride away. "It was a really lovely ceremony," said Mrs. Fisher smiling reminiscently. "We had a little church built by then and we were married there. It was decorated with palm leaves and the natives had laid a path of yellow grasses up the aisle. The king sold a tusk of ivory from his treasury so that he could buy clothes from the traders and he looked very handsome. He gave me away. The natives sang hymns and as we didn't have any church bells, they beat the royal drums instead. We were very happy."

King Kasagama was greatly interested in Christianity and wished to be baptized but there was one serious difficulty. The king, in accordance with his dignity as a native ruler, had four hundred wives. The Fishers explained to him that as a Christian he could only keep one wife. Kasagama had all his wives lined up and walked slowly back and forth making his choice. Finally he picked one girl. "A very fine girl too," said Mr. Fisher. "Handsome, intelligent and goodhearted." They were married in the church and the rest of his wives found themselves other husbands with little difficulty. "I was afraid that some of them might feel bitter about it, but actually they were quite pleased," Mrs. Fisher remarked. "After all, if you're only one of four hundred, you don't get to see your husband often." The royal couple were very happy together, but some months later, they came in great distress to see the Fishers. The girl queen had proven to be barren, and as a result there would be no heir to the throne.

"It was a real crisis," admitted Mr. Fisher. "The old men of the tribe were saying, 'Ah, if our king hadn't adopted this new religion, he could have plenty of other wives who would bear him "legitimate" sons.' Fortunately, I was able to give him a little helpful medical advice and then we all prayed together. A few weeks later, the queen came to us, radiant with happiness. She was going to have a baby."

Mrs. Fisher delivered the child. He was a boy and is now the present king of Toro.

The Fishers were sent next to Bunyoro, a kingdom in the northern part of Uganda. Bunyoro had been ruled over by Kabarega, a great warrior king who had ravished the other native kingdoms for years. His army had at last been defeated by the British troops and the king exiled. Bunyoro was still in an unsettled condition, without any ruler, and troubled by spasmodic uprisings. At first Mr. Fisher went on with two native converts, leaving Mrs. Fisher behind in Toro.

On the way, a native runner with a message in a cleft stick overtook him. The message was from the British authorities in Mengo. An officer who had been sent into the country had just been killed by the natives and Mr. Fisher was urged to return. "But I wasn't going to travel all the way back to Toro without even making an attempt to talk to the people," Mr. Fisher remarked. He and his two converts kept on. They walked into an ambush laid for them by the angry natives. But when the warriors saw that Fisher was unarmed and had no great caravan of porters and armed guards, they became so curious that instead of spearing this strange white man, they came out to talk with him. When they found Fisher could talk their language, they were even more astonished. At last, they led him into Hoima, the capital of the country, acting as a military guard of honor.

Compared to Bunyoro, Toro seemed like a paradise. Starving natives crawled out of their huts to beg the stranger for a mouthful of food and died while crawling. Young girls were wandering about, offering to sell themselves to anyone for a handful of grain. Fisher and his two helpers lived on roots they dug up. "A yam was a great luxury," Mr. Fisher recalls. It had been the habit of the Bunyoro king to mutilate any man who opposed him or violated any of the innumerable native laws. "I don't believe there was a man in the entire country who was not mutilated in some way or other," Mr. Fisher told me. The cultivated fields had been destroyed, the cattle killed, and the people alternated between sullen indifference and a tendency to murder each other on the chance that the victim might have a few mouthfuls of food concealed on his person.

For the first time, Mr. Fisher was forced to admit that he was beaten. With the country in such a condition, there was nothing he or any other man could do. Then his two native helpers came to him.

"Master, we've been talking things over and we feel it is best that you go," they told him. "We will stay. True, most of these people will be dead in the next few months, but there will be survivors. If we stay and work with them, those survivors will be Christians."

"I felt ashamed that I had allowed myself to become discouraged," Mr. Fisher confessed. "Of course, I determined to stay. With such faith as that, what else could a man do?"

Mr. Fisher sent an appeal to the Christian natives in Toro for help. The Toro people were close to starvation themselves, reduced to such a state because of the constant Bunyoro raids on their country. Also, the Bunyoro had carried off many of their wives and children to be sold to the Arab slavers. Under the circumstances, Mr. Fisher had little hope that his appeal would meet with any response. But King Kasagama rallied his people and a few weeks later caravans of Toro porters began to pour into the country carrying loads of food. King Kasagama sent word, "We are now Christians and must forgive our enemies."

The arrival of the food presented new problems. The porters were attacked by the starving people. Mr. Fisher had the loads of food stored in one of the native huts and he and his helpers began the distribution. A few minutes later, one of the helpers rushed out of the hut in a panic. "Master, the place is alive with rats and they're eating all the food." While one of the natives continued distributing the food, Fisher and the other man fought off the famished animals with clubs. This went on for days, the missionary and his helpers working in relays, snatching whatever sleep they could, until the situation gradually grew better.

The country was still in a state of disorder as the various local chiefs were fighting among themselves for the kingship. At last, a group of the tribal elders decided to stop the wars by placing the old king's infant son on the throne. They asked Mr. Fisher to crown the baby. This Mr. Fisher did and peace at last came to Bunyoro.

Mrs. Fisher joined her husband and the two missionaries had the pleasure and pride of watching the first Christian church built in Bunyoro. The church was built on the lines of a huge native hut. "The interior was a perfect forest of poles," Mr. Fisher recalls. The natives contributed the equivalent of £109 (about $500) for its construction. "That was the largest sum that had ever been raised in the history of Bunyoro," Mr. Fisher proudly recalls. The people brought in eggs, chickens, cowrie shells, goats, oxen, and even needles and buttons—the last two items being considered especially valuable as they were in great demand. Then the ceremonial drums, which could be heard for fifteen miles, were beaten and the congregation flocked in to hear Mr. Fisher conduct the opening service.

The Fishers had five children, all but one born in Uganda. "Arthur delivered all the children himself as we were so far from a doctor," Mrs. Fisher explained. "There were complications only once. We were on a mission trip and expected to be able to reach a village in plenty of time before the baby arrived. But we were delayed by floods and other complications. Then Arthur came down with a fever. I didn't expect him to live. I felt that I was indeed in 'the land of darkness and the shadow of death.' The baby came one evening while Arthur was delirious and couldn't help me. I had to do everything myself. Fortunately, Arthur came out of his delirium long enough to wash the baby—she was a little girl—and give me some assistance. But due to the strain of the journey and the poor food we had, I didn't have any milk. I was sure my baby would die. One of our native porters heard me crying. He came to the door of my tent and asked, 'Mistress, what's the matter?' 'I haven't any milk for my baby,' I told him. He thought for a few minutes, and then vanished without a word. Arthur had had another relapse and I felt terribly alone as there was no one to help me. The next morning, the native appeared with a gourd full of milk he had gotten from a native village miles away in the jungle. Every evening during the rest of the journey, he would vanish as soon as we made camp and come back again some time during the night with another gourd of milk he'd gotten—and remember this was after carrying his load all day and performing his other duties. My child lived and she's now married and has a family of her own."

I asked the Fishers if they had ever been attacked by hostile natives during their mission trips.

"Only once," said Mrs. Fisher. "It was on our last station. Arthur was sent to the upper Sudan to a tribe called the Gangs. Of course, I went with him and I had my little girl with me—that was the baby I just told you about. This tribe lived on one of the tributaries of the Nile. We weren't expecting any trouble. We'd really never had any. But as soon as our native paddlers put us ashore, they paddled away in a great hurry and we knew what that meant. Almost at once we heard a great shouting and scores of Gang warriors dashed down on us, brandishing their spears. They were painted in the most terrifying fashion and completely naked. Of all the tribes we'd seen, they were by far the most degenerate—excuse me," Mrs. Fisher instantly corrected herself. "That was a foolish word to use. I meant, of course, that they were the most primitive. I stood very quietly with my little girl—we shouldn't have taken her but there was no one I could leave her with—and Arthur climbed up on an anthill and spoke to them in one of the local dialects which they understood. 'Why do you come against us with spears and shields?' he asked. 'Do you think I wish to harm you? If I wished to harm you, would I come unarmed? Do you think that I covet your wives? I have a wife. Here she stands. Perhaps you think that I covet your children? I have a child. Here she is too. If you intend to kill us, listen first to what I have to tell you, for I bring tiding of great joy to you and to all men.' Then he began to tell them of Our Savior. How He had died to save all men, no matter what color their skins might be or whether they lived in the white man's country or in Uganda. The warriors leaned on their spears to listen. Then they took us to their village. We stayed there two years."

"Our old mission still stands in that country," said Mr. Fisher, smiling reminiscently. "I also introduced the cultivation of bananas into the district. Helped to tide the people over when the other crops failed. We grew very fond of the Gangs and I think they liked us."

"Many years later, Arthur and I attended a meeting in England where problems connected with Africa were being discussed," Mrs.

Fisher went on. "After the lecturer had finished, a native student at one of the famous British universities came up to speak to us. 'Don't you remember me?' he asked. I'm sorry to say we didn't. 'Why, I was one of those warriors who came out to kill you the day you landed,' he said. We did remember him then, we'd seen him several times afterward in the Gang village, and I said, 'I have a surprise for you.' My daughter was there, the same little girl who'd been with us but now she was a young lady. I called her over and introduced her. When our friend heard who she was, he cried, 'Why, you're not a foreigner! You were born in Uganda. You're our little girl!' and he called her by her native name. There were tears in his eyes and in ours too. It was a lovely reunion."

In 1914, Mr. Fisher enlisted in the First World War as an army chaplain. After the war, the Fishers remained in England, as the church authorities decided that his health did not permit him to return to Africa. It would be hard to say when Mr. Fisher officially retired, as he is still very active in church work—a little too active in Mrs. Fisher's opinion, for she thinks he should rest more than he does.

I said to the Fishers, "I've heard many people say that the missionaries did more harm than good and that the natives were better left to their own devices."

"Yes, we've heard that also," said Mrs. Fisher gently. "Yet I can't believe the people who say that ever knew the natives intimately in the early days."

"But aren't the natives still having a very hard time of it today?" I asked.

The Fishers looked slightly bewildered. "Of course they're having a hard time, a very hard time," said Mr. Fisher. "You can't change the whole civilization of a people within fifty years and not have trouble. As soon as you stop such things as the native wars, the famines and the plagues, there is naturally a tremendous increase in population and that in itself causes great problems. Then when you expect a native man, who has traditionally never had any duties except to fight other tribes, to work eight hours a day the man naturally grows resentful. When you send children to school, the parents lose the help those children gave them in the fields and they don't like it. When you curb the power of the native kings, you also destroy their people's respect for authority and that leads to trouble. But these things are unavoidable."

"But enormous strides have been made," protested Mrs. Fisher. "Before we left Uganda, the kings of Baganda, Toro, Bunyoro and Ankole—all hereditary enemies—met together in our church to pray. Think how proud we were!"

"Today, a native minister has my old position in Toro and there is a native bishop in the country," added Mr. Fisher. "Yet when I first started my 'sunagogi' I was assured by white administrators that the natives could never take any responsibility. What a victory for our beliefs!"

When I left, Mrs. Fisher said to me, "As you're interested in mission work, I hope you go to the offices of the Church Mission Society in London and talk to the people there. Arthur and I have been retired for many years now, but there are thousands of young people starting out today who are just like us."

"I certainly hope that's true, Mrs. Fisher," I said.

Daniel P. Mannix

v

Dr. Sir Albert Cook,
Pioneer Doctor

During the latter part of the Victorian era, a bitter war broke out between certain scientists and clergymen. For some time there had been friction between the two groups, and the announcement of Darwin's theory of evolution brought on the battle. So savage was the controversy and so firmly were the lines drawn between the two camps that many men of great good will sincerely felt that there could be no mutual understanding between the rival philosophies. Either you were a scientist—which implied that you were also an atheist—or you were a Christian. For a man to be both a scientist and a minister of God seemed an impossibility, a contradiction in terms.

One of the few men of the period who was able to see the folly of this attitude was Dr. Albert Cook. Dr. Cook was one of the first doctors to go to East Africa and by his knowledge and devotion save thousands of lives. In addition, he was an outstanding research scientist. Although part of his equipment consisted of retorts made from old wine bottles and a charcoal fire fanned by a native assistant for a Bunsen burner, he isolated the virus of relapsing fever and identified the wood tick as the carrier. He discovered the worm responsible for anemia among the natives and did outstanding work in the control of sleeping sickness. He was also a missionary and so intensely devoted that some of the tales about him may sound strange to us today.

I talked to an old-time settler in Kenya who told me the following story about Dr. Cook. "I found that I had to have an operation performed," he explained. "My friends urged me to return to England for it. I said, 'If anyone is going to operate on me, it's going to be Dr. Cook.' I went to his hospital at Mengo. It was built on the order of a native hut—a long, low building with a thatched roof and reed shutters in the windows, as there was no glass. It had only one room with the patients in a double line of native-made beds along the walls. The far end was curtained off with woven bark cloth. That was the operating room.

"Friday was operating day, although naturally the doctor would perform an emergency operation at any time. Dr. Cook started at dawn and kept working until it was too dark to see. Often, after an operation, a native orderly would come out of the operating section carrying an earthenware pot containing an appendix or an arm or whatever and throw it out the door. There was a tree just in front of the door and every Friday morning a big vulture would fly down and take up his stand in that tree. He came only on Fridays, never any other time. That vulture was the disposal system, and very good one. He never left anything.

"After I came out of the anesthetic I was lying on my bed and Dr. Cook sat down beside me. 'Are you saved, my friend?' he asked. I didn't quite know what he meant but I said, 'I certainly am and you saved me.' 'I didn't mean your corporal body,' said the doctor very seriously. 'I meant your immortal soul.' He asked me to pray with him, which I did. Then he went back to the operating room and a few minutes later was hard at work again while the vulture continued to sit on his tree limb, waiting patiently for his share."

Like Mr. Fisher, Dr. Cook came to Africa in answer to Bishop Tucker's appeal for missionaries to help the people of Uganda. The doctor arrived in Mombasa in the autumn of 1896 with fifteen other missionaries, of whom three were young girls. One of these girls, a Miss Katherine Timpson, later became Mrs. Cook and still later Lady Cook when the doctor received his knighthood. Much of the supplies that the party had so hopefully brought from England had to be left behind. Dr. Cook particularly mourned the loss of many of his medical books which were too bulky to be carried by porter to Uganda. The three girls also had to abandon many cherished articles. One of the items that the girls did take with them was a cobbler's set of tools needed to repair the old-fashioned solid type of shoes that proper young ladies wore at the time.

The caravan left Mombasa with two hundred porters and forty-six donkeys and started up the trail to Uganda. It was not known at that time that malaria was carried by mosquitoes and so no precautions were taken against the insects. Within a few days, virtually every member of the party was down with malaria. The three women had to be carried in litters. The men struggled along as best they could.

Dr. Cook was a methodical man and he has left one of the best and most detailed accounts of the problems confronting an African safari in those days. As the porters were able to carry only a small amount of food and water in addition to their loads, the route had to be carefully planned so that every night brought the party to a waterhole or source of food. Ten miles a day was a good average march for the heavily loaded men. If the waterholes in that area happened to be dried up, the party had to push on. But the weakened porters could now only do an average of three miles a day, so reaching the next waterhole took not one day but three. As the men could not well go three days without water, they began to sicken. Every man who took sick required four other men to carry him in a litter and these men also had to carry their loads as well. This additional burden caused the litter porters to collapse and further slowed up the march. It was not surprising that the early caravans were constantly troubled by having porters desert or mutiny.

Trouble with the porters reached a climax near Lake Nakuru, about a hundred miles from Uganda. A native had come into camp and asked Dr. Cook to administer to a local chief who was seriously ill. As the natives had little idea of distance, Dr. Cook couldn't tell whether the sick man was ten miles away or a hundred, but he left the caravan and set out with the native. The chief's village was thirty miles away and by the time the doctor arrived, the chief had died. The doctor had meant to rest a few days in the village, but scarcely had he arrived when a native runner from the caravan rushed in to say that the porters had mutinied and were threatening to kill the Europeans. Dr. Cook hurried back, making the whole journey of sixty miles in less than forty-eight hours, a remarkable feat for an inexperienced white man in African jungles, and was able to quiet the porters and persuade them to go on to Uganda.

The party arrived in Mengo, Mwanga's capital, in February of 1897. Mr. Fisher was not there, having already left for Toro but Dr. Cook met the other missionaries and was heartily welcomed by them.

But a difficulty arose at once which seems incredible to us nowadays. The leader of the missionaries was a hard old man who had headed scores of caravans across some of the wildest parts of Africa and was equally handy with both his Bible and his gun. This sincere but narrow-minded man grimly opposed the idea of a missionary-doctor. "Our work is to save these people's souls, not heal their bodies," the argument ran. "If Cook does his work as a missionary, he won't have any time left to be a doctor."

Incredible as it may seem, the conflict between science and religion had grown so bitter that the other missionaries sided with their leader. To Dr. Cook's great disappointment, he was virtually forbidden to practice.

Now occurred an event which, if it had not been of such a terrible nature, might almost be considered a divine visitation to show these heroic, misguided men their error. King Mwanga had been growing increasingly restless as the missionaries continued to gain adherents to their new faith. The climax came when a group of native chiefs, who had embraced Christianity, decided to outlaw slavery in their territories. Mwanga depended on the Arab slavers for guns and money and this decision was a serious blow to him. The missionaries had done their work so well that Mwanga did not dare order his people to rise against these men, as he had been able to do ten years before. So one night the king picked a hole in the wall of his royal hut and fled, climbing over the series of stockades that surrounded his palace as he was afraid to trust even his own guards.

He fled by canoe and formed an alliance with his old enemy, Kaba-rega, the warrior king of Bunyoro. Together, these two men at the head of an army marched south and attacked the capital at Mengo.

In the fighting that followed, there could be no question of for-bidding Dr. Cook to administer to the wounded. In a single morn-ing, the doctor once treated 150 men suffering from bullet, arrow and spear wounds. The uprising was put down by Emin Pasha's Sudanese troops who were still in the country and were hurriedly hired as mercenaries by the British. By the time the war was over, Dr. Cook's position as a medical man as well as a missionary was firmly established.

In the spring of 1897, Dr. Cook put up a dispensary with the help of the native converts. The building had mud walls and a floor made of hard-packed cow dung. The doctor had discovered that cow dung acts as a deterrent to chiggers and so was far superior to earth. He used his packing cases for medicine cabinets. A fireplace was constructed in the middle of the room and the natives wove reeds together to form the ceiling, as the usual thatched roofs were apt to harbor insects and snakes. The dispensary was finished one morning and Dr. Cook started operating that afternoon, so great was the demand for medical attention.

The dispensary was a magnificent training ground for a young doctor, as virtually every ailment to which the flesh is heir turned up during the course of a day. In addition to the injuries received in battle, the doctor also sewed up wounds caused by lions and leopards, treated patients for snake bite, elephantiasis, venereal dis-eases, malaria, blackwater fever, and even for curses laid on them by the local witch doctors. Like most people of his time, Dr. Cook was at first inclined to ridicule the power of these strange men but when he had a patient actually die of a curse in spite of everything the doctor could do to save him, he was impressed. At that time, little was known of the powers of suggestion but Dr. Cook con-cluded that the men had died of "paralysis of the brain"—a fairly accurate diagnosis.

Dr. Cook kept a diary of his work in Mengo. A typical day reads: "A busy morning as usual. 80 patients and constant distractions.

In the afternoon, saw 50 patients and performed five operations."
Miss Timpson acted as his anesthetist in this work. The crucial
problem was the supply of drugs. Everything had to be carried up
from the coast by porter and this made even the simplest medicines
almost prohibitively expensive. "Oh, if there were only a railroad!"
the doctor moaned time after time. Epsom salts were worth only
a few pennies a pound in England, but the salts were so bulky that
it cost several shillings to transport them to Uganda and finally the
doctor had to rely on other more concentrated drugs. Even getting
kerosene for the lamp in the operating room was a major problem.
The native porters soon discovered that by driving nails in a packing box containing tins of kerosene they could substantially lighten
their load, so the tins had to be packed in layers of soap. In his
efforts to economize, the doctor had no mosquito nets in his ward.
Naturally, malaria was rampant and the doctor was horrified when
he finally received a medical bulletin from England explaining how
the disease was carried.

Mwanga, who had returned to his throne after his defeat by the
Sudanese troops, still regarded the missionaries with hatred and
suspicion. One of Dr. Cook's outstanding triumphs was to cure the
king's little son of infantile diarrhea. The child was so weak that
he had to be artificially fed and this meant keeping him in the dispensary. However, there was an unbreakable rule in the royal court
that the king's son could not be taken outside of the imperial
enclosure, a specially woven type of reed fence which had a religious significance. This problem was finally solved by having a
duplicate fence woven and set up in the dispensary around the
child. The baby lived and Mwanga was deeply impressed. He later
became converted to Christianity, possibly as a result of Cook's
having saved his son, although it must be admitted that Mwanga was
never a particularly devout Christian.

To a European, the natives often seemed to combine an amazing
intelligence and insight with an incredible stupidity and callous-
ness. One of the chiefs became converted to Christianity through
Dr. Cook and ceremoniously burnt his collection of fetishes and
jujus in the village market place. A number of his subjects started

to follow the chief's example but the old man stopped them, saying, "You are only doing this to please me. Wait until you sincerely believe in this new religion before you destroy the old." Dr. Cook, who had been watching approvingly the burning of the idols, realized that the chief was wiser than he. Yet a short time later, the chief asked Dr. Cook if he could watch him perform an operation. Cook said that he could if there was anyone in the village that needed his help. "Oh, I'll find someone," said the chief and gave an order. Happening to glance out the door of the chief's hut a short time later, Cook saw a terrified man running for his life pursued by the chief's guards. "What's that man done?" the doctor asked. "Nothing. He's the one I've selected for you to operate on," said the chief carelessly. Dr. Cook postponed the operation until another day, to the chief's intense disappointment.

In their own way, the natives were often extremely logical but their minds worked along channels bewildering to a foreigner. Dr. Cook found it was impossible to give a native a number of pills and tell him to take one every day. The native would immediately swallow the whole handful, reasoning that this would speed up the cure. A native could easily understand taking medicine for a stomach complaint but he could not understand taking medicine to help an outbreak of boils, even though the doctor carefully explained that the boils were due to an infection. The man, in spite of all instructions, would rub the pills given him on the boils. A man who had been one of the doctor's assistants told me that once he saw a native come out of the dispensary and angrily throw away the precious pills that the doctor had given him—pills that had been laboriously brought up from the coast at the cost of so much pain and trouble. When the assistant remonstrated with the man, the native retorted angrily, "That doctor is a fool. I kept telling him I had a headache and he kept giving me pills for my stomach. I couldn't make him understand that the pain was in my head, not my belly."

A more serious question was the problem of outpatients. At first, the doctor answered every call but he soon found that he was being asked to take a two- or three-day journey through almost impenetrable jungles for the most minor reasons. Yet it was impossible to tell how serious the call might be. A man came in to the doctor, saying his baby daughter had a bad place on her cheek. From the way he spoke, the doctor decided the child had a teething rash. He gave the man medicine and the man departed well satisfied. A short time afterward, Dr. Cook happened to pass through the man's village and saw the child. Half her face was gone. "Oh, yes," said the father. "A hyena got into our hut and bit her cheek off. That's why I went to see you. I told you she had a bad cheek." After such an experience as this, Dr. Cook would answer all calls no matter how far they took him into the unexplored wilds of the country, until he dropped from exhaustion. Finally, at Miss Timpson's suggestion, the doctor decided to charge outpatients ten cowrie shells a visit. Those who couldn't pay were required to do four hours' work at the dispensary. This helped to curb the number of calls.

In talking to the people who knew and loved the doctor, one is apt to get the impression of an almost saintly figure who wandered about the jungle patting picanninies on the head and healing the sick. Dr. Cook was a noble man of great ability but he was also a determined man who permitted no opposition when he knew he was in the right. Once while he was in a canoe on Lake Victoria, another canoe ahead of him was overturned by an enraged hippopotamus. The doctor's paddlers refused to go close enough to help the drowning men. Without a second thought, the doctor grabbed up his kiboko, the rhino hide whip whose use Tippu Tib understood so well, and laid it on. The paddlers were so terrified of the hippo that it was not until the doctor had made the "most liberal use" of this terrible whip that he could bring his canoe close enough for a rescue.

Ever since he first arrived in Uganda, Dr. Cook had wondered what he would do in case of a serious epidemic. Now this disaster occurred. Smallpox broke out among the Kikuyu tribe in central Kenya and, leaping from tribe to tribe, reached Uganda. For a terrible moment it seemed that Dr. Cook might stand by helplessly while the natives died by the dozen.

Then the doctor suddenly remembered that when he was embarking in England his brother, who was also a doctor, had come to the dock to say good-by. As his brother was leaving the ship, he had thrust his hand into his pocket and pulled out two small vials. "Take this. It is a new vaccine that has just been developed for smallpox," his brother had said. "If you get the chance, try it and see how effective it is." Dr. Cook still had the two tiny vials among his medical supplies. He got them out and he and Miss Timpson started inoculating natives. The vaccine was quickly exhausted but the two missionaries made each native promise to come back in a week so they could tell if the inoculation had "taken."

None of the natives bothered to return, and the plague continued to rage unchecked. Then one afternoon while Dr. Cook and Miss Timpson were busy in the dispensary, Miss Timpson happened to glance out the door. She gave a strangled gasp and dropping the tray of instruments she was holding, rushed out. Thinking the girl had at last cracked under the strain, Dr. Cook followed her. Miss Timpson had seen a group of native children run past and one of them was a boy she had inoculated several weeks before. When the boy saw the white woman chasing him, he started to run but Miss Timpson, who did not lack determination any more than the doctor, made a flying tackle and brought him down. She dragged him back to the dispensary and the doctor examined his arm. The vaccination had taken and a blood test showed that the boy had developed an immunity.

To the desperate missionaries, this boy was a gold mine—a source of lymph that could save at least a dozen other people. Using arm-to-arm vaccination, they inoculated a number of other natives and this time kept careful track of them. These natives, in turn, were used to inoculate still others and at last the epidemic was checked. "It was surely God who inspired my brother to give me those two tubes of vaccine," said Dr. Cook later. "Of all the medical supplies we took to Uganda, those little tubes were by far the most valuable."

The little band of missionaries began to feel that the worst was over. Mwanga had given them his grudging friendship. Most of the influential native chiefs were wholeheartedly co-operating. The Sudanese were preserving order and the Arab slavers had at last realized their day was over. There was even talk of building a railroad from Mombasa to Lake Victoria.

In the autumn of 1897, the Sudanese troops suddenly mutinied. They shot their white officers and marched on Mengo, looting and burning the native villages as they came. Kabarega, the warlike ruler of Bunyoro, promptly invaded the country from the north, joining forces with the mutineers. The fickle King Mwanga went over to the invading forces and again fled his capital. Thousands of his subjects joined their king and swore to drive the white men and women out of their country.

The British had virtually no way of quelling the revolt. A small expeditionary force was started up from Mombasa but it would take months to arrive. When word came that the mutineers and the native forces were only a short distance from Mengo, the missionaries knew that all was lost. "I can hardly believe," Dr. Cook wrote in his diary, "that in a few hours our church, the hospital, and our homes will be reduced to a pile of charred logs." Typically, the doctor never considered his own danger. Even more typically, he spends several pages carefully explaining that the Sudanese who were on their way to destroy all his work and very likely kill him had their side of the question. They were miserably underpaid, they had been constantly jerked from one part of the country to another to suppress native wars, and placed under white officers who knew nothing about their needs and prejudices. Dr. Cook also had an amazing understanding of the natives who had accepted his help and yet were now on their way to cut his throat. Because a "lack of gratitude" is the principal complaint brought against native peoples by white administrators, I think something should be said about this extremely disillusioning native characteristic.

In the first place, there is no avoiding the fact that the missionaries, in spite of the great good they did, were interlopers who interfered with native beliefs and customs. In protesting against the constant native wars and the slave raids, the missionaries set themselves in opposition to the local kings, and not only the kings but the people themselves resented this defiance of authority. The missionaries did everything in their power to avoid this issue. In fact, as slavery was the law of the land, they even went so far as to require that their converts return fugitive slaves to the Arab slavers. However, they were opposed to slavery and their influence made itself felt. The natives were loyal subjects and when the king ordered a war against the foreigners, most natives felt their duty lay with their ruler rather than with the missionaries.

In the second place, the natives had only a vague idea of what Dr. Cook was doing when he treated them. One old native was brought in to the clinic with a badly infected leg rotten with gangrene. The doctor had no choice but to amputate. Although the reason was carefully explained to the old man, the native never forgave Dr. Cook. Whenever he met him after that, he would stop and scream, "It was you who cut off my leg!" The natives had never heard of the use of anesthetics, so when the doctor anesthetized patients before an operation, the rumor went around that he had murdered them. Then when the patients appeared, alive and well, another rumor was spread that he could raise the dead. Many of the natives were furious when the doctor unkindly refused to bring their own dead back to life after they'd gone to the trouble of carrying the corpses to the clinic. Another legend sprang up when the natives found that the doctor was cutting people open on his operating table and taking out part of their insides. To the natives, there was only one possible explanation—the doctor was obviously a cannibal selecting the daintiest parts of his patients for food. These rumors would spread by bush telegraph throughout the country and they were extremely difficult to confute.

There was still another factor, extremely hard to explain, and yet of fundamental importance. Our ethical concepts have been so carefully incorporated into our culture that we think of them as being inherent human virtues. This is not so. We are trained to consider lying wrong, but to many African tribes lying is a praiseworthy device, extremely useful in deceiving one's enemies. This difference in ethics is not always in favor of the white man. The Kavirondo, a tribe who live on the east shores of Lake Victoria and refuse to wear any sort of clothing whatsoever, traditionally had a far higher code of sexual behavior than the average European.

Adultery was unknown among them. A young Masai boy was given a spear at twelve years and told to defend the tribe's herds with his life. If a lion attacked the cattle, these children died spear in hand. It probably never even occurred to them to run away. But the native is not inherently a liar, or inherently virtuous, or inherently brave. These characteristics are the result of tribal education.

Among most of the tribes, the virtue that we call "gratitude" was almost unknown—just as cowardice was almost unknown among the Masai. As it was against all custom and tradition for one community ever to help another, there was no way for this virtue to be developed. Colonel Grogan tells of finding a native almost dead from starvation and disease. Grogan fed the man and cured him. The native did not give Grogan a word of thanks (as a matter of fact, there wasn't such a word in his language) but as soon as he had recovered, he stole everything he could find in Grogan's tent and ran off. To the native, this was perfectly proper behavior. He had never heard of anyone helping a stranger. If this white man chose to do it, that was a curious phenomenon—just as it was a curious fact that this man had white skin, wore clothes and carried a stick that made a loud noise and killed game. But it never occurred to the native that Grogan's actions should awaken any particular response in him.

This is not to say that a native was incapable of feeling gratitude. The native who carried Mrs. Fisher for miles on a litter because she had cured his leopard wounds proves that. But a man who could so radically depart from his tribal training was comparatively rare. And when the natives did attempt to show gratitude, they often did it in curious ways. While Dr. Cook was making one of his routine trips to the outlying villages, he came to a community where everyone was suffering from some mysterious ailment. The overworked doctor spent hours trying to find out what was wrong with them. Finally he lost his temper. "I don't believe these people are really sick at all," he snapped to the chief. The chief put his hand on the doctor's shoulder. "We appreciate all the time and trouble you spend trying to help us," he said simply. "When I heard that you were coming, I told my people, 'The least we can do for the doctor is to be sick when he gets here.'" Because they lived so closely with the natives, the early missionaries such as Dr. Cook and the Fishers understood them to an extent very few white administrators ever equaled. As a result, the missionaries refused to condemn the natives for many deeds which others regarded as the actions of a completely degenerate race.

By no means all of the natives deserted the missionaries, but Dr. Cook's diary shows how perilous the situation was.

July 9th. More and more natives are deserting. A group sent to help us have been killed from ambush.

July 10th. Nearly all the native police have deserted. They took their guns and went to join Mwanga.

July 13th. The faithful chiefs began to arrive today. We could hear the sound of their war drums a long distance off. Each chief has his own special beat to identify him. However, many think these chiefs will also go over to the enemy.

July 17th. The next station, Nakanyonyi, has just declared for Mwanga. All business has stopped. I am in the hospital, still operating.

But all was not lost. Word was received that the relief expedition under Major Macdonald coming up from the coast had reached the borders of Uganda. The little outpost waited breathlessly to welcome the troops. A few days later, a single runner staggered into Mengo with a message in a cleft stick. It was from Major Macdonald and addressed "to any white man." The message said that the relief expedition had been trapped in a swamp. The men were running short of ammunition and must retreat. Almost at the same time, another message arrived that Mwanga was marching on the town with a thousand warriors, armed with spears and muskets.

The missionaries held a conference. There was a chance that the women could escape across Lake Victoria in canoes. Miss Timpson, speaking for all the women, said, "We will not leave unless matters grow more serious than they are at present."

Dr. Cook and Pilkington, the brilliant young Oxford athlete who had translated the Bible into Baganda, went with a relief force of fifteen hundred native spearmen to Major Macdonald's help. Major Macdonald moved on to Mengo and later defeated Mwanga and his ally, Kabarega, after a long period of guerrilla warfare. In the fighting, Pilkington was killed.

After the war, Uganda and Kenya, the highroad to Uganda, were established beyond all doubt as British territory. There can be little question that the missionaries in all innocence were largely responsible for this annexation. Although Bishop Tucker had been perfectly sincere when he told Sir Gerald Portal that the missionaries asked for no support, the fact remained that the British public refused to see the work of such men as Fisher and Cook wiped out at the whim of a native ruler who desired to restore the slave trade.

That there was another side to the question we will see in the chapter on Kabarega, and also there can be no doubt that the British government was strongly influenced by the presence of the Germans who were attempting to establish themselves in the country. But the driving force behind the British conquest was not imperialistic ambition. It was the political pressure brought on the government by the Anti-Slavery Society, a group of deeply sincere men and women, who had urged that missionaries be sent out to help the people and later considered it their duty to support the missionaries with troops. From now on, there could be no turning back. The Union Jack had been hoisted and Great Britain had been committed. Even so, the British government took for granted that within a few years the country would be "civilized" and the troops could be withdrawn, leaving behind them a prosperous, peaceful area which would also be a fruitful source of trade.

In 1900, a time of relative peace, Dr. Cook and Miss Timpson were married. There was a moment of terrible uncertainty when the bride's wedding gown did not arrive and the capable Miss Timpson was reduced to tears at the thought of having to be married in her old clothes. Fortunately, the dress arrived the morning of the wedding and everything turned out perfectly. The wedding breakfast was slightly marred because an irritable hippo wandered up from the lake during the meal and chased a native, but such events as this were so common that the guests hardly commented on the unexpected visitor.

In the next few years, Dr. Cook made his two most significant contributions to science. Shortly after his marriage, the doctor wrote a paper on the treatment of malaria which was published in a London medical journal. Later, he received a subsequent copy of the journal with a sarcastic letter written by a research scientist, pointing out that this "missionary who calls himself a doctor" had illustrated his article by sketches of a flagellate parasite that wasn't a malaria parasite at all. Cook had been working under the most primitive conditions with a small, low-power microscope and his critic had obviously not allowed for this fact. Cook, instead of losing his temper, calmly went over his experiments and found that his unknown critic was quite right. But if the flagellates were not malaria, what were they? After a series of elaborate experiments, the doctor was at last able to identify them as a bacteria responsible for relapsing fever and later found that the fever was transmitted by ticks. This discovery established Cook as a prominent research scientist.

Dr. Cook's second important contribution to medical science was the discovery that anemia among the natives was caused by the presence of a parasitic worm. The doctor had suspected this for some time but had been unable to prove his theory because the natives had a superstitious fear of having a post mortem performed on one of their dead. Dr. Cook scrupulously observed the tribal taboos and so, although he knew that the positive identification of the cause of anemia would save thousands of lives, he refrained from performing an autopsy on anyone who died of the disease.

Then one day four native litter bearers dropped a dead woman by the door of the clinic and went away without apparently showing any more interest in the matter. Dr. Cook saw that the woman had died of anemia. Apparently she had no one who was interested in her. Here was the opportunity he had been awaiting. With his wife's help, he performed the autopsy and proved beyond doubt that the woman was suffering from nematode worms, picked up like hookworm through the soles of the feet. He had just completed his work, when the woman's family appeared. They had sent her on by litter while they followed more leisurely. She had died on the way, but they knew nothing of that. There was a terrible scene,

and the family left amid a storm of curses. But Dr. Cook had at
least found the source of the anemia. This second discovery was
even more important than the first.

The doctor had a hospital built, "the finest building in the Protectorate," he wrote proudly. The hospital was 120 feet long by
40 feet wide, with a fine, reed ceiling. Vines were looped back and
forth across the framework of the rough-hewn beds to provide a
springy rest for the mattresses, made of layers of banana leaves.
These beds were so comfortable that they became famous throughout the Protectorate and people traveled for miles to see them.

One night during a violent thunderstorm, Dr. Cook saw a red
glow of light between the reed shutters of his bedroom window.
As he leaped out of bed, he heard the native drums beating the
alarm signal. Rushing out, the doctor saw his beloved hospital
in flames. The thatched roof had been struck by lightning. He
and Mrs. Cook ran to the burning building. Native interns were
already carrying out the sick. When Dr. Cook tried to enter the
hospital, one of the men stopped him. "Doctor, there's 120 tons of
burning thatch ready to fall at any moment," shouted the intern.
"We've gotten the patients out." "There're still my instruments,"
cried the doctor, "the only ones in Uganda." He and Mrs. Cook
rushed into the building which was by now blazing like an ignited
hayrick. The native interns followed them. They saved what they
could and then managed to escape as the roof came down.

Most of the instruments were lost as well as all the blankets and
the medical supplies. Dr. Cook had managed to save his precious
microscope but later found that in the excitement the lens had
been left behind. Many of the local natives had gallantly risked
their lives to help. Unfortunately, it turned out that they had concentrated on carrying out the famous beds which seemed to them
the most valuable articles in the building.

Dr. Cook had spent three years of hard work raising the funds
and getting native support to build that hospital. Now it was gone.
For a time, the doctor doubted if he could ever face the task of
having it rebuilt. But the native community rallied to his support.
The chiefs for miles around came with their followers to help in

the work, Christians, pagans and Mohammedans alike. When Dr. Cook thanked them, one chief said simply, "In helping you, we are helping ourselves, Doctor."

By now the railroad had at long last been put through and the new building was built of brick with a fireproof corrugated-iron roof. It was the forerunner of the modern Mengo Hospital, one of the finest institutions of its kind in Central Africa today.

Compared to the excitement of the early days, life in Uganda after 1900 was almost peaceful. However, some reference should be made to the terrible sleeping sickness epidemic that attacked the country in 1901. Within the next few months, the population dropped from 56,000 to 13,000. As the natives could not count, Dr. Cook asked each chief to send in a twig for every person who died in his village. When the chiefs' messengers came with the twigs, Dr. Cook at first thought they were carrying loads of kindling. Dr. Cook sent a desperate appeal to England for help and was sent a new type of drug, just discovered, for treating the disease. Dr. Cook inoculated forty-five natives the evening that the drug arrived and then stopped his work until the next morning. At daylight, he found that all forty-five had died during the night. The new drug had not been properly tested before being sent out and was actually a fatal poison. I mention this because many people have a vague idea that "science" is somehow omnipotent and never makes mistakes. This error on the part of a few experts in London nearly caused another uprising against the whites and undid much of Dr. Cook's great work.

However, science did save the day. A research commission was sent out from England to study the disease, bringing complete equipment on the new railroad. At that time, almost nothing was known about sleeping sickness, not even how it was spread. Sir Aldo Castellani of the commission was able to isolate and identify the flagellates that caused the disease and later, Sir David Bruce was able to prove that the sickness was being carried by the tsetse fly.

The disease struck its heaviest blows on some of the islands in Lake Victoria. A young woman convert, trained as a nurse, went to one of the stricken islands to help the people, although Dr. Cook warned her that she was unquestionably going to her death. Later, Dr. Cook visited the island and found the heroic woman dying of the fatal disease. He offered to take her to the mainland, but the woman said, "If God calls me, I'm ready to go to Him. If He wants to leave me here awhile to go on with my work, I'm content to do that too." A few hours later she was dead.

Dr. and Mrs. Cook stayed on in Uganda and saw the country gradually change from savagery to one of the most prosperous and advanced districts in Africa. In 1932, the doctor was given a knighthood for his work. He and Lady Cook regarded Uganda as their home and left the country only for occasional visits to friends in England. They attended the coronation of George VI and an old friend of the Cooks told me an anecdote about this occasion. "They had been assigned to rather inferior seats, and Lady Cook insisted that they be given better," he said, smiling. "She was an old lady at the time, but she had no hesitation in expressing her views. Lady Cook actually cared very little about where they sat, but whenever she considered that any slight was being cast on her beloved husband, she certainly spoke out. Needless to say, they got the better seats."

Lady Cook died in 1938 and the doctor twelve years later. They were buried together by the Namirembe Cathedral in Uganda. The funeral service was conducted entirely in Luganda, the language of the country. All the leading native rulers attended.

While collecting material for this chapter, I asked an old-time settler in Uganda if he could tell me anything about the Cooks. The old man thought for a moment and then said, "I've known a great many outstanding people in this country. Some of them did great work, perhaps as valuable in its own way as the work done by Dr. Cook. But in one thing the Cooks were unique. They were the only people I ever met who never had a single enemy."

VI

Kabarega, the Warrior King of Bunyoro

The most difficult task that a writer can undertake is to give an intelligent description of a personality whose emotions and mental processes are completely alien to him. The writer is apt to reason, "If I were in this character's position, how would I think and behave?" This is particularly true of men who write about wild animals and attribute to the animals thoughts and emotions that an animal simply does not possess. It is equally true of authors who write about wild people. A savage does not think along the same lines as a civilized man. In some instances he may seem extremely shrewd and in other situations he may give the impression of incredible stupidity. But in few cases does he go through the same mental processes as his civilized brother. It is this fact that makes a man like Kabarega such a mystery.

East Africa produced very few great native leaders. Even the handful whose names have come down to us seemed to have been men markedly inferior to, say, the great Indian leaders in the United States. Kabarega was an exception. Perhaps the most fitting tribute paid to him was the comment of Sir Frederick Jackson, the British administrator in Uganda, who directed the war against Kabarega for several years. Sir Frederick wrote, "Kabarega never sued for peace, even when hard pressed. He never grovelled to us when he was captured. In fact, he always kept his end up (in spite of his treacheries and cruelties) and was at least a man."

Kabarega's father was Kamurasi, who ruled Bunyoro, the northernmost kingdom of Uganda, during the middle of the nineteenth century. The kingdom of Bunyoro, like most native kingdoms, was composed of a number of isolated villages, each under its own chief who was more or less independent of the king. When Kamurasi became king, a number of these chiefs revolted against him. Kamurasi put down this revolt with great brutality. Attached to the king were the Bugungu, a clan of hereditary torturers, and these highly expert professionals made such a terrible example of the rebellious chiefs that afterward no one dared to question the king's authority. Kamurasi even had his blood brother murdered, an almost unthinkable crime in native eyes.

Kamurasi then went on a campaign of conquest and subdued most of the northern half of what is now modern Uganda. Afterward he settled down to reign as one of the most powerful monarchs in Central Africa.

Kamurasi was at the height of his power when word was brought him that two strangers with a large safari and many armed natives had appeared in the northern part of his dominions. These strangers were unlike anyone ever seen before and were unquestionably potent magicians. Their skins were white and at night they carried stars in their hands to light their way. Three times a day, one of their priests prepared magic brews in pots. One of these strangers the natives called "The Beard." The other, who was younger and clean-shaven, they called "The Little Star." It was thought that The Little Star was probably The Beard's younger brother.

Kamurasi was disturbed at this news. There was a legend among his people that at one time a tribe called the Bacwezi had lived in the country who were also light-skinned and were demigods. The Bacwezi had become so disgusted by the wickedness of the people that they had sailed away into boundless Lake Victoria, with the promise that some day they would return and rule Uganda. These strangers might well be the Bacwezi.

When the strangers arrived, Kamurasi received them in his hut with all ceremony. He had leopard skins strewn on the floor and gave each of his guests a carved stool to sit on. The Beard explained that he was Sir Samuel Baker, an English explorer, and The Little Star was his wife. They had come in search of a great lake, thought to be the source of the Nile. He wanted the king to provide him with porters so he could pass through Bunyoro in his search for the lake.

Kamurasi assured Sir Samuel that he would do everything to help him, but as soon as the couple had left, the king and his councilors had an anxious conference. Obviously, the stranger was lying. Why should a man come so far only to look at a lake? Why should he bring his wife with him, unless he was planning to seize the country and needed her to raise a dynasty? What was this talk of porters? No one in Bunyoro had ever heard of porters. But they did understand demanding a levy of young warriors to be used as troops. This stranger was clearly intending to conquer Bunyoro.

However, Kamurasi naturally did not tell any of his suspicions to the stranger. That would have been foolish. Instead, he was most cordial to him, but gave secret orders that no food or porters were to be supplied. The councilors spent a tremendous amount of effort thinking up new, ingenious excuses whenever the white man wanted to know what was causing the delay. Finally, Sir Samuel lost his temper. Marching into the king's hut, he told Kamurasi, "You must learn that a white man's word is law. If you disobey me, even if you are a king, you must die." As he finished speaking, Sir Samuel angrily knocked out the ashes of his pipe and the ashes fell on Kabarega, the king's little son, who was playing at the foot of the throne.

Instantly every native was on his feet snatching for his weapons, for to throw ashes on anyone was the deadliest possible insult. The astonished Sir Samuel drew his pistol and shouted to his armed troopers. Under cover of their rifles, he managed to withdraw, followed by the furious natives, brandishing their spears and giving their war cries.

Little Kabarega never forgot this incident; indeed, he couldn't very well forget it as he was brought up believing that the white man had cursed him. He swore to avenge himself on the whites.

Kamurasi now decided that Sir Samuel was far too dangerous a person to have in the country. To get rid of the white man, the king supplied him with the porters and food. Sir Samuel departed toward Lake Victoria where the Baganda tribe lived. Sir Samuel thought he had scored a great victory over the Bunyoro but if he could have looked into the future, he would have been more careful where he threw his pipe ashes.

Some ten years later, Kamurasi died. In accordance with native custom, the body was smoked to preserve it. Then a pit was dug and the king's wives forced to sit in the bottom in two lines facing each other. The royal corpse was laid across the women's knees. This was done during the night. When morning dawned, the royal guards seized as many people as possible as they came out of their huts, broke their arms and legs, and threw them into the pit to serve the king in the next world. Then cowhides were stretched across the pit and pegged down. The cowhides were covered with earth, which was stamped hard, and a grass hut erected over the spot. Some of the old palace servants were put in the hut to guard it. They were never permitted to go outside.

As invariably happened after the death of a king, there was a war to determine his successor. Kabarega's brothers had the dead king's jawbone, the symbol of royalty, and most of the tribal chiefs supported them. Kabarega consulted a famous witch doctor to see what his chances were. The witch doctor sacrificed a chicken and after studying the bird's intestines said, "You will become king and be even greater than your father, but there is a spot on the bird's liver and that means you will receive a serious mutilation."

Kabarega cared nothing about a mutilation if he could become king. He gathered together his supporters and marched against his brothers. Every village that opposed him, he sacked and burnt. His brothers also mustered their forces and went out to meet him. In the battle that followed, Kabarega was victorious. His brothers, fleeing through a swamp, flung away the sacred jawbone. Without this jawbone, Kabarega could not be crowned king. However, he managed to capture one of his brothers' councilors who had seen the jawbone thrown away. Under torture, this man told where it was. With the jawbone in his possession, Kabarega was crowned king of Bunyoro.

Kabarega built his capital on the site of modern Hoima. To protect himself, he created a bodyguard called the Bonosoora, composed of escaped slaves. He was confident that this guard would defend him to the death, for if he fell, they would be returned to the tender mercies of their former owners.

Shortly after he came to power, Kabarega's mother appeared before the young king's palace to congratulate her son. Kabarega was shocked and infuriated that she was still alive. "If you were a decent woman, you'd have been buried alive like my father's other wives," he told her. However, there wasn't much he could do about it then, especially as the old queen had a substantial army of her own. The queen left, weeping, and later a tree sprang up where she had stood. Kabarega regarded this as a very ominous sign. Every day he had a man sacrificed at the foot of the tree and built a small, grass temple near the spot.

Kabarega soon had need of his Bonosoora guards. His brothers had fled to King Mwanga, who lived on the shore of Lake Victoria, and enlisted his support. In return for the promise of some of the Bunyoro provinces, Mwanga declared war against Kabarega and sent his army north under the command of his best general. Although he was hopelessly outnumbered, Kabarega went out to meet the attacking force.

The two armies met at the Kafue River. Kabarega led the attack with his bodyguard. In a few minutes, he found himself cut off with only his uncle and one other man. They had two spears and a musket among them, but they stood back to back and held off Mwanga's forces. This desperate resistance could not last long. Kabarega had clubbed his empty musket and Mwanga's men were closing in to wipe out the little group, when suddenly there came the roll of Bunyoro war drums beating the charge and the army of the old queen fell on the enemy's right flank. At the last moment, she had decided to come to the help of her savage son.

Even so, the battle still hung in the balance. Kabarega fought his way to where Mwanga's general stood directing his troops and cut the man down. Then he lifted the dead general's body on a spear so Mwanga's army could see that their leader was dead. The invaders broke and fled, pursued by the victorious Bunyoro forces. Kabarega returned to Hoima in triumph and gave his mother a formal pardon for not having been buried with his father.

He ruled with a heavy hand. Mr. and Mrs. Fisher, coming into the country some years later, said that there was not a single man who did not show the marks of either the knife or the branding iron. One of the native kings, when asked by the Fishers why he mutilated innocent men, answered in surprise, "If I didn't mutilate the innocent, how could I make the guilty fear me?" Kabarega apparently operated on this same principle. If he cut off a man's nose for no reason at all, it gave the victim some idea of what to expect if he really did commit an offense.

Everything was running smoothly in Bunyoro, for the king at least, when Sir Samuel Baker and Lady Baker appeared again. This time, Sir Samuel was in a sense working for the pasha of Egypt as well as his own monarch. The pasha, who was then working in conjunction with the British, was hoping to extend his dominions south to Lake Victoria and Sir Samuel was preparing the way for him.

Sir Samuel had a considerable force of Egyptian troops with him. The spearhead of this force was a group of forty men, all of whom were cannibals and ex-slaves. Baker good-naturedly referred to this group as his "Forty Thieves" because of their tendency to murder and loot whenever possible. Sometimes this carefree lot even got on Sir Samuel's nerves and he then called them "my Satanic escort." Neither they nor Sir Samuel was warmly received by Kabarega.

For a long time, Kabarega refused to meet Sir Samuel as the king had never forgotten the incident of the tobacco ash. But at last, by means of threats, Baker forced an audience. Kabarega received the Englishman sitting on a divan in his palace—a huge, well-made native hut. Baker describes him as "about twenty years old, five feet ten inches in height. His skin was quite light. His eyes were large and projected slightly. He had a broad forehead, high cheek bones, and very white teeth. His hands were beautifully shaped and his fingernails scrupulously clean. He wore sandals of buffalo hide and had a headdress of antelope with the horns attached. He wore a robe of bark cloth, striped with black."

Baker brought in some of Kabarega's minor chiefs who had opposed him and had them flogged in front of the monarch as a gentle hint. Baker also produced an Arab slaver named Suleiman who had, for a bribe, agreed to betray Kabarega to Baker. Suleiman, however, had later double-crossed Baker and gone back to Kabarega. Baker had Suleiman flogged with a rhino hide whip. Friendly relations having now been established, Baker and Kabarega sat down to talk things over.

The forces of the two men were almost equally matched. Although the Bunyoro army outnumbered Baker's little force several hundred to one, they had very few firearms and no discipline. Baker explained that he wanted ivory. Kabarega replied that all ivory was a royal monopoly. "Apparently this savage wanted to keep all the ivory in the country for himself," Baker later wrote. This, of course, could not be allowed, so a compromise was reached for a division of all ivory brought in.

The next morning, Baker had a flagpole erected and ran up the Union Jack, declaring that the country was now under British rule. His band struck up a lively tune and his troops fired a volley into the air. Kabarega thought this was such a pretty show that he presented Baker with two goats and begged him to do it again, but Baker explained that once was enough.

Relations between the two men were now fairly amicable. Kabarega and his court attended a big banquet given for them by Baker in the European's tent. Kabarega was as delighted as a child with the strange things around him. He marveled that the eyes of a photograph seemed to follow him no matter where he moved. Baker gave him two mirrors and Kabarega was charmed when he found that by putting them on either side of a lighted candle, he could make an endless series of reflections of a candle appear in them. Baker also showed this big child his repeating rifles. "I was astonished at the rapidity with which he learned how to load and unload them," Baker indulgently remarked. While playing with the guns, Kabarega chatted to one of his councilors who promptly bowed and left the tent, an incident which attracted little attention at the time.

During the meal, Baker had his men fire off some rockets to impress the natives. Most of Kabarega's staff fled screaming, "The foreigners have set the sky on fire!" Kabarega was unmoved. "That would be a good way to set the roofs of an enemy village on fire," he remarked thoughtfully.

The royal guest finally left. Baker had given him some beads and Kabarega walked away playing with them happily. Baker was very pleased at the success of the party and amused at the charming naïveté of the young king. His amusement did not last long, for one of his men rushed in to report that during the meal, some of Kabarega's men had stolen several of the rifles. This was serious. Baker instantly demanded an audience with the king, but Kabarega explained that pressing matters of state prevented his obliging his new friend. When Baker insisted and threatened to march on the palace, Kabarega sent him word, "You are my guest and a guest stays where his host puts him and doesn't cause trouble."

Baker was in no mood to discuss the ethics of hospitality. With his Forty Thieves behind him, he marched on the palace. Kabarega mustered his Bonosoora bodyguard and went out to meet him. The Bonosoora moved forward with locked shields, their spears thrown back for the cast. The Forty Thieves were in a double rank, the first rank kneeling. When Baker gave the order, the Thieves poured a murderous volley into the advancing spearmen. The Bonosoora broke and fled. Kabarega tried vainly to rally them. He refused to retreat and finally he had to be dragged off the field by his chiefs.

But Kabarega had learned a valuable lesson. This was the last time he ever tried to attack trained troops with a phalanx of spearmen. From then on, he relied on trickery and guerrilla warfare.

An uneasy truce followed. The seemingly simple native villages had always been hotbeds of conspiracy and counterconspiracy that would have interested a Machiavelli. Baker worked hard to encourage the local chiefs and the Arab slavers to attack Kabarega, and the king, in turn, conspired against the European. The slavers, encouraged by Kabarega, attacked Baker. Baker defeated the slavers and then used them against natives as mercenary troops. Kabarega managed to corrupt Baker's trusted dragoman who decoyed Baker into a secret meeting with two of the king's spearmen sent to murder him. Baker escaped only by a miracle of luck. Later, he wrote, "I have broken up the slave trade, freed the people from the despotism of their king, brought peace, and introduced improved agricultural methods which will prevent famines. The disgusting ingratitude and treachery of the negro surpasses the imagination. All good will brings forth evil deeds."

While all this was going on, the two men continued to profess boundless devotion to each other. "You are my son," Baker told Kabarega and the king humbly rejoined, "You are dear father." Baker was constantly making demands on Kabarega for food for his men, porters for his trips and, of course, ivory. Kabarega resisted these demands by every trick ingenuity could suggest although he seldom dared openly to oppose Baker. It is said that once he retorted, "You say that I'm your son and you are my father. Isn't it a father's duty to support his son rather than have the son support him?" But such open clashes were rare. Kabarega relied on trying to have the white man secretly assassinated or to bribe his followers away from him while Baker did his best to cause a general uprising against the king.

Matters reached a crucial stage when Kabarega discovered that Baker was secretly treating with Mwanga and trying to induce that uncertian monarch to invade Bunyoro with the support of Baker's men. An open quarrel broke out between Baker and the king. The situation became so serious that Baker had a stockade built into which his men could retreat if attacked. Kabarega now realized that the crisis had come. Either he must destroy Baker or Baker would destroy him.

The king handled the situation with his usual cunning. He stopped all supplies of food to Baker's men, knowing the European would then have to threaten him with the Forty Thieves. This was exactly what happened. Under the rifles of the troops, Kabarega pretended to fall into a blind panic. He begged for mercy and not only supplied all the food that Baker demanded but also presented him with several gourds full of native wine as a present for his men. Ordinarily, Baker would have been suspicious of such a gift, but the king's terror was so obvious that he believed the gift was simply meant to placate him.

That evening while the Bakers were at dinner, one of his men rushed in to say that the troops had been poisoned. The Bakers rushed out. Half the command were rolling on the ground in agony. At the same time, Baker heard the most ominous of all native sounds —far more deadly in its portent than war drums or battle cries. It was the lowing of the herds, being driven away to a safe spot before an all-out battle.

Fortunately, Lady Baker had some knowledge of pharmacy. She hurriedly made a mixture of salt and mustard which was forced down the throats of the dying men. This concoction acted as an emetic. Then Baker, followed by his sergeant and bugler, left the stockade to see how the rest of the force, camped outside, were faring.

He walked into a carefully prepared ambush. The sergeant was walking in front, Baker's usual position, and the man was instantly killed. Baker ran back for the stockade, shouting, "Sound the tabor!" As he ran, the war drums of the Bunyoros roared out the signal for the attack, mingled with the roll of the military tabor beating to quarters.

He was only just in time. Kabarega hurled his spearmen against the stockade time after time, only to have them repulsed by the steady fire of the defenders. The sick troops fired, vomited, and fired again at the yelling, painted horde that swept around the stockade. Then Baker led a counterattack. The Forty Thieves, firing with disciplined precision, broke the Bunyoro attack. Baker set fire to the town, and then charged at the head of his men toward the king's palace. Here another stubborn resistance had to be overcome, but a few minutes later the huge building, eighty feet high, went up in flames. The soldiers swept the town, looting and killing. When the fugitives attempted to hide in the tall grass, Baker ordered the grass fired. Not until dawn did the bugle sound "Cease fire."

Baker had won only a temporary victory. His losses had been heavy. Many of the men sleeping outside the stockade had been speared in their sleep. Although he could hold the stockade against the natives, his supply of food was limited. Kabarega had escaped and was raising the whole country against him. The situation was indeed desperate.

For several weeks the beleaguered force held out. Once, when they were on the point of starvation, Lady Baker disclosed that while the fort was being built, she had buried six boxes of food under the floor of the main cabin. This food enabled them to hold out a little longer while Baker desperately tried to get messengers through to Mwanga for help.

Finally, Baker decided that he could hold the fort no longer. On the night of June 14, 1872, he resolved to try and cut his way through to Rionga, a village under Mwanga's protection. As soon as it was dark, he had everything that might prove useful to Kabarega put in the main cabin and then set fire to the fort. Led by Baker and his Forty Thieves, the little party set out through the jungles for Rionga. Lady Baker, of course, was a member of the party. It must have been a terrible trip for a woman.

As soon as the light of the burning fort was seen by Kabarega's scouts, the war drums were beaten and Kabarega with his entire army set out in pursuit. Although the natives did not dare to close with Baker's force, they hung on their flanks, shot arrows into their ranks, speared any straggler and dug game pits, lined with dagger-sharp bamboo stakes, in their path. Whenever Baker's cannibal troops caught one of their attackers, they cut out his liver and ate it. Whenever Kabarega's men captured one of the fugitives, he was handed over to the tribal torturers. Baker's terrible retreat across Bunyoro, strongly reminiscent of Cortez's "Night of Tears" when he tried to escape from Mexico City, could never have been accomplished if Baker had not resorted to a clever trick. When his men reached a tributary of the Nile, he had them scatter beads and cowrie shells, the standard currency of the country, in the grass along the trail. Kabarega's men stopped to collect the valuable loot and this gave Baker a chance to get his men across the river. He promptly seized all canoes for miles up and down the bank and captured or killed the paddlers. Kabarega was unable to cross the river and was forced to give up the pursuit.

Baker and his party finally reached Rionga after one of the most brilliant and heroically conducted retreats across a hostile country on record.

Having gotten rid of Baker, Kabarega now settled down to enjoy himself. He replenished his supply of ivory by looting some passing caravans, and exacted a terrible vengeance of any of his chiefs who had supported Baker.

But the influx of Europeans was not to be stopped. Three years after Baker left, Emin Pasha appeared, sent as governor by the pasha of Egypt. At first, Emin and Kabarega got along very well. Emin describes the king as "hospitable and intelligent." Emin was very sympathetic with the natives, too sympathetic, many Europeans thought, and he made no attempt to levy on Kabarega any heavy demands for ivory or supplies. Like Baker, Emin was surprised at Kabarega's ability to grasp new techniques and adopt them to his own use—a characteristic seldom found among the natives. When Emin appeared riding a horse, most of the natives fled in terror, as they had never seen such an animal, but Kabarega instantly began to speculate as to whether zebras could be trained for such a purpose. Emin also showed Kabarega his revolver and explained how it could be taken apart and reassembled. After one lesson, Kabarega was able to do it as well as the German.

Although Emin liked Kabarega, he was violently opposed to the continual and destructive native wars. When Kabarega started the conquest of two tribes on the outskirts of his dominions, Emin protested. Kabarega politely ignored him. Emin then sent one of his most trusted lieutenants, an Italian soldier of fortune named Casati, to argue with the king.

Casati and Kabarega disliked each other almost on sight. Casati describes him as cruel, drunken and arrogant. When Casati's pleas for peace produced no results, the Italian followed the time-honored formula of Tippu Tib and Baker. He begged Emin to encourage Mwanga to attack the country. Kabarega managed to intercept one

A portrait of Tippu Tib. (From in *Darkest Africa* by Henry Stanley)

A Masai corral. (R.N. Watkins-Pritchford)

Joseph Thomson in camp. (From an old engraving in *Joseph Thomson, African Explorer* by Rev. J. B. Thomson.

An Arab of the frontier, Sheik Umar bin haji.

An early frontier fort in the bush country. (Charles Adams)

A native soldier of the Northern Frontier District by one of the frontier forts. (East Africa Tourist Association)

An example of the type of mutilations performed by King Kabarega. (From *Fighting the Slave Hunters in Central Africa* by Alfred J. Swann)

An early photograph of a pioneer safari. (F. H. Clarke)

Transportation for a lady pioneer. (Charles Adams)

Ewart S. Grogan. (From *From the Cape to Cairo* by E. S. Grogan and A. H. Sharp)

A Kikuyu girl, taken by H. Binks, earliest photographer in Kenya. This picture was taken in 1904. (Binks & Co.)

John Boyes as a young man. He was probably "King of the Kikuyu" about the time this photograph was taken. (Courtesy John Boyes Jr.)

James and Mary McQueen.
(Courtesy Mrs. M. McNaughton)

Mr. and Mrs. R. O. Preston. (Courtesy R. O. Preston Jr.)

A Kikuyu warrior. (Binks & Co.)

John Boyes photographed with a group of Kikuyu in his later years. (Courtesy John Boyes Jr.)

The King's African Rifles. (Charles Adams)

The frontier outposts were primitive but held a commanding position.
(Charles Adams)

Mrs. R. O. Preston driving the last spike in the Mombasa-Uganda railroad on the shore of Lake Victoria. The building of the railroad was held up for three months because of man-eating lions attacking the workmen. (R. O. Preston)

R. O. Preston and a man-eater. (Courtesy R. O. Preston, Jr.)

Camel caravan, Northern Frontier. (William Hoey)

Masai spearmen with a recent kill, photographed in 1904. (William Hoey)

Clifford and Harold Hill with a hunting party. (Courtesy Harold Hill)

One of Paul Rainey's early pictures of hunting lions with dogs. (Courtesy Harold Hill)

Harold Hill on his ostrich farm.
(Courtesy Harold Hill)

Dragging a bait to attract lions.

F. H. Clarke, the white hunter, with a rogue elephant shot near the Lado Enclave. (Courtesy F. H. Clarke)

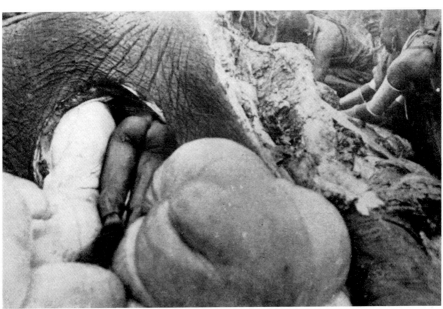

Natives devouring an elephant killed in the Lado Enclave. (Courtesy F. H. Clarke)

Suk Warriors. (East Africa Tourist Association)

Theodore Roosevelt with a Masai band. (Courtesy William Hoey)

Abyssinian raiders. (F. H. Clarke)

British fort on the Northern Frontier. (East Africa Tourist Association)

of Casati's messengers and learned of Casati's plans. He had the Italian seized, tied to a tree and tortured. Then he sent him back to Emin.

Emin was now reluctantly forced to move against Kabarega. He reprimanded Casati for having alienated a friendly king, but determined to avenge the outrage committed on his representative. Organizing the tribes opposed to Kabarega, he led them on Kibiro, one of Kabarega's main villages. The sacking of the town was so horrible that afterward, when the chiefs came to Emin to report that they had followed his orders, Emin could only say bitterly, "That is true, but I cannot find it in my heart to thank you."

Now Kabarega had his revenge. The Mahdi uprising in Egypt cut Emin off from his source of supplies. Kabarega promptly declared war against the governor. He attacked Emin's caravans, ambushed his troops, and looted the villages that had supported the German. Emin was finally released from his precarious position by Stanley with the help of Tippu Tib.

Again, Kabarega was left in undisputed control of his country. But now the British were moving into southern Uganda to support missionaries like Dr. Cook and the Fishers. For Kabarega, this was the beginning of the end.

One of the kingdoms conquered by Kamurasi, Kabarega's father, was Toro lying along the slopes of the Mountains of the Moon in western Uganda. Toro now rose in revolt against Kabarega. The king put down the uprising so efficiently that Toro was virtually depopulated. But the young king of the country was a Christian convert and a friend of the British, and Captain F. D. Lugard, the British representative in Uganda, had sworn to defend him. Lugard had a line of forts built between Toro and Bunyoro, and manned them with Emin's old Sudanese troops who had been unable to follow the governor when he left with Stanley. These troops, left to their own devices, had been wandering around the country as more or less disciplined bandits. As Lugard desperately needed troops, he felt that he was lucky to enlist them.

The Sudanese, left almost entirely to their own devices in the string of isolated forts, promptly entered into an orgy of slave-

catching and looting. One fort was turned into a slave market. The
Reverend R. P. Ashe, one of the Uganda missionaries, reported, "The
horrors and atrocities which they perpetrated upon the people of
Toro and Bunyoro is one of the darkest pages in the book of Africa's
story." He accused the Sudanese of wholesale rape, abnormal actions
resulting in the death of women and children, slave-catching, and
castrating boys. Sir Gerald Portal, one of the British administrators,
wrote in despair:

I would let the whole country go. 15,000 square miles of Uganda have
been laid waste by the Sudanese. Our only friends in the area are the
king of Toro and about 5,000 of his supporters. The rest of the people are
more afraid of the Sudanese than of Kabarega.

What had started out as a benevolent attempt on the part of the
British public to stop the slave trade and bring Christianity and a
higher scale of living to the natives had ended in a miserable mess.
Major Macdonald, one of the British officers, put the matter with
military bluntness:

[In spite of what Sir Gerald Portal had suggested] we cannot now
leave Uganda. The British public would not permit it [because of the
missionaries]. We have sworn to support the people who have trusted us.
We must also control the Lakes [because of the Germans]. If we get rid
of the Sudanese, who after all support themselves, we will have to pay
for troops and their supplies. That is too expensive. The only other solution is to get rid of Kabarega. That is the course we must follow.

Kabarega at this time was a very puzzled man. He even sent
secretly to his old enemy, Mwanga, to ask the king if he could find
out what these white men really wanted. If the British had simply
seized his country, deposed him, and then looted Bunyoro, Kabarega could have understood it perfectly. Instead, the British kept
talking about justice, mercy and the importance of mutual trade
relations—all concepts so completely foreign to the native that there
were not even words in his language to express them. Kabarega
ruled by force and he had never conceived of a king ruling in any
other way. The British claimed they did not rule by force. Then

what were those Sudanese doing in these forts? The British claimed they did not build up one tribe against another as the Arab slavers had done. Then why had they supported the king of Toro against him? The British had ordered the natives not to interfere with the missionaries. But the British were constantly interfering with the native religious rites on which the whole structure of the universe depended. For example, every month when the new moon appeared, Kabarega would have a number of travelers in his country sacrificed to make the moon grow. Without this ceremony, there would be no moon. But the British objected to this custom on the absurd plea that it interfered with caravans passing through Bunyoro. What was more important, a few caravan porters or the moon? The British claimed he should live in peace with his neighbors. How then could he support his Bonosoora bodyguard? He had to pay the Bonosoora by allowing them to loot neighboring tribes, and the Bonosoora were not only a bodyguard but also a standing army and the police force. He certainly couldn't tax his own people to support them. He'd have had a rebellion on his hands.

Captain Lugard made one last attempt to avoid a war against Kabarega. He had the Sudanese withdrawn from the forts and sent a message to Kabarega, telling what he had done and asking for the king's co-operation in bringing peace to the country. Kabarega interpreted this message as a sign of weakness. Within a few hours after he had received it, Kabarega threw his warriors across the now unprotected frontier into defenseless Toro.

That did it. Captain Lugard headed an expeditionary force into Bunyoro. Kabarega was off raiding Toro at the time, but he hurried back with his army as quickly as possible. He had left a strong force under one of his best generals to guard Bunyoro during his absence and this general decided to meet the British at the ford of a river. Captain Lugard knew he could not force the ford under the natives' fire, for by this time the Bunyoros had guns purchased from Arab gun runners in exchange for ivory. Lugard hit on a clever trick. A large part of his force were spearmen, loaned by Mwanga. He had their drummers beat the signal to halt and camp for the night. When the Bunyoro general heard the beat, he also went into camp with his men. As soon as it was dark, Lugard forded the river and with the first light of day, attacked the Bunyoro army and inflicted a serious defeat on them.

Lugard withdrew, but now Kabarega engaged in open warfare against the Europeans and there was no possible doubt that he must be destroyed. Another expedition was sent against him under Colonel Sir Henry Colville. Kabarega's chiefs urged him to submit, claiming that these strangers were certainly the fabled Bacwezi who had returned to rule the country and it was useless to oppose them. "You lie," retorted Kabarega. "But even if these men are the Bacwezi themselves, I'll fight them to the end." Too wise to attack the British force in open warfare, he retreated before them, burning his villages and destroying the crops so they could find neither shelter nor food. Whenever possible he ambushed them in the tall grass or cut off parties of foragers.

Colonel Colville built a line of forts across the center of Bunyoro, put a steel boat on Lake Albert to cut Kabarega off from the supply of guns smuggled in to him from Egypt and burnt the king's capital at Hoima. Kabarega was now reduced to the position of a bandit leader with a small, loyal force hiding in the swamps and jungles. But he still refused to surrender.

Another force was sent against him the year after, directed by Sir Frederick Jackson. This force went up the Nile in canoes with the heavy equipment and, to keep from being ambushed, natives were sent ahead to clear the brush from both sides of the river bank. After the brush-clearing parties had passed on, Kabarega had his men dig trenches in the bare banks. His warriors hid in these trenches until the flotilla of canoes came down the river. Then the Bunyoro warriors suddenly leaped up and poured a murderous fire into the canoes. The flotilla was destroyed.

In 1897, the Sudanese troops mutinied. Mwanga fled from his capital and joined with Kabarega to drive out the Europeans. Together, the two kings marched against the British. Meanwhile, the British had rushed up Indian troops from the coast. The two forces met in a great naval battle on the Nile in which several hundred canoes took part, some of them carrying fifty men. Kabarega and

Mwanga were defeated. With what was left of their forces, they fled to the swamps.

For the last time, the British sent an expedition against him. Mwanga wanted to surrender. "Never!" said Kabarega. "We must all die sometime, let it be now." He had an ox killed and told his craven ally to drink the blood. "Maybe it will give you some strength," he suggested. Colonel Ewart, the officer in charge of the expedition, spent weeks trying to catch the two kings and their followers in the great papyrus swamps. Finally he bribed a native with some beads to betray Kabarega to him.

The native went to the chief of the village where Kabarega was hiding and divided the beads with him. In return, the chief agreed to hold Kabarega there until Ewart could bring up his men. The chief told Kabarega he had received word that the British had left and the fugitive king lay down to sleep. Meanwhile, Ewart's force surrounded the village and then attacked. At the sound of the battle, Kabarega snatched up his spear and rushed out to rally his men.

Mwanga promptly surrendered, weeping and begging for mercy. Kabarega, although he knew it was now hopeless, fought on. His arm was shot off, thus fulfilling the prophecy of the old witch doctor that he would receive a mutilation. He could no longer use his spear. His Bonosoora bodyguard lay dead around him. Still Kabarega remained on his feet, urging his men to fight on. Finally his chiefs tripped him so he fell. The desperately wounded man was unable to get up and the chiefs surrendered to the British.

The two captive kings were taken to Mwanga's capital on the shore of Lake Victoria. As they walked along, Mwanga kept sniffling and bemoaning his fate while Kabarega looked about disdainfully at the low, marshy country so unlike his own beloved mountains. "What you crying about?" he asked Mwanga contemptuously. "If I were king of this rotten country, I'd thank the English for throwing me out of it." Kabarega never lost his arrogance. A doctor was treating the wounds of natives in the Mengo hospital and had just bent over one man when, to his astonishment, he received a hearty kick in the behind. Turning around, he saw that Kabarega had wriggled down to the foot of his cot and had a foot poised for another kick.

"How dare you waste time on a dog of a peasant when a king demands your aid?" he asked indignantly.

Kabarega and Mwanga were sent to the Seychelles Islands in the Indian Ocean. Mwanga died in 1903. Kabarega was returned to Africa but so great was his influence over the people that the British did not allow him to go to Uganda.

In 1923, Kabarega, then an old man, was dying. He begged to be allowed to die in Bunyoro. The British government decided to grant his request and so he started back to his homeland, but he never reached it. He died on the way. The old king is buried at Mparo, three miles from Hoima, his ancient capital which was burnt by Colonel Colville.

The natives deeply mourned him. They regarded this fierce old man as a symbol of their savage but free, wild past. "So great is their hatred of foreign domination, that they glorify even this tyrant," marveled one of the British administrators.

VII

John Boyes,
King of the Kikuyu

I was a young lad, fresh from Scotland, and had been in Kenya only a few months when I first met the famous John Boyes. I had wandered into the bar of the old Norfolk Hotel and suddenly found myself in the center of an unholy row. Riddell, one of the best known of the early white hunters, was leaning against the bar with a glass of straight whisky in his hand and his thumb hooked into his cartridge belt, watching a little man who was jumping about in front of him like a furious terrier and using the most terrible language it had ever been my lot to hear. "Riddell, you bloody fool," shouted the little chap, the Yorkshire accent heavy in his speech, "you'll never make it without me. You'll only make a mess of it."

"Johnny, you don't know a damned thing about Abyssinia," answered Riddell. "I've raised five thousand pounds for this trip and you admit you haven't a bean. Why should I take you along and give you a share in the profits when you haven't a penny to put into the safari?"

"You'll be sorry for this, mark my words," yelled the little man. "I'll go up to Abyssinia myself, buy up every horse and donkey in the place, and make you look like the fool you are."

There was a great howl of friendly laughter from everyone in the bar as the little man stamped out, leaving the air blue with curses behind him.

"Who was that?" I asked a settler standing near the bar.

"Oh, that was Johnny Boyes," the man chuckled. "Riddell has

been planning on this trip to the Abyssinian border for the last two years to bring back a bunch of donkeys and horses to sell in Nairobi. It's across three hundred miles of desert, full of bandit tribes, and most people don't believe he can make it. For some reason, Johnny is convinced that Riddell ought to take him, although what kind of contribution he could make is beyond me. All that talk of Johnny's about going up there ahead of Riddell is so much wind. I happen to know he has only a few shillings. We've had to stand him drinks."

I thought no more about the matter, until about a year later, as I was walking down Government Road in Nairobi, I saw an amazing sight. Along the street came a proper caravan of camels, all laden with some of the finest ivory it has ever been my lot to see. Behind the camels was a long string of donkeys and horses, all seemingly in first-class condition. At the head of this safari, rode John Boyes on a fine stallion, waving to passers-by and telling them to meet him at the Norfolk for a drink.

Later I heard that Riddell, although a man of great experience and ability, had given up the project at Marsabit, halfway across the desert, and been forced to return to Nairobi.

Afterward, John told me the story of the trip himself. After leaving the Norfolk bar that day, he had gone to the old polo field where some of the settlers used to race their horses and started betting. Within a few hours, he had run up his few shillings to four hundred pounds. With this sum, he departed for Abyssinia. He had managed to purchase the necessary stock and had driven them south across the desert to Nairobi with the help of a few Somali herdsmen he'd picked up along the way. At one point along the route, a local district commissioner had asked him to transport several hundred pounds of tusks he had collected from elephant poachers. Hence the ivory-loaded camels. This was the first time on record that a trader had been able to cross that terrible desert, but I will always believe that John performed the amazing feat more to irritate Riddell than for any other reason.

I cannot help but recount an amusing bit of a sequel to this journey. The district commissioner who had engaged John to transport the ivory struck a bargain with him for a certain rate. John charged a high price, on account of the danger of attack from the wild tribes. However, John was in luck and brought the ivory through without trouble. In Nairobi, the district officer and the other officials of the government refused to pay the high rate, arguing that John had been in no danger, so they would pay only the standard rate of a rupee a mile. John refused the money and went off to drink at the Norfolk in a bitter mood.

Now it happened that there was a convention of settlers at the Norfolk who had met to protest certain government regulations concerning sisal growing—sisal being a plant whose fibers are used in the making of rope. John knew nothing about sisal and cared less, but he was always active when trouble was about, and in no time he was virtually in charge of the convention. Finally John mounted to a chair and roared, "Are we going to take this matter lying down? Follow me, men! To the Governor's Palace!"

With the furious settlers at his heels, John led the way to the government building where, presumably, the governor sat quaking in terror. "Let me handle him!" shouted John and rushed into the governor's office while the yelling mob waited outside. "Governor," said John pointing to the open window, "those fine fellows are so furious over the way I've been treated in this matter of the ivory that they've come to insist that justice be done." "My dear Mr. Boyes," said the anxious governor. "There has been some mistake, I assure you. Please let me give you a check now for the amount owing you." John pocketed the check and returned to the waiting settlers. "Men, the governor has promised to look into the matter," he assured them. "Now, as we are all law-abiding citizens, let's return to our homes." The crowd dispersed and John retired to the Norfolk for a well-deserved drink.

John Boyes was born in Yorkshire in 1873. His father was a shoemaker but John had no love for the trade and ran away to sea at the age of thirteen. During the next ten years, he served on everything from a fishing smack to a man-of war and traveled to Brazil, India, Port Said and the West Coast of Africa. While his ship was in Durban, South Africa, John heard of the Matabele War and as John never willingly missed a disturbance of any kind, he jumped ship to take part in it. After the war, he worked his way north, taking any job that came handy, and in 1898 found himself in Mombasa, then a small Arab town.

The Sudanese Mutiny had broken out in Uganda and the army was willing to pay good prices to anyone who would transport food from the coast to Lake Victoria. John started out for Uganda with a caravan of donkeys laden with boxes of food and herded by a few native drivers. Several weeks out, the donkeys died of tsetse fly. John loaded the food boxes on the backs of the drivers and kept on. He developed malaria and while he was delirious, his drivers deserted. Three days later when John came out of his delirium, he found himself in the middle of a jungle, surrounded by his food boxes and a circle of patient vultures waiting for him to die. Many men would have found such a situation discouraging but not John Boyes. He reasoned that other caravans must also have had porter trouble, so he sat down by the trail with his rifle cocked on his knee. Sure enough, in the course of the next few days, a number of porters who had deserted from other caravans trotted by on their way to the coast. These men John promptly pressed into service, loaded them up with his food boxes, and continued on to Uganda.

John sold his food for a profit of two hundred pounds (about a thousand dollars). "It was the largest sum of money I'd ever had," he told me later. But even John Boyes realized that trying to haul food up from the coast was too uncertain a business. He looked around for some closer source of supply.

In the fastnesses of the great Abardare forests that grow on the foothills of snow-topped Mount Kenya, lived the Kikuyu. Today, the Kikuyu have achieved world fame as the originators of that terrible secret society known as the Mau Mau, but at that time virtually nothing was known of the tribe. The Arab slavers, who evaluated the various native peoples as a farmer might evaluate breeds of cattle, had written on their books after the Kikuyu: "So vicious and uncertain as to be virtually worthless." Sir Gerald Portal, who had passed through the country a short time before Boyes, wrote of this area:

We plunged into the darkness of a dense belt of forest inhabited by the treacherous, cunning and hostile Kikuyu. Warned by the state of affairs which we had heard was prevailing at the Company's fort in this district, we were careful to keep all our people together, every man within a couple of paces of his neighbor. The Kikuyu very seldom or never show themselves and run the risk of a fight in the open, but lie like snakes in the long grass within a few yards of the line of march, watching for some incautious porter to loiter a few yards behind. Even then not a sound is heard but the twang of a small bow and the almost inaudible whizz of a poisoned arrow. A slight puncture in the arm, throat or chest is followed almost inevitably by death. Another favorite trick of the Kikuyu is to plant poisoned skewers in the path, set at an angle so they will pierce the stomach of anyone advancing through the under-brush. For a man to lag behind the others, even for a few seconds, means certain death. A group of native soldiers sent out from the fort in the hopes of trading for food with the Kikuyu were all massacred.

But it was known that the Kikuyu were an agricultural people who had great supplies of food. John Boyes determined to go into the Kikuyu country and get some of this food by hook or crook.

By dint of offering huge rewards, he managed to obtain the services of seven local natives, one of whom knew the Kikuyu language, and started out. He hadn't gone far when he was overtaken by a white sergeant with some native soldiers and was dragged back to a fort recently established by the government to protect the caravan route to Uganda. There he found the furious officer in command awaiting him.

"You must be mad," shouted the officer. "I wouldn't go into that country unless I had a Maxim gun and a company of trained troops."

"Nobody's asking you to go," John pointed out. "I'm going."

"You certainly are not."

"I bloody well am."

"I say you're not and I'm in charge of this district."

"Then I'll go round your district and come in from the other side," John bellowed.

And so he did. The trip took several weeks and the sergeant's guard went along with him to make sure he didn't make a bolt into the forbidden area. Once clear of the officer's district, John and his seven natives crossed a pass eight thousand feet high over the Abardares and dropped down into the Kikuyu country.

The Kikuyu country is made up of a series of great mountain ridges with fertile valleys lying between, each valley usually having a little stream running through it. When Boyes came to the first of these valleys, he met some Kikuyus on the way to their "shambas," as the patches of cultivated land are called. The natives took one look at the stranger and fled, giving their alarm cry of "Hue—he-ee, he-ee, he-ee!" In an incredibly short space of time, the cry was taken up throughout the entire valley and tossed from ridge to ridge to rouse the distant villages. As Boyes went on, he could see the warriors hurriedly assembling on the mountain slopes on all sides of him, their bodies painted with red and white clay and their great head-dresses, formed from the pelts of the black-and-white colobus monkey, making them appear nearly as tall as their spears. Each man carried a huge shield, painted in bright colors, and wore a rattle on his leg. As the warriors advanced on the little group, they began stamping their feet in unison and the sound of the rattles rolled through the valley like thunder.

John hid his rifle under a bush and came forward with bunches of grass in his hands to show he was on a peaceful mission. In a minute, he was surrounded by more than five hundred warriors. Through his quaking interpreter, John asked to be taken to the chief.

The leader of the warriors asked John where the rest of his expedition was.

"There is no expedition," said John.

"Where are your guns?" was the next question.

"I have no guns. I have come on a peaceful mission."

"I will take him to our chief," said the warrior leader to the interpreter.

Under guard, John was marched to the village. The Kikuyu people were broken up into a number of clans, somewhat like the old Scottish clans, and these clans were constantly at war with each other. The villagers were even forbidden to keep roosters for fear that the crowing of a cock in the early morning might betray the

position of the village to an enemy force coming up through the
forest. The roosters used for breeding were kept in coops hidden in
the bush. The village to which John Boyes was led had been built
on a rise of ground and the brush cleared around it to give an area
of fire for the defending forces' poisoned arrows. The village was
surrounded by a high boma or wall made of thorn bush. The only
entrance was through a tunnel made of slabs of wood bound together with vines. John had to crawl through this tunnel on his
hands and knees while his captors followed. Inside the boma, John
found himself in a village of thatched huts and little granaries made
of mud and wattle, built on stilts to protect their contents from
insects. He was promptly surrounded by a crowd of curious women
and children. They exclaimed over his white skin, long straight hair,
and pulled at his clothes to see if they were part of him.

John was taken to the principal hut in the village. There he was
met by the chief, an intelligent, middle-aged man by the name of
Karuri.*

John explained that he had come to trade for food. Karuri refused.
"We are afraid that if we give the white men food, they will settle
in this country and take our land away from us," he told Boyes.

John was amused by this idea. He tried to explain to Karuri that
the white men were not interested in settling in Kenya. All they
wanted was a trade route through to Uganda. He also assured the
chief that even if the whites ever did settle in Africa, the last place
they would select was the cold Abardare Mountains or the great
swampland below it that the Masai called "Nairobi—the place of
water."

The chief still refused to trade. He did, however, allow one of

* The Kikuyu had no chiefs in the ordinarily accepted use of the word. They
were governed by a council of nine elders who acted somewhat like a supreme
court, deciding on cases brought before them. In addition, each clan had its
own council of nine who decided local problems, and each subclan a similar
group. Also, each valley had its own council, made up of representatives from
the different villages in the valley. Karuri was the principal member of the
council in that particular valley. The fighting men had a similar system of
government, operating independently of the civil administration. The whole
arrangement was extremely complicated and for purposes of simplification, I
have used John Boyes's method of referring to the various local leaders merely
as "chiefs."

his women to bring the thirsty John a gourd of water. Automatically, John dumped some fruit salts into the water. These salt crystals were thought to purify water, as does chlorine.

When the water began to bubble from the action of the crystals, the assembled natives screamed with astonishment. "Look, he drinks boiling water!" they shouted.

"Won't it kill you?" asked Karuri in astonishment.

"Certainly not!" said John. "Don't you know that it's impossible to kill a white man?" This wild statement was later to cause John Boyes serious trouble.

After drinking the water, John sent one of his porters back for his gun. When the gun arrived, John pointed to a big baobab tree in the village. These trees are enormous things, often six feet in diameter, but they are hollow and the soft wood offers little resistance to a bullet. John fired at the tree and, as he expected, the bullet went completely through. When the natives screamed with astonishment, John said carelessly, "The bullet not only went through the tree but also through that mountain over there. My bullets never stop."

The chief was impressed but not impressed enough to trade. John went to bed that night in a hut, thinking his mission had been a failure.

He was awakened at dawn the next morning by the sound of war whoops and the screams of men, women and children. Snatching up his gun, John dashed out of the hut. The village had been attacked by a rival Kikuyu clan. The boma was in flames and the enemy had forced their way inside. Karuri was desperately trying to rally his warriors to meet the attack, but the village was already burning and the enemy were in the streets, spearing everyone in their way.

Bellowing like a bull, John opened fire on the hostile warriors. The sight of this strange, white apparition and the terrible effects of his soft-nosed bullets made the enemy force falter. The pause gave Karuri time enough to gather his men and charge. The attackers broke and fled, pursued by Karuri's men, stabbing and clubbing everyone they could catch.

After the fight was over, John said to Karuri, "You know what this means. Those men are bound to come back to avenge their dead. Without me and my gun, you don't stand a chance of fighting them off. Now, will you trade?"

"I have no choice," said Karuri grimly.

John doctored the wounds of the injured men with iodoform, the first disinfectant the natives had ever seen. Usually after a fight, a wounded man took for granted that his cuts would infect and he would lose an arm or leg from gangrene. When the natives found that their injuries healed normally, they were determined to have this strange, new magic substance. John bought all the food he wanted, exchanging enough iodoform to cover a man's thumb nail for twenty pounds of flour.

When John returned to the fort with his loads of food, he found that the railroad which the British were putting through from Mombasa to Uganda had reached the outskirts of the Kikuyu country. Thousands of Indian coolies had been imported to work on the roadbed and these men were in desperate need of food. John sold his loads of flour and made four hundred pounds (about two thousand dollars). To the young Yorkshire lad, this seemed a fabulous sum. He hurried back to the Kikuyu country as fast as his porters could go.

Karuri and the people of his valley had now definitely accepted John not only as a friend but also as a protector. By exchanging their surplus grain for the trade goods that John brought in, they began to grow enormously prosperous by native standards. But the other clans regarded the whole affair with jealous hatred. John's porters were being constantly ambushed. Several of the other Kikuyu chiefs had begun to band together to loot and wipe out this thriving community. John knew that with only Karuri's followers and one rifle he could not hope to stop a determined attack.

Then some of Karuri's men came in with the report that one of the other clans had attacked and massacred an Arab caravan and had seized a hundred rifles. The thought of these guns fired John's imagination. "With that number of guns, I could go anywhere in the country," he told me. Selecting a hundred of Karuri's best men, he set about training them as troops. In the rear rank, he put a body

of picked bowmen and taught them to fire all together, like the
English archers at Agincourt and Crécy, although John got his idea
from watching trained British troops volley-firing in the Matabele
War. In the front rank, he put his spearmen and showed them how
to advance behind a wall of shields, in the manner of the old Roman
legions—although I doubt if John Boyes had ever heard of the
Romans. But to John's shrewd mind, this seemed the logical way
to handle his little army, and he was quite right. He had the spearmen kneel while the bowmen behind them discharged their volleys
of poisoned shafts. Then, at a signal from John, the spearmen leaped
to their feet and charged before the enemy could recover from
the deadly hail of arrows.

At dawn one morning, John led his army against the village that
had looted the Arab caravan. The attack was so completely unexpected and delivered with such order and discipline that the
villagers made no attempt to resist. John seized the guns and withdrew without losing a man.

To his great disappointment, John found that only thirty of the
guns were in working condition. The Kikuyu, knowing nothing
about firearms, had simply thrown the guns on the ground and
most of them were hopelessly rusted. With those that were left,
John formed a bodyguard from the most intelligent and bravest of
Karuri's people. With this group, plus his company of spear- and
bowmen, he now had a force that could successfully fight off any
enemy attack.

The cost of maintaining this standing army—especially as the
riflemen had to be supplied with cartridges which, at that time,
were virtually worth their weight in gold—was a heavy strain on
the little community. So John was glad when several of the neighboring valleys asked to join with Karuri's people so that they also
could obtain some of the valuable trade goods and have the protection of the army. This opened new sources of grain which John was
able to sell to the railroad section gangs to help defray the cost of
his troops. But soon these outlying valleys began to be raided in
their turn by the clans opposed to John and Karuri. Naturally, the
villagers demanded protection. John was in a quandary. Although

his force was large enough to repulse any direct attack, he did not have enough men to patrol the borders of the entire area and prevent spasmodic raids. If he increased the size of his army, he would be right back where he'd started—in other words, his overhead expenses would be greater than his profits. John was discovering on a small scale the great, basic problem in empire-building.

Karuri had a simple solution. "Let us go out and exterminate these people," he argued. "That will solve the whole business." But John was reluctant to start a full-scale war. Instead, he sent messengers to the enemy clans, urging them to sign a peace pact and agree to stop raids. The rival chiefs regarded this as evidence that John was afraid of them. A few days later, they made a large-scale attack on one of the outlying valleys that had joined John's confederation. Several villages were burnt and scores of goats and young girls captured.

Karuri and John sent a message to the enemy clans demanding that the goats and girls be returned and that the people killed in the raid be paid for at the standard rate of one hundred sheep for a man and thirty for a woman. The chiefs responding by sending in a few old women, "not worth ten sheep apiece," as John contemptuously told me afterward. This was a deliberate insult and meant as such. Karuri and John gathered their forces and marched off to war.

Although they were greatly outnumbered, the disciplined forces backed by the rifles of John's bodyguard won the day. After the battle, John was astonished to see the two sides sitting down happily together, sharing food out of the same bowls, and chatting over the high spots of the fight. This convinced him that it was possible to confederate the various clans into one, peaceful unit.

During the next months, with a small group of warriors John traveled from one tribe to another, interviewing the paramount chiefs and urging them to form blood brotherhood with him and with each other. At last, a great meeting was arranged. After many speeches and ceremonies, the pact was signed. John returned to Karuri's valley confident that his troubles were over.

Now came the great crisis in John Boyes's career, which established him as king of the Kikuyu.

John had convinced the Kikuyus that white men had a special power. They had believed him. Now a clan who controlled John's principal caravan route attacked a safari passing near their area. Everyone in the safari was killed, including three Goanese traders. The death of these white traders electrified the whole Kikuyu people. Instantly uprisings against Boyes began to burst out all through the Abardares. The clan that had killed the traders, called the Chinga, led the insurrection. It could not have come at a worse time. John, with only a handful of followers, was on his way through the Chinga country taking out a shipment of ivory and food to sell at the fort.

When he heard of the massacre of the Goanese traders and the Chinga uprising, John left the main body of his caravan with its armed guards and hurried on ahead with four men. John was riding a mule and since even this small group couldn't keep up with him, he finally went on alone. John was confident that by a personal talk with the Chinga leader he could stop the uprising and restore peace. On the way, the mule suddenly refused to keep on the trail and insisted on turning off at an angle. John let the animal have its way. The mule trotted along for a few hundred yards parallel to the main track and then turned back on it. John thought the incident curious but unimportant. By evening, he reached a native village on the outskirts of the Chinga country.

The chief of this village was called Bartier. He was in a sweat of terror. He assured John that the whole country ahead was up against him. The Chingas were marching to meet him with an army of several thousand warriors and their skirmishers were already in the area. The Chinga witch doctors had assured the tribe that the three dead traders were John's brothers and that the tribesmen could kill John as easily as they had these other white men. Bartier assured John that to go on would be suicide.

While John and the chief were talking, two of the four men John had taken with him staggered into the village. They had fallen into an ambush set by the Chinga skirmishers along the trail and the other two men had been speared. John realized that his mule had scented the men lying in ambush and, by avoiding the trail, had probably saved his life.

The rest of the caravan now came in, having been too powerful for the Chinga skirmishers to attack. John had not been expecting trouble on this trek and so had brought only a small guard to protect the ivory and food. He could expect no help from Bartier. The chief was shaking with funk and refused to allow the caravan to stay in his village. He was not, he explained, unfriendly to John, but he intended to observe a strict neutrality in the coming conflict.

Not wanting to cause additional trouble, John and his men left the village and built a strong boma of thorn bushes some distance away. Even while they were building it, they could hear the patter of bare feet on the dried leaves in the forest that meant the Chingas were gathering around them. More and more men kept pouring in. John could hear their war cries as they arrived, the sound of their rattles, and the clashing of their spears on their shields as they prepared for the attack. Mingled with the noise came the howling of hyenas, for these scavengers knew from long experience what the cries foretold.

For perhaps the only time in his life, John Boyes came close to panic. The Chingas were dancing around outside his little fort, carrying the heads of the Goanese on poles and wearing pieces of the dead men's clothing. Later he told me, "I felt terribly lonely. I had been in the Kikuyu country now for over a year without ever seeing a white man and I couldn't even speak the language. I worried over having betrayed the natives who had trusted me. The Chingas had begun to chew narcotic roots and drink native beer to prepare themselves for the coming attack. I tried walking about to steady myself but I felt that I was on the edge of hysteria."

Confident that the little party could not escape, the Chingas built a big fire out of gunshot of the boma and began an orgy of drinking and feasting, screaming out insults to the beleaguered men and telling them of the tortures to which they would be submitted before the night was over. They were slowly working themselves up to a frenzied charge that would carry them into the boma in spite of losses. Finally, John could stand the strain no longer. He gathered his men around him and prepared for a sally.

"Even if the Chingas are on top of us, I'll shoot the first man who gives a war cry or throws a spear before I give the signal," John warned his men. Then a passage was opened in the boma and the men stole out, the rattles on their legs stuffed with leaves to deaden any sound. They crept through the forest until they came to the fire where the Chingas were competing in describing the ghastly tortures they would inflict on their captives.

When all his men were in position, John fired his gun, the signal for the attack. Instantly a volley of arrows was poured into the astonished Chingas. Back-lighted by the fire, they made perfect targets for John's men hidden in the forest. The Chingas rushed about, trying to find their weapons, getting in each other's way and tripping over the bodies of those already fallen. Another volley was poured into them. Then John led his spearmen in a charge. The Chingas broke and fled. John and his men burnt as many of their bows and spears as they could find and then retired to the boma.

John knew this was only a temporary victory. The main Chinga force was still on the way and against this he would have no chance. Meanwhile, runners had come in to say that Karuri and the other chiefs had heard of his plight, and were coming to his aid with a large army. John was afraid that they would arrive too late. He decided to bury the ivory, abandon the loads of food, and try to fight his way back to meet the relief force.

For a time, the return trip went well. Then the party came to a ravine filled with grass higher than their heads. "I knew that if an ambush had been laid, it would be here," said John later. The natives went forward slowly, parting the grass ahead of them with their spears while John covered them with his rifle. Suddenly an arrow whizzed by. Then another and another. Black forms began to appear in the grass. John fired whenever he could. He heard his men around him yelling as they began to engage the enemy. Then the Chinga war cry went up. The grass became alive with charging black warriors, and the fight was on.

John fired as fast he could jam fresh cartridges into his gun. A huge warrior rushed him, spear thrown back for the death blow. John shoved the muzzle of his rifle against the man's chest and fired. The giant black stood there, spear still poised, and John put three bullets into him before he fell. Gradually, the little party began to retreat. Looking up, John saw that the slope of hill behind them was covered with black forms; hangers-on of the main force, hoping to rush in when John and his men were overwhelmed.

Slowly, John and his men cut and shot their way into the open. Then John gathered his followers around him and charged up the hill. The Chingas on the slope scattered and ran. The exhausted men made their way back to Bartier's village.

But now Karuri and the rest of John's blood brothers were coming to the rescue. Within the next few days, a force of several thousand Kikuyu warriors had assembled around Bartier's village. Screaming their war cries, drugging themselves on beer and narcotics, this force worked itself up to a fighting pitch. Then, with John and his trained troopers leading them, they entered the Chinga country. They swept through the land from one end to the other and when they had finished, the Chinga had virtually ceased to exist.

John Boyes was now king of the Kikuyu. His caravans could travel throughout the country in perfect safety. The chiefs consulted him on every major issue and his orders were unquestioningly obeyed. None of the clans dared oppose him and John took good care to guard against an uprising. He learned to speak Kikuyu fluently, but when dealing with an uncertain clan, he preferred to talk through an interpreter. The natives, not realizing that he could understand them, would talk openly among themselves while John listened. He also soon found out that the witch doctors, although professing to be a unified group, were split up into various factions, each group bitterly jealous of the others; the rain-makers distrusting the medicine men and so on. By playing off one group against another, John learned everything that was going on. The Kikuyu had bands of strolling minstrels that wandered from one valley to another, singing songs. John subsidized these minstrels and through them kept in touch with events in different parts of the country.

One day, while on a tour of inspection of the villages, John saw a Kikuyu bearing the unmistakable signs of smallpox. Epidemics of smallpox and other diseases were not introduced by the white man but were common among the primitive African tribes and as the natives had no idea of hygiene, these plagues took a fearful toll. John explained to the villagers that the man had a disease that could kill hundreds of them. The Kikuyu were shocked and begged John to shoot him. John refused—"If I had done so, I would have saved thousands of lives," he admitted later—and told the villagers to keep the man under strict quarantine in a hut.

A few weeks later, John saw the same man wandering about in another village. It turned out that the Kikuyu, after guarding the man for a few days, had gotten tired of the whole business and turned him loose. John had him locked up again but it was too late. The plague began to break out through the entire Kikuyu country.

John sent to Mombasa for vaccine which, since the railroad had now been put through, arrived in a few days. Together with some native helpers, John set about a vast program of inoculation. Although he vaccinated thousands of Kikuyus, other thousands died. Before the epidemic could be brought under control, whole districts were wiped out.

In the middle of the epidemic, a serious drought developed. The drought was most severe in the lowland area and there starvation began to set in. To make matters worse, one of the great swarms of locusts that still make African farming a problem settled on the area. Grogan speaks of walking for four days through a swarm that was so thick he couldn't see the sun. The locusts ate what little crops were left. Then, as a final blow, an outbreak of rinderpest greatly decimated the Kikuyu sheep and goats.

Such disasters were part of native life and, in nature's grim way, even served a certain purpose by keeping the population in check. But for four of them to occur simultaneously was most uncommon. The lowland Kikuyu, who had suffered the most, began to migrate in great numbers to the mountains where there was still food. On the way, these miserable people were attacked by the other clans who robbed them of the few possessions they had left. When John heard what was going on, he organized a relief force and hurried to the aid of the refugees.

He found them in a pitiful state. Already weakened by the effects of the smallpox and starvation, the miserable people were dying by the score. He found groups of natives huddled around tiny fires, cooking their skin garments in the hope of getting some sustenance from them. He even heard of cases of cannibalism, which was most unusual among the Kikuyu. John, in his usual brisk manner, took control. He gathered together what few sheep and goats the refugees possessed and every day had a limited number slaughtered, enough to keep the starving people alive. He sent runners back to Karuri and the other chiefs, telling them to make arrangements to feed and house the desperate host when they arrived. Gradually, traveling only a few miles a day, he managed to get the people into the still fertile mountain valleys and distribute them among the various villages where they could receive care.

When the drought was over, John tried to move the people back to their old homes. The people refused to go. They were living quite comfortably on the relief provided for them by John and the hill clans and had no intention of going back to work. But the hill clans had not the slightest intention of supporting their kinsmen indefinitely and finally, after much arguing and pleading, John had to use his army to drive the refugees out of the hills and back to their former areas.

One day runners rushed into Karuri's village with the news that two strange white men, carrying a brightly colored piece of cloth on the end of a stick and followed by a large number of natives with guns, were entering Kikuyuland. From their description, John realized that these men were British officers, come to take over the country in the name of the queen. He was wild with excitement. Now at last his troubles and responsibilities were over. He could go back to peaceful trading and the administration of the country would be taken over by properly authorized and experienced officials. He summoned a conference of the paramount Kikuyu chiefs and told them that a new era was starting for their people. Roads would be built, schools opened. The epidemics would be stopped.

That afternoon, John was marched in under guard to the officers' tent. One of them rose and read from a paper in his hand:

"I charge you, John Boyes, that during your residence in the Kenya district, you waged war, set shauris [made treaties], personated Government, went on six punitive expeditions, and committed dacoity."

"I should warn you that conviction under any one of these charges is a capital offense," the officer added.

John considered the accusations.

"What's dacoity?" he asked.

"Banditry," explained the officer.

"That part's a lie!" roared John. "I was never a bandit in my life."

John was sent to Nairobi for trial under the supervision of the native sergeant and ten men. Meanwhile, the officers, through an interpreter, set about getting evidence against him from the amazed Kikuyu. The trip to Nairobi was ludicrous. The native sergeant had been given a folder containing the charges against John, but the man promptly handed John the folder and asked him to keep it, explaining that he was afraid he might lose it. In every community they passed, the inhabitants turned out in full fighting regalia to welcome their king. The sergeant and his men were so terrified of these wild people that they made John go ahead of them and calm the crowd down before they would venture near the place.

When they arrived in Nairobi, John went to see the subcommissioner with the charges. A supercilious clerk told him that the subcommissioner was too busy to see him and to come back later. John wandered around the town for a few hours and finally managed to get an audience with the subcommissioner. This official casually accepted the bill of charges and glanced through them. The next instant, he froze to attention.

"You're a dangerous criminal," he snapped. "I must send you to Mombasa for trial immediately."

John was put on the train, this time guarded by a white officer and six Indian soldiers with fixed bayonets. In Mombasa, he was thrown in the old Portuguese fort which had been turned into a prison. After a long delay, his case came up for trial.

During the trial, the Crown produced witnesses who testified that Boyes had tortured them by pricking their arms with needles and rubbed in a strange, magic fluid. Others swore that Boyes had wrongfully slaughtered their sheep and goats. True, these animals had been fed to their starving fellow tribesmen, but, as one Kikuyu pointed out, "I still lost my goats." Others claimed that while they were living happily in the hills, Boyes's soldiers had made them go back to work.

At last the judge broke into the proceedings. "It would seem to me that Mr. Boyes did the best he could under the circumstances. Case dismissed."

No matter how officialdom felt about John Boyes, they soon found that they couldn't do without him. When one of the Kikuyu clans began to raid passing caravans and the British sent an expeditionary force against them, John Boyes acted as guide and interpreter. After the expedition, the officer in charge gave John a letter saying that the success of the campaign was due in large manner to John's tact and fair dealing with the tribe and that he would bring the matter to the attention of the authorities. As a result, John was given a thousand-acre farm on the outskirts of Nairobi, which today is being cultivated by his son. I should like to mention that none of this land was ever Kikuyu country. It was part of the open plains area where the Kikuyu, because of their dread of the Masai, never ventured and was inhabited only by wandering herds of game.

John Boyes died July 21, 1951. Many of the leading men in the colony walked humbly behind the coffin of this amazing little man who had once been the king of the Kikuyu.

I believe John Boyes was the only man in the history of East Africa who performed a major feat with no money and no support. John was always completely on his own. He was a remarkable combination of courage, ability, and sheer bluff—at which last quality, I should add, he was a past master. Under somewhat different circumstances, he might well have been another Rhodes or Clive. As it is, his name will never be forgotten in Kenya. I am proud that I had the privilege of knowing such a remarkable man.

John A. Hunter and Daniel P. Mannix

VIII

The Scotch Family McQueen

For many years, James and Mary McQueen, together with their six children, lived a life as closely approaching that of the famous Swiss Family Robinson as can be imagined. I can remember, when I first came to Nairobi, seeing the family on one of their rare visits to the town, all solemnly walking down the main street in a long line—"Indian file" I think it is called—for they were so used to traveling on narrow paths they never thought of walking side by side. First came James McQueen, his full-length beard down to his waist and his rifle over his shoulder. Next came Mary McQueen, a handsome, sturdy woman who would have thought anyone mad to go to a doctor for a little thing like having a baby. Behind them, walked the young McQueens who chatted to each other in Kikuyu, a language which came more naturally to them than English. The eldest boy, John, was the first white child to be born in the Nairobi area. I regret that we "new arrivals" (the year was then 1908) did not take more interest in the McQueens but it is only recently that Kenya has become conscious of its history and pioneers.

What causes certain men and women to leave the comforts of civilization and live in a wilderness? With the Fishers, it was a great religious enthusiasm. With Colonel Grogan, it was a young man's desire for adventure. A desire for profit sent my old friend John Boyes into the Kikuyu country. None of these factors affected

157

James and Mary McQueen in their decision to go to Kenya. They had no desire to convert the natives. The prospect of adventure did not lure them. James McQueen was a somewhat solid, unimaginative man who was the village blacksmith near my old home in Dumfries, Scotland. They did not go to Kenya in hopes of great riches, for there were none to be had. What then caused them to build a home in the wilderness?

I think I know the answer. Deep within every man is the desire "to get away from it all"—to drop everything and go and live on a desert island where the manifold complications of civilization can be forgotten. James McQueen was sick of shoeing farmers' horses, of touching his hat to the squire, of knowing that until the day he died he must get up at the same hour, perform the same chores, and live the same, predestined way of life that Victorian society forced on a man of simple means. He wanted to go where a man was master of his fate and needed to rely on nothing but his ax and gun. So he picked Kenya.

He could not have found a better partner for such an enterprise than his wife Mary. Her picture at the time shows her as a sweet-faced young girl but she was also a woman of great physical strength and quiet determination. As a farmer's daughter, she was used to hard work and as a devoted wife, she was prepared to go anywhere that her James might lead. So this couple left their home and, in 1896, landed in the port of Mombasa, prepared to make a home for themselves upcountry.

The McQueens had read glowing accounts, written by the early explorers, of the fabulous White Highlands in the heart of the country. Although almost on the Equator, these White Highlands offered an almost ideal climate. The Highlands are a great plateau region, so high that the climate never grows too hot and yet snow and bitter cold are unknown. In this earthly paradise, the McQueens had decided to build their home.

In Mombasa, they hired a small group of porters. The heavy wooden boxes, in which Mary McQueen had carefully packed their few possessions, had to be broken open and everything split up into sixty-pound loads for the porters. At the last moment, they were lucky enough to get two donkeys, then most rare and valuable animals.

They started northwest along the old caravan route. Almost from the beginning they were plagued by petty thieves. James lost a set of fine razors, a family heirloom. He was so infuriated by the loss that he swore never to shave again—and kept his word. There were other problems as well. Dysentery broke out and many of the porters died. James buried them while the waiting hyenas stood watch. While crossing the Tsavo district, one of the porters went out in the early morning before light to saddle the donkeys. He saw a dark shape and walked over to slap the saddle on it. There was a furious roar. He had tried to saddle a lion. Shortly after, the porters deserted. The McQueens loaded what goods they could on the two donkeys and went on alone. A few days later, James fell on the uneven trail and sprained his ankle. Mary carried him on her back until they reached one of the British forts. At night, Mary cooked their meals on a piece of flat iron laid across three stones. They washed themselves when they happened to cross a stream. So they went on until they reached the White Highlands, the promised land.

They built their first home in what is now the suburb of modern Nairobi. It was made of mud and wattle with a thatched roof like the native huts they had seen on the trip up from the coast. James constructed a strong boma around it as a protection against the wild beasts and the wilder men. One night a Masai war party happened to pass the spot on their way to raid the Kikuyu. They made a demonstration around the boma, yelling their war cries, throwing their spears in the air, and rattling their huge shields. Mary McQueen was in the throes of childbirth but her husband could do little to help her and he was forced to stand, gun in hand, waiting for the expected attack. After a time, the Masai went on their way. Mary McQueen delivered her baby but the little thing was dead.

After this terrible tragedy, the McQueens no longer had any heart for Kenya. They determined to leave the country and go on to Uganda. So they tramped on to Lake Victoria. Here they hired native canoes and went on to Basugo, not far from Mwanga's capital at Mengo where Mr. Fisher had his mission station. This canoe trip was even worse than the long trek up from Mombasa. The mosquitoes settled on them in great clouds. The canoes were constantly being threatened by crocodiles and aggressive hippos. When they finally reached Basugo, they found that the native wars had put the whole country in a tumult. The Sudanese troops that the British government had sent up to restore order had mutinied and were looting the country. Kabarega, the warrior king of Bunyoro, had sworn to drive all white men out of the country and was close to fulfilling his threat. Famine was so prevalent that it was next to impossible to find food and a plague was raging. Totally discouraged, the McQueens returned to Kenya.

Here they decided to try their luck again. After much scouting about, James McQueen finally selected a spot on the bank of the Mbagathi River, a small, gin-clear stream that flows from the high slopes of the Abardares. He cleared the land with his ax and built a long, low, bungalow-like house, with three large rooms. This building was also made of mud and wattle with a thatched roof, but was a far superior structure to the first simple hut. The walls were covered with a white clay that hardens like plaster, shutters were made and fitted into the windows to keep out the cold night air, and a fireplace was built in the main room. This was the family's home for many years. The McQueens called the place "Rhino Farm" because every morning and evening several of these huge creatures could be seen drinking at the river in front of the house or taking mud baths along the low bank.

Here the six children grew up, two boys and four girls. The family were cut off from the rest of the world. The children never knew what a toy was and had no friends. But they had one of the most beautiful parts of Africa as a home and they had the mountains and the forest as a playground.

Although I never had the pleasure of knowing the McQueens, I had heard that their children were living in Kenya. My friend, Daniel Mannix, made inquiries and found that Madge McQueen, now Mrs. McNaughton, is still living on the old farm where her father first cleared the bush and shot the elephant and rhino that threatened his crops. As my duties made it impossible for me to

visit Mrs. McNaughton myself, Dan Mannix did it for me and I will
let him tell of the interview.

(Dan Mannix now takes up the story.)

The old McQueen farm is still in what seems to me fairly wild
country, although of course nothing to what it must have been fifty
years ago. After driving some miles on a country road through the
bush, I saw the sign "RHINO FARM" and turned off on a lane. The lane
led between a double row of magnificent Cape chestnuts, some of
the finest trees I'd seen in the Nairobi area, and finally came to a
comfortable farmhouse overlooking the Mbagathi River, which is
really a wide stream. Mrs. McNaughton, a slender, attractive woman,
welcomed me. With her was an older, thickset man with a somewhat
whimsical twist to his lips. Madge McNaughton introduced him as
her famous brother, John McQueen, the first white child born in the
Nairobi area.

"A great honor, although I must admit I didn't have much to say
about it," said John McQueen, offering one of his big hands. "Come
inside and sit down. We'll try to make ourselves as interesting as
possible."

We walked into the large, cool living room. "This isn't the original
house," said Madge McNaughton, seeing me look around. "I'm afraid
that's gone now. My husband and I live here and John has his own
place a few miles away, but still on the farm. We're the only ones
on the old place. The rest of us are all scattered about."

"I remember reading about people who lived as you did in *The
Swiss Family Robinson* and *Robinson Crusoe*," I began. "But as I
remember it, both the Robinsons and Mr. Crusoe had the good sense
to be shipwrecked in ships carrying a good store of the necessities of
life. I don't understand how you could live completely on your own
in a wilderness."

"That's because you didn't know father," said John McQueen,
grinning. "If you gave that man an iron mine, I believe he could have
built a battleship. He made everything in the house himself. Some
of the furniture Madge and I are still using. When he needed nails
he forged them, just as the Masai forge their spears. He even made a
pair of scissors so mother could cut our hair. He made a Dutch oven

out of baked clay for mother. She baked in that and fried food over the same flat piece of iron she'd brought up from the coast. Very good food she made, too."

"What did you do for food?" I asked.

"I think we were as completely self-sufficient as any family could be," said Madge proudly. "Father shot whatever meat we needed to eat. We raised all our own vegetables. The vegetables were more of a problem than the meat, though. Father had some wheat, barley and oat seed and he expected a fine crop but none of them did well. The elephants would walk through our fields at night on their way to the river and the next morning we'd find holes two feet wide and two feet deep through the crops. Father shot eleven elephants in one day, but they still kept coming."

"And very fine ivory some of them had," remarked John. "I wish we had it today. But I think the herds of game were worse than the elephants," he went on, turning to his sister. (By game he meant zebra, antelopes and gazelles.) "Hundreds of them would go through a field and trample it flat. But our potatoes did well. We raised potatoes as big as your head. Not even the baboons could get at the potatoes."

"Oh, those baboons were a nuisance," Madge admitted. "One of the tasks father set us was to keep the baboons away. They'd come up from the forest in hordes, led by the old males, with the babies riding on their mothers' back just like a man riding a horse. We had to take a nap in the afternoon and the baboons seemed to know it, for that was the time they'd pick for a raid. One of us always kept an eye on the open window and when he saw the baboons coming, he'd give the alarm. Then we'd all rush out with our two dogs. When the baboons saw us coming, they ran for the forest with us after them. As soon as they got far enough away from the farm to feel safe, they'd stop running and start chasing us. We ran, too. A big male baboon is a very savage animal. He has teeth as long as my little finger."

"I don't believe the baboons ever really attacked us, though," remarked her brother. "It was the dogs that they hated. They'd go right past us to get at the dogs. A dog has no chance against a baboon. We'd have to rush to the help of our dogs with sticks and finally Father or Mother would hear the commotion and come out with the gun."

I asked if the children had ever been attacked by wild beasts.

"No, I suppose we were lucky but I don't really think wild animals are as ferocious as people think," Madge told me. "Of course, a cow rhino with a calf doesn't like to be disturbed and things like that. But we got to know about them just as city children learn to avoid busses and trains. I know they never troubled us."

"Just speak for yourself," said her brother. "I remember as a boy I was out in the woods once, trying to shoot some meat and ran into a pack of wild dogs. They're about the size of a wolf with big, hyena-like ears. They ran back and forth around me, getting closer all the time. I went up a tree. The whole pack collected underneath, and some of them put their forepaws on the trunk and started barking at me. I shot several of them. It must have been the first time they ever saw a gun and they didn't know what was happening. Finally they ran off and I scrambled down and ran for home."

"How about the snakes?" I asked.

"The snakes were terrible," John said. "I don't know where they all came from. There're still a few around; I saw one only the other day. The mambas were the worst. A mamba is no thicker than your thumb but it grows to be eight feet long. Very quick. A cobra, now, will hiss and spread his hood. He's a gentleman. But you never know where you are with a mamba. Father killed them whenever he got the chance. Once I was in bed, taking my nap, and a mamba crawled up the side of the house outside. Father fired at him. The charge went right through the mud wall of the house and father nearly got me as well as the mamba."

"My sister Jean was absolutely fearless with animals," added Madge. "There were big porcupines in the bushes around the farm and when we chased them, they used to go down holes. Jean would crawl down after them. She'd grab a handful of quills and try to pull them out but the quills always came out in her hands so I don't think she ever got a single porcupine. I really don't know what she'd have done with it if she had gotten it. I'm sure they can't make nice pets. But Jean used to carry snakes around in her pockets. I suppose some of them must have been poisonous, but they never bit her. It was really a miracle that Jean was never hurt. I remember one night when she was about thirteen, we heard one of our pigs squealing. We had pigs by that time. Nairobi had been established and Father got them from a trader there. We knew a leopard must have him. I wanted to wake Father, but Jean said, 'Why bother Father?' She jumped out of bed in her nightgown and bare feet, grabbed Father's rifle off the wall, and was out the window before I could stop her. She didn't get the leopard, though. He was too fast for her and escaped with our pig. But another time, a leopard grabbed one of our dogs and ran off with him. Jean chased the leopard and made him drop the dog."

"You say Jean was in her nightgown," I asked. "Where did you get clothes?"

"Well, before Nairobi was built, we did have trouble with clothes," said John, leaning back in his chair and smiling. "That awakens painful memories. Madge, do you remember that old piece of striped material Mother brought up from the coast with her? Mother made us all clothes out of it. By heavens, how we hated that striped material! But she used it, down to the last inch. Then one day Father came back from Nairobi with some khaki cloth he'd gotten. Ah, that was a big day! Still, I should be grateful for that old material, or we'd all have been going around in skins."

"None of us had shoes until we were ten years old," said Madge.

"What did you do about schooling?" I asked her.

"Mother taught us at home in the beginning," she said. "And then when we were older there was school in Nairobi. Every Sunday, we'd play church. We would fix ourselves up as best we could, put flowers on the table, and Father would read to us from the Bible. Actually, as kids, it didn't occur to us to regret the absence of school and such-like. We have a lovely home. Father planted a line of Cape chestnuts on either side of the lane running through our farm and they grew into magnificent trees. You may have noticed them on your way in. Then once he managed to get some young grapevine shoots. He built an arbor and we trained the young vines over it.

I can't believe there was ever a finer arbor in the world. It was fifty feet long and heavy with grapes. We plucked them and they were a great treat. You'd be surprised to know how few edible wild plants there are here. The only ones we ever found were the gooseberries and tomatoes. Even they weren't native. They'd been imported from Europe and planted in South Africa. They were eaten by birds and rooted here in the birds' droppings."

"Wild honey was something we could find," remarked her brother. "I was a great boy for finding honey, and so would you have been if it was the only sweet you ever had. Well, I was cured of that. I remember finding a bee tree one afternoon so I got some dried grass to make a smoke and some leaves to stop the hole and up the tree I went. I set fire to the grass, put it inside, and plugged up the hole. Then I sat down to wait until the bees were stupefied. Well, there was another hole I didn't know about, but the bees did. I never realized there were so many bees in the world. I started down the tree as fast as I could but the bees were around me like a fog and finally I couldn't stand the pain any longer. I let go and fell. I was lucky I didn't break my legs. Then those bees would have had me at their mercy. I ran for home, with a tail of bees a hundred yards long after me. I was in bed for four days, completely blinded. They say bee stings are good for rheumatism. All I can say is that if I ever get rheumatism, it'll be a miracle."

"What did you children do for play?" I asked.

"Oh, we had plenty of amusements," said Madge. "We made up a lot of games."

"As a matter of fact," said John, "our favorite game was stealing the beads off dying women."

I must have looked surprised and a bit incredulous, but John, though he spoke with a twinkle in his eye, obviously meant to be taken at his word. "It requires a quick hand and a steady eye. You must watch out for the hyenas too, which gives zest to the whole business. You see, the Kikuyus believed that any hut where a person had died was polluted and had to be burned down. Well, building a hut was quite an undertaking, so when grandma or grandfather got old and weak, the family would carry them out into the bush and leave them there for the hyenas. In this way, the old folks didn't die in the hut and it could still be used. The dead men weren't of any use but the women were covered with bead ornaments. We used to go around and collect the beads. Yes, it was first the McQueens and then the hyenas. The poor vultures never had a chance."

"We had a very happy, innocent childhood," said Madge Mc-Naughton primly. "We girls used to make beautiful designs with the beads. They were our only playthings."

"When the Swahilis came up from the coast, they spoiled our fun," went on John with a great show of bitterness. "They agreed to dispose of the sick and the dead for two cows each. They got the beads too. Yes, civilization is a terrible thing."

"Let's talk of something else," said his sister. "I think it is rather nice to know that although we children wandered all over the country, the natives never bothered us in any way, even when they were drunk. The Kikuyu had great dances during which they'd drink amazing amounts of 'tembo,' the native beer. They'd put sugar cane in hollowed-out tree trunks and beat it with poles to extract the juice. Then they'd cook the juice all night over a slow fire. It was very potent. They used cattle horns for drinking cups like the old Norsemen. Those dances were really frightening. Men and women, stark naked and mad with the drink, leaping up and down in a circle, screaming and waving their arms. We'd hear the noise and slip out of the house at night. The older children would help the little ones and when we got to the dance, we'd all sit in a line and watch. The natives were always very nice, and no one ever molested us."

"Of course our lives weren't all play by any means," John remarked. "Our parents saw to that. We had to muck out the barn, sweep the house, and cut the wood. Our big job was carrying water up from the river. Later, Father got a donkey named Joe and I may add I was most glad to meet him. Then we could load our water barrels on Joe."

"Oh, but we had plenty of time to play," said Madge, smiling reminiscently. "And even though we didn't have any toys, we had plenty of pets. Do you remember our monkey, John?"

"How could I forget him?" said John. "He belonged to Jimmy, that monkey did. I had pigeons. The monkey used to climb up to the nesting boxes, reach under a pigeon so neatly he never disturbed her, and steal the eggs. He used to rush into the house while we were eating, too, and snatch food off the table. Then he'd be off again before anyone could grab him. On cold days, he'd sit by the fire in the forge where I was helping Father. He was a clever little chap, but he never did learn not to grab a hot piece of iron."

"Then we had a little bush buck that used to sleep in bed with us," Madge went on. "And we had a pet mongoose. I think Father and Mother got us the mongoose hoping it would help protect us from snakes."

"What happened when you got sick?" I asked.

Madge and John shook their heads. "We never seemed to get sick," said John. "Remember that most diseases are spread by humans and there was no way a germ could get to us unless it took a three-month safari. The natives had diseases but we didn't have much contact with them. We didn't know what a cold or a sore throat was. We could get soaking wet in the river, play around all day long in wet clothes, and it never did us any harm."

"Tell me something more about your parents," I suggested. "They must have been remarkable people."

"They were remarkable people," said John, while his sister nodded agreement. "We have a picture of them somewhere, taken before they left Scotland. Where is it, Madge?"

Madge burrowed through some old keepsakes and produced the picture. It was an old daguerreotype, somewhat faded but still surprisingly clear. "Mother looks as though a breath of wind would blow her over in this picture," said John, regarding it affectionately. "You wouldn't believe that she was six feet tall, would you?" I admitted that I certainly would not. "And strong!" added her son. "Even when she was an old lady, I've seen her pick up a two-hundred-pound sack of oats and carry it like a peck measure. And what that woman didn't know about a cow wasn't worth knowing. I've been a veterinarian all my life but Mother had as much practical knowledge about cattle as I have."

"Did you know that even when Mother came to Kenya she had

lost the sight of one eye?" asked Madge. "It was some weakness of the optic nerves. Toward the end, she became completely blind but she knew the farm so well she could go anywhere. She insisted on working up to the end."

"How did your mother get on with the natives?"

The brother and sister hesitated slightly. Then John said frankly, "Neither Father nor Mother ever had any trouble with the natives, but Mother was never particularly fond of them. She'd worked hard all her life and she expected other people to do the same. You can't really expect a native man who's never done anything but coat himself with oil and polish his spear to have any great love for hard work. We realized that, but I don't think Mother ever did. Of course, in the beginning Father and Mother did all the work themselves. Later, when crops had to be taken into Nairobi, the native women had to carry them, as the men considered it beneath their dignity to act as porters. That sort of thing was hard for Mother to understand."

"The natives couldn't understand Mother either," added Madge with a smile. "Once we found a charm they'd put under the doormat. Mother didn't know what it was, but we did. It was a love charm. They'd put it there to make her more easygoing."

"Father seldom showed his feelings," John went on. "I only saw him lose his temper once. Leakey, a missionary here in the early days, sent over two donkeys for Father to shoe. The animals had never been shod in their lives and had hoofs a foot long. While father was filing their hooves, one of them kicked him on the head. I thought the animal had killed him. He fell flat on the floor and lay there half-stunned. He got up slowly, never saying a word and brushed himself off. Then he grabbed that donkey by the legs and slammed him down on the ground. He filed off the hooves and slapped on the shoes and the donkey never budged."

"Like Mother, Father was also tremendously strong," added Madge. "But he moved so slowly and quietly you weren't really conscious of it."

"He was so strong he couldn't understand that what was simple for him might be too much for others," said John, nodding his head. "When I was young, a man brought in a big Clydesdale mare to be shod. Father sent me to do the job. I couldn't even lift one of the brute's feet off the floor. When Father came out later and found I hadn't even begun, he gave me a look as much as to say, 'You lazy little shirker.' Then he went ahead and did the job himself. Father wanted me to be a blacksmith but as I stood there watching him I thought, 'If that's what being a blacksmith needs, I'm going to be a veterinarian.' And so I did."

"Did your parents ever regret coming to Kenya?" I asked.

"Never," said both McQueens together. Madge added, "They never went back to Scotland, not even for a visit. They loved the farm so well they stayed here until they died. Mother passed away in 1940 and Father two years later."

It was noon, and Madge McNaughton rose to turn on the news broadcast. The broadcast was delivered by a young, native announcer in the Kikuyu language as many of the tribesmen have radios but do not speak English. I noticed that several of the native servants, who had been quietly waiting outside, sat down on the porch by the open door to listen. The only words in the broadcast I could understand was the oft-repeated "Mau Mau." Once Madge and John spoke to each other quietly and I noticed that they were unconsciously speaking in the same language. Seeing my surprise, John remarked, "We were just saying that the announcer has a very poor accent. These mission-trained boys try to make Kikuyu a musical language, whereas it's really guttural with plenty of clicking noises. Of course, the different clans have different accents, like Cockney and a Scotsman's brogue."

After the broadcast, I rose to go. "How do you feel about the Mau Mau?" I asked.

Again the brother and sister looked at each other. John answered. "Well, the Kikuyu say this was their land. All I know is that when our parents came here, there wasn't a hut or a stray goat or a broken bit of pottery or any other sign of human habitation. Father cleared the forest, built the buildings, and we've spent a good part of our lives carrying on. If we were thrown out, where would we go? Back to Scotland? We know nobody there. How would we make a living? Scotland is overpopulated already. I have nothing against the natives. Neither my sister nor I ever carry a gun. But we were born here, this is our home, and we wouldn't leave without a struggle."

"After the hardships you've endured, I can understand it," I admitted.

Brother and sister looked at me in amazement. "What hardships?" asked Mrs. McNaughton. "We had a glorious time."

John A. Hunter

IX

R. O. Preston of the "Lunatic Line"

What it will cost, no words can express,
What is its object, no brain can suppose.
Where it will start from, no one can guess
Where it is going, nobody knows.

What is the use of it, no one can conjecture
What it will carry there's none can define,
And in spite of George Curzon's ° superior lecture,
It clearly is naught but a lunatic line.

This poem, which appeared in a London newspaper in 1896, gives
one a fair idea of the public reaction when it was announced
that plans were under way to build a railroad from the coast to the
central lakes. There was much to be said for the opinions expressed
by the unknown poet. Nearly a thousand miles of track would have
to be laid across deserts, through jungles, over rivers that were in
flood during the rainy season, and among mountain passes inhabited
by still untamed tribes. These difficulties seemed well-nigh insurmountable for the engineers of the time, yet a small group of men
determined to go ahead with the project. Yet I doubt not that if these
men had known that, in addition to their other problems, the "lunatic
line" would be held up for three months by man-eating lions, they
would have reconsidered. But they did not know, so the railroad was
begun.

° George Curzon was Undersecretary for Foreign Affairs at the time.

171

But, the reader may ask, why build such a railroad at all? The answer is that by the close of the last century, the British found themselves definitely committed in Uganda, and the cost of putting down the native wars far greater than had been anticipated. Hundreds of troops were in the country and their clothes, ammunition, and often even food had to be carried up from the coast by porters. Then, too, the main business of the country—slave-raiding—had been abolished. The population was rapidly increasing and some way had to be found to get the country's produce down to the coast. Formerly, the goods had been carried by slaves who were then sold along with the goods. That was no longer possible. The only solution was a railroad.

I have decided to tell the story of this remarkable line through the eyes of an old friend of mine, R. O. Preston. Preston followed the railroad from its start in Mombasa until the day, eight months later, when his wife drove in the last spike on the shore of Lake Victoria. To Preston also goes credit for killing at least one of the man-eaters who bid fair to stop the line's construction. I had the pleasure of knowing this quiet, capable man very well and I take pleasure in telling of his exploits.

At some time in the 1870's, two lonely and frightened children were put in an orphanage in India. Their father was a prominent British official of the country. Of their mother, little is known. The children were a boy and girl, the girl several years the elder of the two. The girl married a sergeant in the British army and she and her husband did everything possible to help the little boy. They saw that he received the best education available in India at the time, and was able to gratify his great interest in engineering. This boy was R. O. Preston.

Preston worked on several important projects in India, including the Madras Harbor, where reinforced concrete was first used on a large scale, and the famous Godavari Bridge. In 1896 he was called to Kenya to start work on the new railroad. Preston left India in charge of three hundred Punjabi coolies, utterly ignorant men pressed into service because it had been discovered that African natives refused to do the back-breaking work required in building a railroad. His wife accompanied him and went all the way to Lake Victoria.

When Preston and his gang of coolies arrived in Mombasa, they found the place was still an Arab seaport village, totally unequipped to receive the cargoes of steel rails, engines, and other bulky materials due to arrive there. When the men unloaded a small, two-wheeled refuse cart, one of the inhabitants asked curiously, "Is that the railway?" There was no dock. The ships came in as close to the shore as they dared at high tide, dumped their cargoes into the bay, and left the coolies to retrieve the goods when the tide went out. Living conditions were extremely primitive. The only hotel was a native hut. Food was almost impossible to secure. Preston's servant once proudly laid down two steaks in front of him. "I was lucky," the boy remarked. "I found two dead camels beside the road so I fought off the vultures and got these steaks." On another occasion, Preston stopped to examine some large, black currants a native woman was selling. He reached down to pick up one of the "currants," whereupon the whole lot flew away, revealing a tiny bit of meat underneath. As all water was contaminated, everyone drank coconut milk to avoid dysentery.

Preston's greatest problem was handling the men. Each construction gang had a few natives assigned to it whose duty was to shoot game as food for the crew. A few days after he arrived, Preston saw one of these natives bolt out of a tent and start running for his life. An instant later, another native stepped out of the tent with a rifle in his hands and shot the man dead. "He owed me four annas [about ten cents]," the man remarked casually when Preston protested.

"To show you how desperate we were for food," Preston recounted, "the echoes of the shot had hardly died away when a crowd of my coolies came running up, thinking a buck had been shot. When they found nothing but a dead man, their only reaction was disappointment. I started toward the murderer with some idea of putting him under arrest. He turned toward me with the cocked rifle in his hands. I decided that my shoelace needed tying instead."

The coolies were being paid regular daily wages. The men decided that as long as they got the same sum at the end of a day no

matter what they did, there was no use working. When the morning
bugle was sounded, it turned out that every man in the crew was too
sick to leave his tent. After considering the matter, Preston had the
bugler blow "mess call." Instantly, there was a rush to fall in line.
Preston then addressed the men. "Instead of hiring you as day
laborers, I've decided to promote you all to subcontractors," he told
them. "Now how much will you charge per mile of track laid?" After
a consultation, the men named a rate about three times as high as
their wages would have been. Preston finally managed to persuade
the company to approve this new plan and the work got under way.

The ten-mile strip along the coast is a tropical, well-watered area
and here the crews met with little difficulty. Then they reached bush
country. The only water lay in depressions in the soil or holes in the
outcroppings of rock. These puddles were full of decaying vegetable
matter and crawling creatures. When the men tried boiling it, it
turned into a substance like very thick pea soup and could not even
be filtered through a cloth. To make the mess taste better, Preston
tried dropping some fruit salts in it. To his pleased surprise, the
action of the fruit salts precipitated the matter so that it floated on
the top in the form of a scum. This would be drained off and the
clear water drunk.

Even so, the water was not of the best. Within a few days, thirty
men came down with blackwater fever. Another twelve were limp-
ing about with running sores, probably caused by the bad water and
poor food. There was great rejoicing when the line reached the
Chumvi River. The water was brackish, but drinkable. But the land
around the river was swampy and the mosquitoes rose in clouds
every evening. For several days, virtually every man was laid up
with malaria.

The Chumvi was finally bridged. The building of this bridge,
without the use of derricks, tackle or jacks, was a fine example of
engineering under primitive conditions but to these men it was
simply a routine job. Then the line went on across the Taru Desert.

Laying the tracks here was simple, but the crew that had been
sent ahead to clear out the bush with "pangas" had left the sharp
stumps of the thorn scrub sticking up. Walking among these stumps

was like walking among porcupine quills. The coolies developed ulcers on their legs which quickly infected. On either side of the right-of-way, the bush grew so thick that three men who were sent to shoot guinea fowl for the crews were lost within two hundred yards of the rails. They wandered about for hours until by great good fortune they happened to hear a section gang chanting as they laid the rails.

Preston was not a bushcraftsman and made no pretense to be. He knew nothing of Africa and told me several amusing stories to show his inexperience. While he was out in the bush, hoping to shoot some meat for his crew, he saw the long necks of several giraffes sticking out above the low scrub. "I thought I'd run into some of the giant serpents that Sindbad the Sailor described," admitted the Indian-raised Preston. "Then the animals moved out into the open. Of course, I instantly knew what they were."

Preston good-naturedly told another joke on himself which I take the liberty of recounting here because every outdoor man has had a somewhat similar embarrassing experience. Later on in the trip, he shot a duck and the bird fell in a shallow lake of muddy water. Preston waded out to retrieve his prize. He happened to look down and saw a snake attacking him. Preston fired at the reptile but missed. In something of a panic, he fought his way back to shore, the snake following him and striking at his legs. Crawling up the bank, he clubbed his gun and began to beat the creature. Then he saw that the supposed snake was really one of his leggings which had gotten untied and was trailing out a yard or more behind him.

Although Preston had had no experience in the African bush, he was a remarkably clear-thinking man. I mention one story to show this ability. While out after meat for his men, he became lost in the Taru bush. This was a serious situation. Preston had been trusting to the steady wind, which always blows in the same direction at that time of year, to guide him. But in the deep bush, there was no wind. Then a fowl rocketed up above the scrub. Preston shot it and watched how the feathers of the dead bird floated. With that as a clue, he found his way back to the line.

New complications arose almost daily for the men. Rhinos walking over the line left deep potholes along the roadbed. When the rains came, these filled with water and caused the embankment to sink. As a result, trains turned over. In one accident, two men were killed and twenty-seven injured. Under the fierce desert sun, the rails became so hot that the men couldn't handle them. A certain type of fly attacked the men, sticking its long abdomen under the skin and laying its eggs there. The eggs soon turned to maggots. "But the cure for this was easy," Preston explained. "We soon found you had only to squeeze the boil thus formed and the maggots popped right out."

The Taru Desert was passed and on September 28, 1897, the line reached Voi, about halfway from the coast to the site of modern Nairobi. The railroad was a single-track line and so far the men had not been able to put in a triangle so trains bringing up supplies could turn around. Hence a train had to back all the way to the coast. This meant that the coal dust and smoke constantly blowing in the driver's face constituted a real peril. Now at last the triangle was installed and the line went forward rapidly to the Tsavo River.

"I'll never forget the sight of the Tsavo," Preston told me. "After weeks of the most terrible suffering, it seemed like paradise. The water was clear and cool. Palm trees overhung the banks. Great herds of game grazed on the soft grass. Here was all the food and water a man could want. We thought our difficulties were over. Yet it was at Tsavo that the line nearly came to an end."

The first hint of trouble appeared that evening when the native scouts turned up in a body and announced that they were leaving. The white men thought they were mad. The scouts had stayed with the construction crew all through the terrible desert journey and now, in this modern Eden, they were leaving. In reply to questions, the scouts would only say, "This place is haunted by evil spirits. None of you will get through the Tsavo district alive."

"We begged and pleaded with the men," Preston recalls. "We told them that the white man's magic was more powerful than that of any evil spirit. We offered to hire a witch doctor to protect them. They retorted, 'No witch doctor is fool enough to come near this place.' At last they departed, leaving us cursing the superstitious native."

The river was bridged and the rails pushed on. To Preston's intense annoyance, the Indian coolies appeared to have been affected by the wild tales of the natives. First one man and then another deserted, vanishing in the night without a trace. Finally, Preston called a meeting of his crew. He explained to the men that no one could get back across the desert alone so the men had simply gone to their deaths. He explained the folly of the idea of evil spirits and pointed out that for the first time on the entire trip the crews were well-fed and healthy. "If you have any complaints, don't desert but come to me," Preston ended. "We'll try to work them out together."

The coolies cheered him and returned to their tasks. The next morning, two more men were missing.

An Indian foreman brought in a sandal belonging to one of the missing men. This puzzled Preston. Why should a man desert without taking his sandal? The next day, the mystery was finally solved.

Another coolie had vanished during the night. One of the man's friends, a hillman with some knowledge of jungle craft, tracked him a short distance. He found the missing man's loincloth and brought it back to Preston. "Sahib, a fool might desert with only one sandal but no one would desert naked," he pointed out.

Preston knew this was true. Taking his rifle he set out to track down the missing coolie with the help of the hillman. A few hundred yards away in the forest they found the Indian's skeleton. There was virtually no flesh left on the bones. Beside it was the pug mark of a lion.

"At first, I could scarcely believe the evidence of my senses," Preston admitted. "That a lion could take man after man in this manner and without having the victims give a single cry to warn their friends sleeping around them seemed absolutely incredible."

I can well understand Preston's astonishment, but I know from many experiences with the brutes that a man-eater is a creature of great determination and cunning. An unarmed human being has less chance against one of these animals than a mouse has against a cat. A lion often breaks the neck of a sleeping man with one blow of his paw, and the stroke is delivered almost soundlessly. Then he picks up his victim in his jaws and trots off with him. As a lion can easily carry a full-grown cow, the weight of a man means nothing. If the ground is hard, there is no spoor and it would take an experienced hunter to know what had happened.

All work was promptly stopped and Preston led a party back to the former camps to search for the bodies of the other missing men. One after another they were found—or rather what was left of them. Then precautions were taken against a recurrence of the tragedy. Thorn bomas were cut every night and the men took refuge inside of them. Great fires were kept burning and guards posted. "I knew now that we were safe," Preston told me. "I soon forgot all about the lions in my efforts to get the line through."

For two nights, nothing happened. Then Preston was awakened by the yells of the sentinels and the screams of the camp. Grabbing his gun, he rushed out. "The camp was a madhouse," Preston recalled. "Everyone was screaming, guns were being fired off indiscriminately, men were dashing about beating on kerosene tins and buckets. I finally quieted the disorder. Then I found that a lion had leaped the boma, seized a man, and jumped back over it again so quickly that he was gone before anyone quite knew what had happened."

Tracking the beast at night was impossible. At dawn, Preston went out and found the dead coolie's body. All the flesh was gone from the face, leaving only the grinning teeth. The body was buried and that night Preston had even a bigger boma built and doubled the guards.

There were six thousand men engaged on the railroad. Building bomas to enclose this number of men every night was a major problem. Preston knew their best chance was to get out of the haunted district so he pushed on the construction of the line as hard as possible.

The next day, Preston was returning from a fishing trip when he saw a white contractor who had come up to inspect the line sitting in a tree wearing his pajamas. Rightly considering that this was a bit unusual, Preston went over to question the man. The contractor not knowing about the lions had pitched his tent some distance from the boma. During the night, a lion had leaped on the tent and torn a hole in the canvas, trying to get at the man. The terrified contractor had managed to crawl under his bed and the lion had grabbed the mattress, evidently thinking that was the man. He carried it some distance off and had then begun to tear it to pieces, obviously believing that his prey was inside. The contractor had managed to crawl to the tree and climb it while the lion was busy with the mattress. After discovering his mistake, the lion had return to the tent and followed the man's spoor to the tree. He had then taken up his position underneath and waited until dawn. He had probably left at daylight, but the contractor had been afraid to come down until Preston arrived.

The next man killed was a white man by the name of O'Harra, in charge of road construction. He was sleeping in a tent by his wife's side. There were also two children in the tent, in another cot. Evidently profiting from his previous experience with the contractor, the lion entered the tent and grabbing O'Harra, started to carry him off. The woman's screams and the man's struggles apparently disconcerted the beast, for he dropped O'Harra and ran off. He returned a few minutes later to make a better job of it, but by this time Mrs. O'Harra had gotten a gun and by repeatedly firing at the animal, managed to hold him off until dawn. Unfortunately, this brave woman's heroic effort was to no avail. O'Harra died as a result of the mauling he had received.

Preston describes the funeral as the most pathetic sight he ever witnessed. The corpse was carried on a litter to the grave, followed by the widow. She was carrying one child and the other toddled along beside her, holding on to her skirt.

The lion—or rather lions, for it turned out that there were several of the man-eaters—had now killed eighteen men. The coolies built platforms in trees and on top of watertanks and slept there. However, not all could find such accommodations and the rest had to rely on the frail protection of the bomas. It is almost impossible to build a boma so strong that a determined lion cannot force his way through it. Even the trees did not offer complete protection. The lions learned to take up their position near the bomas and roar. Within a few minutes, the terrified men would rush out and climb the nearest tree. As more and more men climbed the tree, those who had gotten there first would be pushed out on the end of the branches. After awhile, the branches would begin to bend down, with the horror-stricken men clinging to the ends like bunches of fruit. When these bunches were only a few feet above the ground, the lions would come out, pick the fattest individuals as it were, and then carry off their screaming victims with a minimum of trouble.

Only a few of the men with the construction crew had guns and these could not be everywhere. Also, it is almost impossible to see a lion at night, especially in thick forests, whereas the lion, guided by his sense of smell and his natural ability to see even on the darkest night, can move about with complete freedom. So it was decided to trap the animals. No spring traps being available, a very ingenious device was constructed.

This trap was a great box. It was divided into two compartments by a grille of steel rails. One compartment was made with a heavy door which fell into place when the lion entered. The other compartment was to hold the "bait." As a man-eater becomes so wedded to his human prey that he will not often touch anything else, the bait in this case had to be live men. Three of the coolies were persuaded to act as bait. This took considerable persuasion. However, the men were finally induced to get into one compartment of the cage, the door to the other compartment was lifted, and the trigger that would release it after the lion entered set in place. In order to prevail on the men to get into the cage, each had to be given a gun so he could defend himself in case of a mistake. Then other men with rifles were posted in trees around the cage, ready for any emergency.

Night closed down. The watchers in the trees and the men in the cage remained alert for many hours, but nothing happened. At last, it became obvious that the man-eaters had attacked some other spot or were not hungry that night. Everyone dozed.

A few hours before dawn, the men in the trees were awakened by a tremendous racket in the cage. The lion had gotten in and been caught, but instead of being frightened by this state of affairs, he was calmly trying to hook the coolies out of the other compartment with his paw. He could just get his paw through the opening in the rails which acted as bars between the two compartments and this did indeed make matters brisk for the coolies. Grabbing their rifles, they opened fire. In the darkness and their panic, their shots went nowhere near the lion, but they did very nearly bag several of the men in the trees. These men were so busy crouching behind tree trunks to avoid the fusillade of bullets that they were unable to come to the coolies' rescue. This went on for some time until finally the coolies, who never did manage to hit the lion, shot away the hinges of the door. The lion, thoroughly disgusted with the whole business, went away leaving a group of sweating coolies who later swore that they wouldn't go through such an experience again for a ten-pound note.

With every new success, the lions became increasingly aggressive. They would force their way through a boma, grab a victim, and go out by the same opening as casually as a woman doing her afternoon shopping. Preston was astonished at the ease with which these fearsome animals could crawl through the great masses of heavy thorn bushes he had had erected, but the lions were used to living in bush country and thought nothing of it. "Their only problem seemed to be getting the man out through the hole on the return trip," he told me. "Their victims kept getting caught on the thorns and the lions would have to shake them loose, growling irritably in the meanwhile. At first, only one lion would go in at a time while his friend waited outside. But soon the beasts learned to go in together and each would seize a victim. They no longer carried their prey off into the bush, but devoured their quarry within a few yards of the boma. The terrified coolies within could hear the crunching of bones and the screams of the victims, mixed with the loud purring of the huge cats as they set about their evening meal."

Constant efforts were made to track down the man-eaters. Once Preston and three of his men set out on the trail of one of the brutes. As they forced their way through the scrub, they heard a growl and saw the lion crouching in the dense bush only a few yards away. He was still at his meal. Preston fired and hit him, but the light bullet only infuriated the animal. He charged the men at the terrible speed which, I believe, only a lion is capable of attaining in a short rush. Preston and his gunbearer both fired again. Then the lion was on top of them. The cat grabbed the gunbearer and began to maul him, while Preston desperately reloaded. "With absolutely incredible courage, another of my Indians actually pushed the lion aside to get his fallen companion's weapon," Preston recounted. "He pressed it against the animal's side and pulled the trigger but he had forgotten to cock it. Then I was able to fire and the lion fell dead. My gunbearer was still alive but he died a short time later of his wounds."

A few men had miraculous escapes. A hospital orderly, hearing a noise at the entrance to the hospital tent, went to see who was there. He found himself face to face with one of the man-eaters. The lion instantly sprang at him and the man fell backward into a cabinet full of medicine bottles. The crash of glass disturbed the cat and he left the semiconscious orderly to find another victim. Many others were not so fortunate. As the bomas had proved ineffectual, a stockade was constructed around one of the camps. During the night, a lion jumped the stockade so easily and lightly that the guards did not even know that the animal was inside. The lion padded around the tents looking for a suitable victim. Finally the man-eater reached under a tent and grabbing a sleeping men by the foot, began to haul him out. The unhappy coolie awoke, and screaming for help, grabbed a heavy box. The lion dragged him and the box along until the pressure of the canvas side wall pulled the box out of the man's hands. As the man was pulled clear of the tent, he seized a tent stake. The stake broke in his hands and the lion bore him off into the night.

By this time, some thirty men had been killed by the man-eaters and the coolies went on strike. They told Preston that they had come to Africa to build a railroad, not to provide food for the local lions. For three weeks all work on the line stopped. A large group of the coolies stopped the next train coming up from the coast by throwing themselves across the rails. Then they climbed on the cars and refused to get off again until they were taken back to Mombasa.

How many of these man-eaters there were in the Tsavo area it is difficult to say. J. H. Patterson, an engineer on the line, shot two lions generally believed to have been the principal man-eaters. Their skins were sent to the Field Museum in Chicago, U. S. A., and now form part of a group there. Preston also shot a lion which may well have been another of the man-eaters. His son still has the mounted head in his living room. However, there were many lions in the district and it is hard to identify a man-eater positively unless he is caught in the act or systematically spoored down. In my own opinion, there was not one or two "man-eaters of Tsavo" but a considerable number. I think the condition in Tsavo may have been caused by the fact that when a coolie died, the burial parties hired to inter the corpse would often simply leave it out in the bush to save themselves trouble. Lions are great scavengers, and the lions soon learned to follow the camps to pick up these easy meals. Thus they developed a liking for human flesh and when the mortality rate among the construction crews dropped, due to better food and water, the lions turned on the living men. This is a handy theory, and yet I must say that even today the lions in the Tsavo region have always had a curious tendency to become man-eaters. I myself have been called in by the game department to deal with several of them. Why this should be, I cannot imagine unless there is some vitamin deficiency in the game in the region that gives the lions a craving for human flesh. Possibly it is a lack of salt. The human body is very salty.

The construction crews were not the only sufferers from the man-eaters. As the line progressed through Tsavo, stations were established at intervals of thirty miles or so and each of these left in charge of an Indian stationmaster and an assistant. Some of these stations were held in a virtual state of siege by the lions. Preston has recorded several of the amusing but somewhat pathetic telegraph messages sent out by these men in moments of stress. It must be remembered that these stationmasters were simple men, newly imported from India, who had probably never seen a wild animal bigger than a jackal and were completely isolated and unarmed. I give two of the messages.

Two lions on platform. Train approaching and signal man up water-tank. Lions won't let him down. I very nervously frightened and secure in office. Cannot give "line clear" signal to oncoming train. Please arrange matters own personal satisfaction and dispose of lions who greatly bane my existence.

Another read:

Please inform station-master Makindu serious mix-up. Approach with caution or beware troubles and life dangers. Four lions with consorts aggressively on platform and completely in charge of my official functions. Regret impossible perform duties necessary. Please therefore arrange grave matters under report as said lions and consorts making fearful roars and acting savagely. Am in terror of own life.

Lions were not the only trouble that the construction crew had to face. Word was sent to them that the Germans, hearing of the line, were rushing through their own railroad across Tanganyika to Lake Victoria. If this road were completed first, it would mean that the riches of Uganda would be syphoned off into German ports instead of to Mombasa. Preston received a message that a German engineering official was coming up the line to inspect his crew, which was the advance gang. Preston was in despair. Most of his coolies were on strike as a result of the man-eaters and the crew was laying only a few yards of tracks a day. Preston did some hard thinking. The biggest delay in laying the rails came from the rusty bolts which fastened the plates that held the rails together. The rains had started and these bolts had rusted so badly that it was hard to force the nuts over the threads. Preston stopped all work on the line and for two days he and his men feverishly cleaned and oiled the nuts and bolts. When the German inspector arrived, he found the crews busily slapping down the rails and fastening the plates in record time. While he watched, the men laid a mile of track with no apparent trouble. The German returned to Tanganyika and reported that the British were going forward at such a rate that it was hopeless to compete with them. As a result, the German railroad was abandoned. "Our German friend never knew that the strain of cleaning those bolts and laying that mile of track was so great that I had to give everyone two days' rest afterward," Preston remarked.

As new problems kept cropping up, the construction crews solved them as best they could. Once a message came through from the engineer of a train carrying much needed supplies that the train couldn't proceed because millions of caterpillars were crawling over the rails and their crushed bodies were so slippery that the wheels couldn't get traction. That problem was solved by stationing men with buckets of sand on the catcher in front of the engine and sprinkling the tracks. Another time, a train was stalled near Preston's crew because a herd of antelopes had gotten bogged down in the soft mud of the embankment. Preston had his men make lassoes out of their turbans and drag the frantic animals loose.

Near Makindu, some two hundred miles from the coast, the supply of coal for the engines ran out. Wood was used as a temporary make-shift and the work went on. Here the Wakamba, who are still famous throughout Kenya for their skill with bows and poisoned arrows, attacked the line and had to be beaten off with rifles. A few days later, word came in that a Captain Haslan, a veterinarian who had gone ahead to look after the draft mules, had been killed by the Kikuyu. This information arrived at a time when the entire crew was laid up with malaria and a fresh gang had to be brought up from Mombasa. "Malaria was our constant companion," said Preston afterward. "The men would work a few days, be sick a few days, and then go back to the job."

The rainy season broke. The constant floods washed out the roadbed and traffic was halted. High winds capsized two cars. One train was wrecked because guinea fowl, scratching around the ties for white ants, had thrown the rails out of alignment. They were out of the man-eaters' district by now, but wild animals were a constant problem.

"Once a rhino charged a train," Preston recalled. "And when he found that he couldn't make any impression on it, he galloped along-side snorting and looking for another chance. We had some Wakamba hunters riding in one of the cars. We'd hired them after the fighting was over to get meat for the crews. They started shooting the rhino full of arrows, but he still kept on. My crew was in a camp beside the tracks with some of the other gangs and saw them coming.

The idiots all turned out as though watching a race, cheering and shouting. It never occurred to them what would happen when the train and the rhino reached them. We section foremen rushed for our rifles. When the rhino charged into camp, we started shooting while the men scattered in every direction. Fortunately, someone managed to drop the beast. Otherwise, there'd have been a shambles."

On May 17, 1899, the line topped the Athi Escarpment and reached the White Highlands. "We broke records laying track across those flat plains," Preston recalls, "eight thousand feet a day—literally rushing along."

A few days later, the construction crews arrived at the spot where Nairobi now stands. Preston describes it as "a great bog, bleak, soppy and wind-swept." There were no signs of human habitation. "The Kikuyu were all up in the mountains hiding from the Masai raiding parties," Preston believes. Great herds of game wandered about the country, so thickly packed that when the animals moved away to let the men pass, the ones farther away had to bunch up. The old slave route skirted the bog, leading on to Uganda. Ahead, lay the foothills of the Abardare Mountains where John Boyes was reigning as king of the Kikuyu. But the construction gang knew nothing of that. To them, the mountains were simply another obstacle to be surmounted.

"By this time, the only thing that didn't need repair was the foreman's whistle," Preston observed. A halt was called—an important decision in the history of East Africa, as it later turned out. Tents were put up and crude shacks knocked together. After several days of repair work, the crews moved on, leaving behind the abandoned shacks. Other travelers, coming up from Mombasa, used the old shacks and built some of their own. So Nairobi, now the largest city in East Africa, was "founded."

Crossing the mountains, the crews found themselves on the edge of the great Rift Valley. This astonishing formation, running from Egypt to South Africa, is a great crack in the earth's surface, several miles across and walled by perpendicular cliffs hundreds of feet high. It had been planned to take the tracks down the side of this escarpment on a series of long trestles, supported by steel girders. But the girders failed to arrive.

There had been a strike in the steel mills in London so everything was delayed. Ordinarily, a construction crew under such circumstances would simply have sat down and waited until the strike was over. These men could not do that. They had a small army of workers scattered about in a country inhabited by hostile natives. The autumn rains, not too far away, would make work next to impossible and the Germans were still eyeing the new line with considerable interest. To get the trains down the escarpment without the girders seemed impossible but something had to be done.

At length a brilliant if dangerous plan was hit upon and I think my friend Preston at least contributed to its conception. It was decided to run the rails straight down the side of the escarpment and slide the engines and cars down by means of heavy steel cables. There remained the problem of how to get a car up the escarpment again once it had gotten down. To do this, a double track was laid. A cable was attached to a loaded car going down the escarpment and the cable looped around a steel drum at the top and then led down the other track and fastened to an empty car at the bottom. As the loaded car went down, it pulled the other one up.

Laying the tracks down the side of the escarpment was the most difficult problem the crews faced on the entire trip. The escarpment dropped fifty feet in one hundred feet. Even emptyhanded the men could scarcely keep their footing. If they dropped a rail, it simply shot down the slope and disappeared. The ties had to be held in place while the rails were spiked to them. Most of the work had to be done almost blindfolded as the low hanging clouds often kept the men from seeing more than a few feet in front of them.

When the tracks began to reach the bottom of the escarpment, some of the coolies complained that a rogue elephant in the valley below was chasing the crews. Preston took his rifle and went after the animal with a native tracker. While the men were crawling on their hands and knees through the bush, Preston saw what he thought were two tree trunks ahead of him. He made his way toward them. Suddenly the tree trunks moved slightly. Looking up, Preston found himself face to face with the rogue. The supposed tree trunks were the elephant's front legs. Preston fired for the animal's shoulder. With a scream of rage, the bull charged. The old-fashioned black powder threw up a cloud of smoke and under cover of it, Preston rolled away. The rogue rushed past him and an instant later, Preston saw the animal go down on his knees. Thinking he was mortally wounded, Preston hurriedly reloaded and rushed up. Then he saw that the bull had caught his tracker and was trying to gore the man. Preston fired again. The bull flung the tracker over the bush with a flirt of his trunk and rushed away. Preston found the man with five ribs broken but still alive. He later recovered.

The tracks had almost reached the floor of the valley, when Preston, entering his tent one evening, found two dead Kikuyu lying on the floor. The men bore the unmistakable signs of smallpox. The epidemic which struck John Boyes's Kikuyu had broken out. Work was pushed forward desperately to escape the infected area, for here was something far worse than man-eating lions. But the epidemic continued to spread until vaccine was brought up from Mombasa. With the epidemic came a new menace. Leopards began to enter the camps at night, possibly in search of dead bodies. One of the engineers, who was living in a shack made of planks with a corrugated roof, was awakened during the night by something scratching on the door. He opened it and was confronted by a leopard. Hurriedly slamming the door, he snatched up his rifle and fired through it, killing the leopard.

Work was suspended while the men with rifles went out to kill these pests. With Preston was a giant Hindu who walked along through the bush screaming insults to the leopards and daring them to come out and fight. The men hit a fresh spoor and started off on it. The shouts of the Hindu redoubled and finally Preston got sick of the racket and went back to remonstrate with the man. He found the Hindu flat on his back with the leopard tearing bits out of his turban. Preston shot the brute.

The tracks crossed the Rift Valley and started up the west side.

This incline, although not so precipitous as the eastern one, still offered many problems to the engineers. A series of great viaducts had to be built to carry the tracks across ravines and folds in the hills. Within a few miles, twenty-seven of these viaducts had to be constructed from timber cut down by the crews in the forests. The viaducts varied from 156 to 188 feet long, and were from 37 to 111 feet high. It was now the autumn of 1900 and the rains started again. There was an average of six derailments a day. Logs were tied across the front of the engines so when they went off into the mud, the log acted as a buffer and kept the engine from turning over on its side. The trails became almost impassable. The men took the wheels off their wagons and dragged them over the mud like sleds.

They were still working on a grade and as the tracks became coated with the slippery mud, the trains had trouble stopping. Even with the brakes on, the engine and cars continued to move. The crews ran alongside, hurriedly unloading the flat cars as the train slid along. This state of affairs led to a curious and nearly fatal accident. When the line had crossed the west side of the valley, a director of the line came up from Mombasa to see how the work was going. After his visit, he was given a comfortable chair on the rear platform of a string of four cars so he could enjoy the scenery on the return trip and Preston was sent to arrange for an engine to be coupled to the cars. There was a delay in getting the engine and Preston went back to apologize to the director. When he reached the tracks, the four cars had vanished.

Preston called over a workman. "What happened to the cars?" he asked.

"The sahib has gone off with them," said the man, pointing down the track. There, sure enough, was the string of four cars going quietly back down the line toward the embankment with the director sitting happily in his chair admiring the magnificent vista spread out ahead of him.

Preston leaped into a handcar and pumping madly, set off in pursuit of the cars. As the cars approached the embankment, they began to gather speed. Soon they were doing thirty miles an hour and Preston couldn't keep up. In a few minutes, they were out of sight. Preston kept on, expecting at every turn to find the cars crumpled up in a heap with the body of the director in the wreckage. Finally, to his intense relief, he came on the director sitting in the mud beside the tracks, irritated but uninjured.

"When those cars started gaining speed, I waited for a while and then went back to give the engine driver a piece of my mind," he explained. "When I saw that there wasn't any driver or engine either, I was distinctly annoyed. The cars were going so fast by that time, I didn't dare jump but I didn't dare stay with them either. At last I jumped. Thank heaven for this mud."

"Those cars went several miles before they finally left the tracks," said Preston proudly. "A great tribute to the way we'd laid the rails."

Once the Rift Valley was passed, there was nothing but smooth country to Lake Victoria. But at this time an accident occurred that deeply affected everyone on the line. The rails had been laid along the borders of the Kikuyu country and telegraph wire strung up beside the tracks on poles. This wire was a recognized form of currency among the natives and no woman considered herself properly dressed unless she had several yards of wire twisted around her arms and legs. The natives were therefore surprised and charmed to find that the thoughtful white men were hanging up miles of this valuable substance within easy reach. Naturally, they cut down the wire, thus severing all communications.

In December, 1901, the lake was sighted. Two of Preston's best friends, Nesbitt, an engineer, and Turner, a signalman, took an engine and started back with the good news. Not knowing that the telegraph was down, they took for granted that a signal would be sent through if the line was not clear. Unknown to them, another engine was coming up the track from Mombasa. There was a head-on collision. Preston rushed to the scene of the accident in a handcar. Turner was dead, his body so mangled it could hardly be recognized. Nesbitt was still alive. Preston tried to persuade the mortally injured man that he would be all right. Nesbitt smiled. "We've built our last bridge together," he said and died.

On December 19, 1901, the line reached Lake Victoria. Mrs. Preston drove in the last spike. The railroad was finished. It had been started in February of 1897.

Like many another man, Preston found it impossible to leave Africa. After the completion of the line, he bought land near Nairobi and settled down as a farmer. He died a few years ago, one of the best-known and most respected men in the colony. His children and grandchildren still live in Kenya.

Preston was a retiring, unassuming man who was never one to push himself forward. I am glad to be able to give him some of the credit he so greatly deserved.

Daniel P. Mannix

x

Lord Delamere–the Opening of Kenya

The railroad, which was supposed to solve all East Africa's prob- lems, only brought new ones. The supply of ivory in Uganda soon dried up and the other products of the lake district didn't pay for maintaining the line. The railroad fell into such disuse that Colonel Grogan called it "two ribbons of rust." But the road couldn't be abandoned. It had cost too much to build and, besides, the in- habitants of Uganda, now completely weaned away from their old style of life, needed the line to import and export goods—even though these goods weren't enough to support the railroad.

Then the powers-that-be in London had a brilliant inspiration. Why not turn over sections of farming land along the tracks to would-be settlers? This would serve several purposes. The settlers would ship their produce by rail, thus making the line a paying proposition. A vast area would be opened to cultivation and the food raised help the starving people of Europe and the Orient. In addi- tion, this plan would drain off the overpopulated areas of the world and provide new homes for the underprivileged. The natives, too, would profit. The settlers would be taxed and the taxes used to build schools, hospitals, and provide famine relief for the tribes. Looked at from any angle, the plan had only advantages.

So far, every suggestion made about East Africa had met with violent opposition. The missionaries had been denounced, the build- ing of the railroad protested, and responsible men had even seriously objected to stopping the slave trade, arguing that it would upset the economy of the country. But introducing settlers was a happy idea that no one disapproved. There was unlimited land, for wasn't this Africa? A safari could travel for days over magnificent farming country and never see a native. Other great stretches could be reclaimed by irrigation and digging boreholes. So the settlers came, in answer to enthusiastic ads run in the papers.

Everyone was welcome. The Indian coolies who had built the railroad stayed on and sent for their wives, children and relatives from the congested slums of Calcutta and Delhi. A great wagon train of Boers, forced out of South Africa, arrived and took up holdings. A group of Finns migrated to Kenya and settled down. There was even an attempt by some enthusiasts to start a "New Zion" for the persecuted Russian Jews. A large party of Russian Jews did go to Kenya but they were attacked by the Masai and, after a terrible experience, returned to the coast announcing that they'd rather take their chances in Russia. But there were many others to take their place. What America had been to these people's grandparents, East Africa was to them.

One of the first of these settlers was Lord Delamere. No other man, or any single group of men, did as much for Kenya as this erratic, irritating, courageous little English aristocrat. He sank his fortune into the country and proved that it was, as he said, a "white man's country"—meaning that white men could live and prosper there. At that time, it was thought by some that white men could not possibly live for any length of time in a country lying across the Equator. Delamere proved that the colonization of Kenya was possible. Today, his statue stands in the center of Nairobi. The people of Kenya could have selected no better man to honor.

Lord Delamere was born in 1870 in Cheshire. He grew up on his family's ancestral estate, Vale Royal, owned by the family since 1277 and complete with deer park, ivy-covered walls, formal gardens and a stable full of purebred hunters. His father died when the boy was seventeen and so, at a very early age, he became Baron Delamere.

The strict upbringing of most upper-class young Englishmen produced little effect on young Delamere. He thought nothing of losing a month's income on a single bet at the races. He had a violent

temper that stayed with him all his life, along with an almost patho-
logical recklessness. Once while driving a four-in-hand, he lost his
temper with the spirited horses and simply flung the reins over their
backs shouting, "Oh, go to hell!" Naturally the horses bolted and
both Delamere and a companion were nearly killed. His favorite
sport was going downhill at full tilt on a bicycle toward a stone wall
and jumping off at the moment the bicycle crashed. He was pas-
sionately fond of sport and a reckless rider. At an early age, he took
a fall that nearly killed him and gave him trouble with his back for
the rest of his life. He had no apparent sense of responsibility. He
spent money like a drunken sailor and, among other pranks, once
broke into a shoestore and amused himself throwing the shoes
through the windows.

He was a small, slender boy, rather ugly. He had a big nose, red-
dish hair and keen blue eyes. He was intensely nervous and could
not keep his hands still. He had many companions and no friends.
He delighted in making cutting, sarcastic remarks, aimed with
uncanny accuracy at some foible in a person's nature. But, when
the mood seized him, he could be most ingratiating. He often used
his surprising ability to understand a man's temperament in order
to charm him and then, as like as not, a few minutes later would
make some remark of such calculated brutality that the victim was
left hurt and numb. Frequently after one of these verbal attacks,
Delamere would go to great trouble to look up the man and
apologize so sincerely and winningly that his victim would be won
over a second time.

The young lord spent little time at Vale Royal. His passion for
shooting took him on trips to Norway after elk, to India after tiger,
and to Africa after lion, elephant and other big game. With three
other wealthy young bloods, he went to Somaliland, north of Kenya,
where they hired a white hunter to take them out. This man wrote
a number of letters to Delamere's trustee. In them, he gives a description of the trip. He remarks, "Never in all a very varied life have I
seen such disorder, wanton waste, selfishness and utter want of self-
control as these young men daily and hourly show." He went on to
say that although the sportsmen had brought an extravagant amount

of luggage, they had nothing to wear and had to use his clothes. Also "if a thing is left on the ground, it is not picked up, it is kicked aside. Ten times my salary should not again induce me to go with such a crowd of undisciplined, foolish, wasteful, reckless youngsters. I object to a man who tells me on all occasions that I am 'only a servant' and 'not entitled to have an equality with gentlemen.' I am a servant but I am not a 'God damned liar,' or 'a bloody fool.' It was very hard to bear."

The hunter did note that Delamere was much better than the others. On several occasions, Delamere apologized to him for hasty speeches and "spoke in a frank and manly, yet shy, way which I very much appreciate."

The hunter also, somewhat reluctantly it would seem, admired Delamere's nerve. The young lord amused himself hunting wild boars on horseback with a lance, shot five out of the ten lions killed, and although so sick that the hunter thought he was dying, insisted on keeping on. The roughest country and the most aggressive action on the part of the wild tribes produced no effect on him. When his companions gave up and returned to England, Delamere stayed on.

Delamere was so delighted with East Africa that he made five trips there. On his last trip, he went from Abyssinia across the great northern desert to the highlands of Kenya. Delamere is thought to be the first man to make this trip. He fell in love with the cool, pleasant, fertile highlands. When he returned to England, he spoke longingly about them and became increasingly less interested in his magnificent estate.

During this time, an incident occurred that produced a profound effect on the reckless young man and may have influenced his entire life. Between two of his Somaliland trips, he was hunting in England and took another serious tumble because of his wild riding. The fall laid him up for six months. The young doctor in attendance tried to amuse his noble patient by reading to him and for the first time Delamere was treated to something besides the *Sporting Times*. Curiously, he was fascinated. He learned to take a keen interest in science and heard about the work done by Cecil Rhodes in South

Africa with growing excitement. Rhodes's dream of empire became his dream. Delamere decided to return to Kenya and do for the colony what Rhodes had tried to do for South Africa.

Delamere had married a pretty, aristocratic young lady who cannot have known the life she was in for. They arrived in Mombasa in 1903 and went by rail to Nairobi, by now a tiny frontier town.

Lord and Lady Delamere settled near Lake Nakuru. The country there is rolling pasturelands, flanked on one side by the foothills of the Abardare Mountains and on the other by a line of extinct volcanoes which forms the borders of the Masai reserve. There were no natives in the area and even the pastoral Masai never grazed their herds there—a fact which might have made Delamere suspicious if he had ever stopped to think, which at that time he never did. He can hardly be blamed, for the leading agriculturists of Europe would have sworn that these rich, fertile hills were ideal for farming. Delamere decided to raise sheep. He had become interested in the business on a visit to Australia. He imported a number of prize Border Leicesters and Ryelands, together with an experienced Scottish shepherd and his collies to take care of the flocks.

The sheep throve on the fine grass. The climate was ideal—no bitter winters and no hot summers. Lord and Lady Delamere lived in a grass hut and spent every penny they could raise in expanding their flocks.

Then something happened. For some curious reason, the ewes had no milk for their lambs. The lambs died. Then the older sheep began to go into a steady decline. The sheep were not sick. They were fat and apparently healthy. What was wrong?

Delamere called on science to help him, for his talks with the enthusiastic young doctor had convinced him that science can do anything. The scientists he imported found the trouble at last, although only after long and costly experiments that nearly ruined Delamere. There was a vitamin deficiency in the grass. The beautiful pastures were almost as worthless as green excelsior.

The experts agreed that the only cure was to plow up the entire district and plant clover. Delamere mortgaged the income from

Vale Royal to raise the money. In the virgin soil, the clover seemed almost to spring from the ground. The sheep magically recovered and produced perfect offspring. The next year, the clover died.

What was wrong now? New experts were called in. More expensive research showed that the local bees couldn't get into the foreign clover blossoms to fertilize them. So hives of English bees had to be imported and set up.

The clover did well—too well. After the rains, it grew so fast that the sheep were wandering about in green jungles of giant clover. They developed foot rot. Four-fifths of them died before they could be moved to new areas. Here they picked up diseases from the game animals to which the native game was largely immune but the sheep were not. They became so weakened that flies laid eggs in their eyes and nostrils. More died.

By this time, Delamere was close to bankruptcy. From what has been said before, it might seem that Delamere was an enormously wealthy man. So he was, as most English lords went. At home he lived in a great house, had vast estates where respectful cottagers touched their hats to him, and wanted for nothing. But the actual cash income from his estate amounted to less than ten thousand dollars a year. At that time when servants worked for virtually nothing and the upkeep of the estate was met by contributions from the local tenantry, ten thousand dollars a year was a lot of money for a young man to throw around. Champagne was seventy-five cents a bottle and even his most elaborate trips cost only a fraction of what they would today. But to undertake a series of costly experiments in order to develop an unknown country was another proposition. Nowadays, only a wealthy government would attempt such a project.

Delamere did not care a jot about such details. He had never paid any attention to money and he went on with the comfortable assurance that his distracted mother, back in Vale Royal, would pawn the family jewels or raise the necessary cash somehow.

There was another factor involved in Delamere's desire to develop Kenya, equally important, and yet hard to state convincingly. If Kenya was to be opened, someone had to put up the money for experimentation. A modern American would take it for granted that the government would do it. But Great Britain did not have the enormous sums available that the United States does today. The young lord had a tremendous sense of responsibility. So he kept on.

Sheep having been a failure, Delamere tried cattle. While in Abyssinia, he had noted the Boran cattle—hardy animals that were apparently immune to disease and quite capable of roughing it. He decided to try a cross between these animals and imported English cattle. This new stock was promptly wiped out by East Coast fever, which was unknown in Abyssinia. Again, Delamere was faced with ruin. Meanwhile, Lady Delamere, the daughter of an earl, was still living in a grass hut and trying to support herself and her husband by raising chickens, pigs and ostriches from which she clipped the plumes to sell to milliners for ladies' hats.

Now for the first time, Delamere had a little luck. One morning he found a deputation of Masai leaning on their spears waiting to talk to him. The Masai, fanatically keen herdsmen, explained that they had been watching his efforts with considerable interest. If he'd asked them, they could have told him all along that his ranch was in an area unfit for cattle. By a process of trial and error, they'd discovered long ago that the grass was worthless. If Delamere wished, they'd give him a hand, show him sections of grazing land where his livestock could live, and, in brief, run his cattle business for him. Delamere gratefully consented. He never forgot the Masai's co-operation and later became their great champion in rows between the tribe and the government. A group of warriors attached themselves to him somewhat as a bodyguard and the sight of the small man hurrying down the streets of Nairobi followed by the tall, half-naked warriors with their long spears became familiar.

Although the Masai were able to salvage what was left of Delamere's stock, they could not put the business on a paying basis. There were still too many problems, such as wild beasts, rinderpest, East Coast fever, anthrax, bovine pleuropneumonia, foot-and-mouth disease and tsetse fly, which served to keep the stock down. The Masai frequently lost two-thirds of their own herds from such causes. However, the fortune Delamere spent in research was not thrown away. The discoveries he made laid the foundations for subsequent work which has today gone far to eliminate these scourges.

Delamere next turned to wheat. He started off by plowing with a new tractor engine which had proven most successful in Canada. Unfortunately, the Kenya soil turned out to be so light that the heavy tractor forced it into a hard-packed mass that choked the young shoots. Delamere then tried plowing with oxen. He imported Boer farmers from South Africa to teach him how to handle the unruly beasts. The famous Delamere temper was still in evidence and once when two settlers stopped to laugh at the sight of the little man trying to use a long bull whip and getting the lash tangled around himself, Delamere promptly turned and began lashing them with the whip. In those days when everyone carried guns, this was a risky procedure, but apparently the settlers took it in good part and ran off still laughing.

The wheat did no better than the cattle. One of the great problems was the herds of wild game still wandering the country. No fence could stop them once they were on the move and they would trample a field of wheat flat in a night. Delamere resorted to his gun but the British government stopped him. They would not permit the settlers to slaughter these animals as the American frontiersmen had slaughtered the buffalo. How then, Delamere asked, could he raise wheat? The government did not know, but they refused to allow shooting. Delamere, in his usual determined way, told the government where it could go and continued to use his gun to keep the animals away. But even this was only a partial solution. Various types of wheat rust appeared, which were beaten only after another long series of subsidized researches. At last a rust-resistant variety of grain was developed and this "Equator wheat," as it came to be called, made wheat farming practical in Kenya.

By now, no one could have recognized Delamere as the gay, mad young nobleman of a few years before. To protect the back of his neck from the sun, he wore his hair so long that it hung over his collar. He dressed in old khaki breeches and a sweater. He rose before dawn, dressed by lamplight, and ate a hurried breakfast. As soon as it was light, he would start out on his rounds. At first he rode a mule. Later, he used an elderly Ford. He spent the morning checking his wheat for signs of rusts or damage by game, dosing sheep for worms, arranging for the breeding of his cattle, or helping his native boys dip livestock to kill ticks. After a quick lunch, he went over the reports of his researchers and checked the farm accounts. Then he interviewed his Masais and listened to their problems and suggestions. In the evenings, he would meet with other settlers to discuss politics, for political questions were becoming of vital importance to the growing colony.

He seldom went to bed before midnight and was always up by five. He needed surprisingly little sleep, and his energy was inexhaustible.

Occasionally he was forced to make quick trips to England in order to raise more money on his already heavily mortgaged estate. A letter that Lady Delamere wrote him at this time gives an idea of the life they led.

I suppose you have heard of our scare. The Sotik looted two Masai villages on the other side of the line from here. Wiped them out, I understand. Then the government sent word that another party of Sotik were coming. So I borrowed 200 cartridges from Mr. Clutterbuck. Personally, I never thought they would come here but thought it as well to get more cartridges.

I wish you had told me to look after the pigs as one pig produced only one small pig last night. The boy swears she never had more but I think he is lying, at least it seems strange. I have been ploughing with the bullocks but not to my satisfaction. They go round two and a half times a day which is better than nothing but not much.

The rain has been awful and the cold intense. I hope you won't be annoyed but I couldn't stand it any longer and have bought the materials for a little house and have hired a carpenter to build it. I could not stand the cold any longer.

Delamere continued to pour every penny he could raise into his farm. He built pipelines to the mountain streams in order to irrigate. He continued his researches in controlling livestock diseases until finally the raising of livestock became practical on a large scale in Kenya. He experimented with flax, coffee and sisal. By 1910,

Delamere had milked Vale Royal dry and was heavily in debt to the Nairobi bank. But at long last, the farm was beginning to pay. Not only that, but farms throughout the highlands were also beginning to pay, largely through Delamere's tireless work in finding out which were the best crops to grow and his development of new breeds of cattle better adapted to life in Africa. The colonization of Kenya was now assured.

As the colony continued to develop, a new problem gradually took form—a problem so serious and complex that it has now culminated in an armed uprising, forcing the British government to send troops and bombing planes to Kenya. This problem was the "native question."

The settlers had little trouble with the warlike tribes in Kenya. After a few sporadic uprisings, tribes like the Masai realized that they had no chance against firearms and retired to live on their reserves. The economy of these tribes had been based largely on raiding the weaker and more prolific tribes around them. When the British stopped these raids, the tribes that had been the victims of the Masai began to increase at an alarming rate. The most outstanding example were the Kikuyu. Within a few years, the Kikuyu doubled in numbers. Then they tripled. A shrewd people, famous for their ability to accomplish by cunning what other people could not do by force, the Kikuyu found civilization to their liking. They were protected from their enemies and the old bogies of famine, disease and insect plagues were largely checked.

As the Kikuyu increased in numbers and as the people began to have a better understanding of their legal rights, they started agitation for more land. The whole question of land rights in Kenya is very involved, but briefly, this was the situation.

When the series of disasters which John Boyes witnessed hit the Kikuyu, the lowland clans moved into the mountains to escape the stricken areas. When the whites arrived, they found large sections of land apparently vacant. Some of this land was occupied by the settlers. Later when the Kikuyu returned, they found white farmers on their former property. As there was plenty of land at that time, the Kikuyu simply moved into other districts but later as the population increased, they demanded the return of these lands. This was the beginning of the trouble.

There were other problems. The Kikuyu had left large areas as "buffer states" along the edges of the forest between them and the Masai. Many of these buffer sections had been occupied by the settlers. Now the question arose, who owned these areas, the Kikuyu, the Masai or the settlers? Still another problem occurred when, as a result of the stopping of the Masai raids, the Kikuyu were able to move onto the fertile plains where they had never been before. This area had been listed as "unoccupied land" and given to settlers who were coming out from England to farm it. When the settlers arrived, they forced the Kikuyu to vacate. The Kikuyu felt that they had been made to leave land rightfully theirs as they had first occupied it.

Attempts were made to find the Kikuyu more land. A commission was formed which, after long investigation, decided that about 110 square miles of Kikuyu land had been occupied by settlers. As a result, 156 square miles of land was added to the Kikuyu reserve. However, the Kikuyu protested that part of this new land was inferior to the land taken away from them. The commission then investigated again and agreed that the Kikuyu claim was just. So an additional grant of land was made which, in the opinion of the commission, more than compensated the Kikuyu for any land lost to them. The Kikuyu did not agree. They continued to feel that the whites had taken the best land in the highlands and that they had been badly treated.

The British government was frankly on the side of the natives and against the settlers. In a famous white paper, the government stated flatly, "The interests of the natives must be paramount . . . if the interests of the immigrants should conflict, the former should prevail."

This doctrine of "paramountcy" as it was called brought the settlers of Kenya to their feet as one man. The settlers had been having a hard time. One of them turned up at Delamere's farm with a bale of hay, his whole crop that season, hoping that Delamere would buy it. He had walked eight miles carrying the bale on the chance. These men had at long last been able to get their farms on a paying basis and they regarded the highlands as their property, not as an area where native interests were to be paramount. Delamere led the revolt against the government.

At that time, the East Indians were even more of a problem than the natives. Ever since the building of the railroad, immigrants from India had been pouring into the colony until now they outnumbered the whites three to one. The British government felt strongly that the Indians should have full representation in the Kenya legislation. The settlers felt, even more strongly, that this would mean Kenya would become an Indian colony. The Indians would work and live under conditions that the English settlers would not and there was strong feeling between the two groups.

As a result of the Indian-native question, the governmental officials in Kenya and the settlers became strongly antagonistic groups. Delamere was the settlers' champion. His impetuous temperament, his biting tongue and his aristocratic background perfectly fitted him for this position. The settlers loved, and still love, to tell stories of Delamere's engagements with officialdom. The officials seldom won.

As with all bureaucrats, the Kenya officials tended to live in a snarl of sacred red tape and it required weeks to obtain permission to so much as cut down a tree or shoot a lion that was killing cattle. Once Delamere obtained permission to put up a mill on a section of land and after the mill had been partly built, the Land Office rescinded the permit claiming that the title to the land was not clear. Delamere told them to hurry and check it as he could not hold up construction indefinitely. There was a long delay, and finally Delamere marched into the Land Office, followed by his Masai bodyguard and demanded action.

The Land Office gave him what is now known as the "brush off." Delamere was a hard man to brush off and he left swearing that he would make the officials sit up and take notice. They smiled in a superior way and returned to drinking their tea.

The Land Office was on the second floor of a new building and the first floor was empty. A few minutes later, a clerk, happening to pass the stairway that led down to the first floor, stopped with a gasp of horror and shouted, "Look!" The rest of the office staff hurried to his side. Delamere's Masai had filled the ground floor with faggots and Lord Delamere was busily engaged in setting fire to the pile.

At that time, there was only one policeman in Nairobi and he, being a man of great intelligence, invariably left town for a long safari into the blue whenever Delamere arrived with his Masai bodyguard. The distracted Land Office feverishly made out the necessary papers in record time while smoke was curling up through the cracks in the floor. According to several old settlers, this was the only time in history that Kenya officialdom was known to do a quick, efficient job.*

Pranks like this, no matter how much the settlers might enjoy them, did nothing to win over the officials to the settlers' cause. Ill-feeling grew so intense that, according to one old Kenya legend, the governor once said "Good morning" to a clerk who, without bothering to look up, burst into a string of curses. When the clerk saw whom he was addressing, he exclaimed apologetically, "I beg your pardon, sir. I thought you were one of those bloody settlers."

One incident after another added to the tension. A settler, finding some natives stealing his sheep, fired at them and killed a man. He was later acquitted by a jury of settlers. This case aroused so much feeling in Great Britain that the settler was finally forced to leave the country. A law was passed limiting the settlers to a twenty-one-year lease on their lands. Only after a long fight on the part of the settlers, spearheaded by Delamere, was the law changed.

As a speaker, Delamere was excellent. His arguments were well reasoned, well presented, and tinged with just enough sarcasm to sting. On rare occasions, the tough little planter indulged in tricks

* Many of the early officials in Kenya would seem to have been an irritating lot with their contemptuous manners and love of form. Not only the settlers, but such travelers as Evelyn Waugh speak of them bitterly. I think it is only fair to say that during the time I was in Kenya, I had many times to go to government agencies for old records and information, and seldom have I met men so obliging and so willing to go to a considerable amount of trouble to help a journalist.

that the settlers considered uproariously funny but which must have infuriated the officials almost beyond control. Once the governor gave a long and somewhat pompous oration and waited for Delamere to reply. The Baron gravely took out a red bandana handkerchief from his pocket, wrapped it around his head like a woman's scarf, and began to mimic the governor.

The settlers were very like American frontiersmen. Nairobi in those days resembled a Western cowtown. After spending months in the bush fighting nature, wild animals and not infrequently native cattle thieves, the settlers came to Nairobi for a good time. A favorite stunt was to gallop down the main street and shoot out the kerosene street lamps with revolvers. Another pastime was to pull the tiles off the roofs, throw them into the air and shoot at them like clay pigeons. Often a white hunter, bearded and filthy from a long trek upcountry, would walk into the Norfolk Hotel, throw a tusk of ivory down on the desk and say, "Let me know when I've worked my way through that." Then he'd move into the best suite with a case of whisky. Delamere loved this kind of life and these people. He would deliberately start general fights in the Norfolk Bar and then, when the going got good, climb up on the bar, take a run down the length of it, and jump feet foremost into the middle of the riot, flailing with both fists.

If the settlers played hard, they also worked hard. The nine thousand Europeans, who had built up their farms from the raw bush, were by 1920 paying over two and a half million dollars a year in direct and indirect taxes. Most of this money was spent by the government on schools, medical service and famine relief for the native tribes. The tribesmen were also taxed. They paid a "hut tax" of about a dollar a year on each native hut. This tax money was carefully earmarked for projects intended for their benefit. Although there were then some five million natives and thirty thousand Indians in Kenya (who also paid taxes) their combined contributions amounted to less than the sum paid by the settlers. Naturally, there was another side to the picture. The two most profitable crops (coffee and sisal) were a settlers' monopoly and the wages paid the natives were very low—at that time about a dollar and a half a month. The settlers, however, were not making any great sums of money. Most of them were living very simply and even today few of them can afford the expense of sinking boreholes on their lands even though irrigation during the dry seasons is a vital necessity. Although it would have been quite possible to gross large sums farming in Kenya, the numerous restrictions, mainly designed to protect the natives, and the top-heavy government required to administer these regulations, made big profits almost impossible.

In 1923, the Colonial Office in London embarked on a policy that was clearly aimed at eventually turning over Kenya to the natives and allowing the settlers to remain there only under sufferance. The situation had always been tense. Now the settlers began to prepare for open rebellion. They formed "vigilance groups" and made plans to seize the railway, cut the telegraph lines, and occupy Nairobi.

Hoping to keep the peace, Delamere led a committee of settlers who went to London to protest the government's policy. Delamere put up the money to rent a house for the group in fashionable Grosvenor Place. They must have made a strange spectacle in that chaste atmosphere. Delamere with his long hair hanging down over his collar, one of the delegation wearing an old coat covered with red mud from his farm, and two Somali servants. The Colonial Office received this committee with good-natured contempt. The idea of a handful of settlers threatening armed rebellion against Great Britain seemed absurd. Then the office received a cable from Mombasa. The telegraph wires to Nairobi had been cut. It was believed that the governor had been seized by the settlers and the whole country was rising.

This news put the Colonial Office in a terrible situation. The settlers were few in number but they were tough, determined men, all first-class shots and experts in guerrilla warfare. To send an expeditionary force to put down an uprising would be a long and fantastically expensive undertaking. It was even questionable whether British troops would fire on the settlers. Worse yet, if the settlers were put down by force and made to leave the country, Kenya would be in a hopeless state of chaos. It was all very well for enthusiasts to speak of the natives' interests being paramount, but no one, including the natives themselves, seriously wanted Kenya to return to the conditions of fifty years before. Delamere understood the quandary of the Colonial Office perfectly and handled the situation with the skill of an expert politician. Already, he pointed out, the young Masai moran were whetting their spears and looking forward to a descent on the hated Kikuyu. He reminded the Colonial Office that during the First World War when the line of "Beau Geste" forts stretching across the North Frontier District had had to be abandoned, the wild tribes from the north had poured into Kenya looting, burning and carrying off slaves into Abyssinia where slavery was still legal. In the bush country south of Nairobi, the Wakamba were preparing the poison for their arrows and getting ready to reoccupy parts of their country which they claimed had been given illegally to the rapidly increasing Kikuyu. If the settlers left, what did the Colonial Office intend to do?

The Colonial Office didn't know. It had been their idea to ease the settlers gradually out of Kenya, meanwhile taxing them for the benefit of the African tribes. The cost of developing and maintaining peace in the country without the help of the settlers and the settlers' taxes would be more of a burden than the British public could stand. To simply abandon the country, leaving it in a state of intertribal wars, was from a political point of view impossible. Some other great power would simply move in—such as Italy, which had occupied Italian Somaliland and was beginning to show signs of the imperialistic dreams which finally resulted in the invasion of Abyssinia. There was nothing to do but come to terms with the settlers.

Delamere had been lucky. As it turned out later, the telegraph wires between Nairobi and the coast had not been deliberately cut. They had come down in a heavy storm. Before this discovery was made, however, a new colonial policy had been drawn up. It was a compromise between the various parties—settlers, natives and Indians. No one was satisfied but at least the threat of a settler rebellion passed.

A few years after the great battle with the Colonial Office in

London, Delamere suffered a nervous breakdown. When he recovered, he still remained prominent in politics and worked hard at his farm, but he was now growing old. He still retained plenty of his old spirit.

A London official who went to Kenya to discuss the settlers' problems described him at this time as "part politician, part poseur, part Puck, but the greater part patriot." Although eventually he was able to make his farm one of the most successful in Kenya and recoup his fortune to a large extent, he continued to live very simply. He slept in a small outbuilding originally intended as a garage and never bothered to use sheets on his bed, merely rolling himself up in blankets. He continued to plow back all the money made on the farm into new improvements and research. Lady Delamere had died in 1914 and in 1928 he married Lady Markham, daughter of the Hon. Rupert Beckett. Fortunately, the new Lady Delamere was as enthusiastic about Kenya as her husband and enjoyed being a farmer's wife.

To get along with Delamere, you had to be a Kenya enthusiast. One of his employees remarked, "Lord Delamere is a fine man if he feels you're mad for Kenya and will go all out to develop the place. If not, he's apt to have a violent temper. Afterward, if he feels he's in the wrong, he'll come back and apologize." Nothing could ever persuade Delamere that Kenya was not the country of the future. He thought of it as the finest part of Africa, and of Africa as the potentially richest continent in the world.

During the last years of his life, Delamere became so universally recognized as the settlers' spokesman that he was reluctantly forced to spend much of his time heading committees and presenting settlers' grievances to the British government. He always begrudged every hour he was away from his farm and regarded politics as a nuisance that kept him putting all his energies to new pipelines, fresh cattle-breeding experiments and the development of better types of grain.

In November of 1931, Hugh Cholmondeley, the third Baron Delamere, died on his beloved farm. He was buried, at his own request, on a little hill overlooking the lake. The farm is now the property of his son, John Cholmondeley, the present Lord Delamere.

It is hard to believe that the colonization of Kenya could have been carried out without the inspiration and financial help of this exceptional man. Since his death, no one else has been able to take his place as leader of the white community.

XI

The White Hunters

No more colorful group of men have ever existed than the white hunters of East Africa. They have been immortalized in fiction by such men as Rider Haggard and Ernest Hemingway. Today, the motion picture industry has set out to do the job all over again. To my mind, the early white hunters well deserve all the praise they can receive. I can hardly claim to belong to their ranks. But I am proud to say that I knew them. In this chapter, I make no pretense of cataloguing all the white hunters who have made Kenya history. I cannot even say that I have attempted to record all the outstanding ones. I will merely mention a few who happened to be good friends of mine and in whose stories I believe the reader will be interested.

The white hunters differed greatly. Some were as flamboyant as any role played by Errol Flynn. Others were moody and frequently sullen. Still others were hard-headed businessmen. Some of the best were mild little men who seemed incapable of saying "boo" to a goose. Yet there was one trait they all had in common—absolute courage. Even this quality showed itself in many ways. Some men were suicidally reckless. Others never took an unnecessary chance. I know of one man who seemed to be on the point of a nervous breakdown if he saw an animal larger than a Thomson's gazelle but at the last moment he always came through. What impulse drove them to this dangerous and difficult life it would be hard to say. No doubt there were as many impulses as there were men.

How did the white hunters originate? To answer that, I must tell the story of Harold and Clifford Hill, for I believe these two men were the first of the white hunters in the sense that we now use the term. Luckily they are both still alive and living contentedly on their farms near Machakos.

Harold and Clifford Hill are cousins who came to Kenya from South Africa in 1904 to start an ostrich farm. At that time there was a great demand for ostrich feathers to be used on women's hats but in South Africa a good cock ostrich was worth two hundred pounds. In Kenya, the birds were running around loose, to be had for the catching. The Hills obtained a strip of land from the government near Machakos, the same ranch that they have today. Although the Hills did not know it at the time, the government gave them the land to serve as a buffer between the Wakamba and the Masai, hereditary enemies who were constantly at war. The government had built a fort at Machakos which had several times been attacked by the natives and the officials thought that the presence of some settlers would have a quieting effect on the tribes.

The Hills had little trouble obtaining ostriches and started their ranch with high hopes. Unfortunately, the ostrich happens to be the lion's favorite food and the area was full not only of ostriches but also of lions. The lions quickly learned that the Hills were obligingly keeping these birds in pens, apparently for their special benefit. As a result, they began to raid the pens and the Hills were soon faced with ruin.

Neither of the Hills was a sportsman nor greatly interested in shooting. They regarded the lions simply as vermin. One night Harold went out and shot five lions that were killing his birds— a routine, unpleasant task that had to be performed. But the lions became such a nuisance that the Hills were forced to embark on a policy of extermination, much as a farmer might set out to destroy foxes that were killing his chickens.

The Hills are both gentle, quiet men, Harold being several inches shorter than his tall, slender brother. Talking to them, one finds it hard to believe that they not only originated the romantic profession of white hunting, but that both have distinguished war records—Clifford especially having a string of war medals from the relief of Mafeking in the Boer War to a D.S.O. from World War I. The Hills find it mildly amusing that anyone should consider it unusual for two young men, equipped with old Snyder rifles, to engage in a war against one of Africa's most dangerous wild animals. The war was not without its casualties, as you will read.

A lion had broken into the ostrich pens and killed twenty birds. The next morning, the Hills went after the animal. With them were two of the neighboring farmers, named Pease and Grey. The hunters split up into two groups. Grey stayed with Harold and Pease went with Clifford. All were mounted except Harold.

The lion was found in a "donga," a gully full of bushes. Clifford and Pease rode around the donga to cut off the animal's retreat. The lion was bolted with dogs but instead of running toward Clifford and Pease as expected, he went in another direction. Grey started after the beast at full gallop. The other men expected him to dismount as soon as he came within range but Grey kept on. Finally Clifford and Pease began firing, hoping to turn the man. Grey kept on until he was within a few yards of the lion before dismounting.

"He was still shaky from his long ride," Harold Hill explained. "As he took aim, the lion charged. Grey missed. Before he could fire again, the lion was on him. Cliff and Pease galloped up but they didn't dare to fire for fear of hitting Grey. Finally Cliff shot the lion high through the body. The lion, in a spasm of pain, tossed Grey up in the air and then turned on the other men. They both fired, killing him instantly."

Grey was carried on a litter to the train and a doctor rushed down from Nairobi. Harold held a lamp while the doctor worked over the unconscious man. It was useless. Grey died five days later.

"He should never have struggled with the lion," Harold remarked. "That only angers a cat. I remember once when a leopard jumped me while I was after guinea fowl. I had only birdshot in my gun, so I just fell on my face and give him my arm to chew. After a while he got tired of it, and left me. My arm infected and the doctor who came out was drunk. He wanted to cut it off, but I wouldn't let him. In three weeks, it was as good as new."

The Hills became very expert at shooting lions. Their reputations spread, and soon other ranchers who wanted a day's sport came out to see them. Then travelers began to arrive in the country who wanted to say that they'd shot a lion. They were always told to go out and see the Hills. At last, this became a nuisance. The Hills began to charge visitors for their time and trouble. Thus white hunting was started.

A few months after the Hills had established themselves as professional hunters, an American by the name of Paul Rainey arrived in Kenya with a pack of hounds. Rainey intended to use the hounds on lions. Rainey was also a photographer and had one of the first motion picture cameras ever to appear in Kenya. He particularly wanted a picture of a charging lion and, as there were no telephoto lenses in those days, he wanted the lion shot within a few feet of the camera.

Harold Hill at first refused this assignment. Then Rainey said impressively, "I'll give you fifty pounds."

"I hadn't seen fifty pounds for years," Harold Hill admits. He only made one proviso. If he were killed, Rainey would have to support his wife. Rainey agreed.

Harold's quiet manner, not at all what one would suspect of a famous hunter, began to worry Rainey. The American asked suspiciously, "Say, you are a lion killer, aren't you? Have you got a gun?"

Oh yes, indeed, Harold had a gun. He went and got his old Snyder. Rainey exploded with scorn.

"You call that thing a gun?" he demanded.

"It's a good gun," said Harold, very hurt. "The only thing is that after you press the trigger, you have to keep holding your sights on the target because it takes it a second or two to go off."

Rainey took a deep breath. "Well, you're not going out with me carrying that old gaspipe," he said determinedly.

However, that being the only gun that Harold had, they went out. The hounds tracked a lion down into some cover and then rushed in to bolt him. Meanwhile Rainey set up his camera and Harold took up his stand beside him.

"When do you want me to shoot?" he asked.

"When he gets to that little sapling over there," said Rainey with a jerk of his thumb.

The sapling was only a few yards away from the camera. Harold said nothing, but he knew that at such a close distance, the momentum of the lion's charge would carry him on top of them even if it were a mortal wound. The bullet from a modern, heavy rifle hits a lion with such force that it will knock him off his feet but Harold's old Snyder had no such "shock" power. He had to hit the charging beast in exactly the right spot and then trust to luck.

Suddenly Rainey said, "Suppose your wife marries again, do I still have to support her?"

"No," said Harold. "In that case, you're free of obligations."

"Good," said Rainey. "Then let's start throwing in stones to bolt him."

The lion, already maddened by the yelping hounds, required only a few stones. Suddenly he burst from the cover and charged the men, the hounds screaming on his tail.

I believe no animal moves as fast as a lion charging for twenty yards or so. The animal comes at you in a series of great bounds, seemingly as fast as a shell fired from a cannon. It is most difficult to hold him in your sights and you have only a few seconds to draw a bead. Harold did not dare take his eyes off the charging beast to see when he reached the sapling. He waited, thinking Rainey would speak, but Rainey kept turning the crank of the camera. Finally, Harold fired. The lion leaped in the air and rolled over like a shot rabbit. When he stopped moving, he was nine feet from the camera.

In the next few years, Harold and Clifford Hill took out many of the world's greatest sportsmen, including Theodore Roosevelt, who pays the cousins several fine tributes in his book *African Game Trails*.

I should like to mention one slight incident connected with the Hills that may seem of small importance to most but meant a great deal to me. The game department had commissioned me to ex-

terminate the rhino in the Makueni district near Machakos, in order
to open the area for native cultivation. With the stopping of the
native wars, famine control, and the distribution of free medicine,
the Wakamba tribe had increased nearly fivefold and new land had
to be found for them. In this great hunt, the largest of its kind in
history, 1088 rhino were killed. Many of the settlers were strongly
opposed to this wholesale slaughter, although how they expected the
Wakamba to support themselves on their old tribal lands I cannot
imagine. Many of the white hunters were particularly outspoken in
their condemnation both of the game department and me. I think it
not unfair to point out that they had a personal interest in this
matter as the extermination of the rhino in this area made it much
harder for them to find suitable trophies for their clients. The Hills
were especially hard hit, as they lived so near Makueni. In the midst
of the controversy, Clifford Hill walked up to me in Nairobi and I
braced myself for the inevitable criticism.

"J. A., I want you to know that both Howard and I realize that the
area has to be cleared," he said. "When we first came out here, there
was a famine among the Wakamba and the hills were white with
their bones. That sort of thing can't be allowed to happen again.
You're doing a fine work."

A little thing, perhaps, but I have never forgotten it.

Although the Hills stood second to none as hunters, they regarded
the business merely as a way of obtaining money which they could
put into their farms. As soon as possible, the cousins retired as professional hunters and devoted themselves to building up their coffee
plantation, now one of the finest in Kenya.

A different type than the Hills was Arthur Hoey, who took out
some of the first big safari parties in Kenya. Arthur Hoey was a born
hunter and he would rather hunt than eat or sleep. He was also an
extremely able businessman. Arthur came up from South Africa at
the same time as the Hills, not to farm but to hunt elephants for their
ivory. He traveled through the then unexplored northwest regions of
Kenya among the Suk, Turkana and Karamojo—some of the wildest,
most aggressive tribes in the country. Like everyone else in those
days, he had continual trouble with his porters. However, Arthur hit

on a way to handle it. He would make note of the ringleaders and when his safari reached a cannibal village, Arthur would call out the chief and ask him, "How much ivory will you give me for these men?" The chief would feel the porters' ribs, compute their weight, and make an offer. "It was usually a very good offer too," Arthur remarked. "I hated to turn it down." After that, he had no more trouble with the porters.

When the wholesale shooting of elephants for ivory was made illegal, Arthur Hoey turned to white hunting. Much has been said about the modern "luxury safari" and of "shooting lions from taxi-cabs," but in those days there was little luxury connected with a safari and much difficulty and danger. Hoey took his clients where they wanted to go and some of them made remarkable requests.

In 1909, a wealthy sportsman named N. C. Cockburn wished to cross Abyssinia, going up by way of Lake Rudolph and then east to Addis Ababa and the coast. At that time, Abyssinia was notorious as the home of armed tribesmen who lived by slave-catching, cattle-stealing, and the looting of passing caravans. Before starting out with Mr. Cockburn, Hoey spent months in London with him, care-fully checking all available maps of the district, old accounts, the position of the stars and the customs of the people. Although not a pound of unnecessary luggage could be taken, Hoey insisted on including six rockets in waterproof tin cases. These rockets later saved all their lives.

The safari crossed the deserts around Lake Rudolph and entered Abyssinia by bribing the border tribes with a gift of rifles. Here they entered mountainous country and their camels began to die. One load after another had to be discarded and, much to Hoey's regret, three of the rockets had to be left behind. Halfway to Addis Ababa, they were attacked by a wild tribe called the Danekel. The safari built a boma and managed to hold off the natives with their guns, but the Danekel were now mustering in force and obviously pre-paring to attack as soon as it grew dark.

Hoey knew that the Danekel were fierce, determined fighting men and when the rush came they would not be turned aside by rifle fire. He could see their small, round shields, made of buffalo hide and covered with gold and silver studs—looking much like the targets of the old highlanders—shining in the gathering darkness as the tribesmen gathered for the charge. Hoey thought of the rockets.

"There was just one little detail about those rockets I'd overlooked," Hoey admitted. "How to get the damn things out of the welded, tin boxes. I didn't have much time to do it. The rush was going to come at any moment. Finally I found an opener and set to work. I cut my hand open with the bloody thing before I got the tins open. Then I fired off the rockets."

There was a dead hush as the rockets soared up and exploded in a mass of stars. Then the tribesmen fled, screaming with terror. The next morning, the safari moved on without opposition.

In those days, a client who decided to take a shooting tour in Africa had to be a man of courage and ability. Not infrequently, a white hunter's life depended on his client when dangerous game had to be faced. One of Arthur Hoey's clients was a clergyman, the Rev. Dr. Rainsford. He and Hoey were hunting lions from horseback. Hoey had just shot one lion when another leaped up from the same spot and began to run. Hoey mounted his horse and set off in pursuit. In the excitement of the moment, he forgot to reload his double-barreled rifle and left his bandoleer behind. The lion was heading for a swamp and when he got within range, Hoey jumped off his horse and fired. He hit the lion, but only wounded him. Instantly the lion turned and charged.

Hoey's horse bolted and he was left to face the charge with an empty rifle and no cartridges. At that moment, he saw Dr. Rainsford galloping up. It was touch and go whether the doctor or the lion would get to him first. Hoey saw Rainsford dismount at 280 yards and take aim at the lion. Hoey thought, "The damn fool! He can never hit anything at that distance." The clergyman fired and the lion rolled over dead. Hoey considers it one of the most remarkable shots he has ever seen.

As time went on, more and more sportsmen came to Kenya and many of these men were frankly not of the caliber of Cockburn or Dr. Rainsford. They wanted their bag and they wanted it in a short length of time and with a minimum of danger. Some of the old white hunters refused to take these men out. Arthur Hoey was a business-man and considered their money as good as anyone's.

"I had a mule and a horse that were great friends," Hoey recalled. "Wherever the horse went, the mule would follow. I'd put the client on the mule and I'd ride out on the horse. When we found a lion, the cat would usually run. I'd ride after him until the lion was so exhausted he'd lie down, snarling. I knew the client would have to follow me as he was on the mule and the mule never let the horse get out of sight. When the client arrived, the lion was so exhausted that he could get within fifty yards of the beast without trouble or danger."

By no means all of Hoey's clients were cowards. Once he guided a Mr. Wright and his pretty daughter, Gladys. A rhino, wounded by a hunter, had gone mad and was attacking natives. The natives asked Hoey to kill the animal. Hoey set out following him on horseback. Happening to look around, he saw Gladys Wright following him on another horse. "Go back," he told her. "This is dangerous." "Don't be silly," said Miss Wright. "You'll have to follow that animal into cover and you'll need someone to hold your horse for you." Arthur went on, feeling rather annoyed with Miss Wright. He spoored the rhino down and managed to get a shot at the brute. The rhino whirled and charged. It was close quarters, but Hoey stopped him. He turned around, fully expecting that both Miss Wright and the horses would be speeding toward the horizon. Instead, there stood the girl a few feet behind him, quietly holding the bridles of the plunging horses.

"I decided that I'd better keep someone like that in the family," Arthur explained. So he married her. Today they are living in a lovely, modern home on the beach near Mombasa. Arthur is an enthusiastic yachtsman and Mrs. Hoey an equally enthusiastic gardener.

There can be little doubt that the most colorful of all the white hunters was Fritz Schindelar. From the point of view of the motion picture industry or of a romantic writer, old Fritz was the ideal white hunter. He was very handsome, had a mysterious past, was irresistible to women, and brave to the point of foolhardiness. Of

Fritz's early life, little is known and he would never discuss the matter. He was an Austrian and had been an officer in an aristocratic Hungarian Hùssar regiment. After his tragic death, a large photograph was found among his possessions showing Fritz as a boy of about seventeen with his troops. For a boy so young to be in command of a swagger regiment argues that he was of noble blood. However, Fritz had certainly been many things in his remarkable career, including a headwaiter, a hotelkeeper and a luggage master so it is difficult to say what his background actually was. Certainly he was a magnificent horseman and a crack shot, qualities seldom found among headwaiters and luggage masters.

Why Fritz left Austria is unknown, but according to rumor there was some scandal over a lady. When I knew him in Kenya, Fritz was one of the best known of the white hunters. He wore an imperial mustache, the ends well waxed, and dressed in spotless white riding breeches and gleaming boots. He was a great gambler and could often be seen at the Norfolk Hotel with several hundred golden sovereigns lying on the table before him. I have seen one of his old scrapbooks in which, together with snapshots of some of his record heads, he also includes pictures of ladies, usually labeled "The Countess Soandso" or "The Dutchess of That." The ladies had the wasp waists and elaborate coiffures of the period and were striking languishing poses.

Fritz was altogether a strange fellow. When he was guiding H. Barclay of Barclay's Bank and his two daughters, a rhino charged the elder girl and put her up a tree. She screamed for Fritz who galloped up on his white stallion, dismounted, and then played tag with the infuriated beast around the trunk of the tree before shooting him. On another occasion, he was reputed to have thrown an empty beer bottle at a lion to make the animal charge.

Fritz did many curious things which would require a psychologist to explain. As every hunter knows, a mortally wounded lion is a terribly dangerous beast. On one occasion, Fritz shot a lion and then, while the beast was dying, Fritz took the lion's head in his lap and fondled the beast until it expired. A photograph of this remarkable business was taken and hung for many years over the Norfolk Bar, though it has now disappeared. Fritz wrote across the bottom of the picture, "Dying in my arms."

I remember an argument that took place under this picture in the Norfolk Bar between Fritz and another white hunter. The discussion grew violent and finally the hunter said grimly, "One more word out of you, Fritz, and by God, you'll be dying in my arms." Fortunately, the two men were separated, for in those days the country was far rougher than it is today and everyone carried arms.

Fritz was in great demand as a hunter, especially by aristocratic sportsmen, for Fritz could meet these people on their own terms. He was an excellent bushcraftsman and was prepared to go anywhere or do anything that his client required. To say that Fritz was desperately brave is an understatement. He seemed positively to welcome the idea of death and courted it as expertly as he courted the attentions of beautiful ladies. Fritz did not pay much attention to the local girls and never married.

In 1913, Paul Rainey, the American photographer, returned to Kenya to make some more motion pictures of lion hunting with hounds. Again he employed the Hills to help him, but this time Rainey's requirements were so extreme that the Hills, after discussing the matter in their usual quiet manner, decided that no amount of money could recompense them for the dangers involved. I wish to add here that Rainey was well liked in Kenya and was always perfectly frank and straightforward. He wanted certain things done and was prepared to pay top prices to anyone who would do them. He himself was far from being a coward and it must be remembered that in most of these stunts, if the hunter was killed, Rainey would most likely be killed with him. He and the Hills parted company with mutual expressions of sincere good will. Then Rainey went to Fritz Schindelar.

Rainey's great problem, as it is with all wildlife photographers, was to have the lion charge the camera across an open space where the animal could be photographed. The lion was usually bayed by the hounds in dense cover and although he could often be flushed, it was impossible to say where he might break out. Rainey was using a camera mounted on a heavy tripod and hand-cranked. Once this apparatus was set up, it could not be moved and so the lion had to come directly for it. This was difficult to arrange.

Fritz talked the matter over with Clifford Hill. "Cliff, I think if I went into cover on horseback, I could make the lion charge the horse," he told him. "Then I could lead him out and toward the camera."

"Dangerous work, Fritz," Clifford remarked.

Fritz grinned. "For what Rainey is willing to pay, it's worth the chance."

Shortly after this conversation, Fritz went out with Rainey to put his plan into effect. Fritz was riding a white mare, trained as a polo pony. The horse was not only remarkably fast but could turn on a shilling. For what happened then, I will quote a letter written by Mr. Herbert Harvey, a rancher who was an eyewitness to the event. Mr. Harvey wrote this letter to Harold Hill, who has most kindly allowed me to use it.

Our party consisted of the following: Rainey, Fritz, Klein, May and Mrs. Tuscon and myself. There were also the two mounted camera boys, the Masai hound boy, and Fritz's Somali syce [groom].

The lion was located in the mouth of the Ngasawa Gorge and from there he gave us a pretty run over that low range of hills between the gorge and Longonot. The going was extremely rough and our party split. Rainey, the Tuscons, and Klein on one side and Fritz and I on the other. Fritz and I reached the top of a ridge overlooking a wide valley. We saw the hounds following on the heels of a large male lion which was headed for a patch of bush. Every once in a while he would turn on the hounds and make them scatter. He looked extremely active in comparison with the one of the previous day. [This lion had been so gorged that he refused to charge.] I recollect distinctly remarking to Fritz that we were up against a totally different proposition. His reply was, 'He's alright, youngster. We should get some pictures today.' As soon as the rest of the party joined us on the hill lip, we waited for the two camera boys and then all rode down to the valley to where the hounds were baying up the lion in the bush. The cameras were set up about 20 yards from the edge of the bush and then we all discussed ways and means of getting him to charge the camera that Rainey was operating.

It was Fritz's suggestion to ride into a thin part of the bush and attract the lion. This he did at right angles to us accompanied by his syce. It is a gross lie to suggest that he did this in response to a taunt by Rainey of cowardice. [This story is still widely believed in Kenya.] Fritz was a brave man and Rainey would never have sent anybody to do a thing that he would not do himself. As a matter of fact, Fritz was warned by all of us not to go too close. What happened afterwards took place in a matter of seconds. From where we were we could see Fritz cautiously entering the bush. He couldn't have gone more than a few yards when there was a rustle and out bolted the lion. Fritz had already turned his horse to gallop away when the lion was on him. It partly knocked the pony down with a mighty buffet. Fritz landed on the ground on his feet with his double barreled rifle in his hands. He fired one shot at point blank range but missed. The lion was on him in a minute, and bit him twice in the stomach and left him and returned to the bush where he was lying before he charged. We were already half way into the bush by this time and when he charged us we filled him with lead. Fritz was in great pain and we squirted permanganate of potash into his wounds and then bandaged him. A stretcher was improvised with saddle blankets and I with the four Africans started to carry him to camp. Rainey raced back to camp where he had his car and made all speed to Naivasha. There happened to be a doctor in the Rift Valley Hotel. After ordering a special train, he returned with the doctor. It was not until late in the day that we were able to get Fritz to Naivasha where the special train was waiting.

Fritz was always inclined to be a bit rash and I am sure he misjudged his distance. I also think he placed too much reliance on his sporting pony. I am sure he had no idea that the lion would charge out on him at sight especially as he was being bayed up by the hounds.

The chief photographer on the Rainey expedition was Herbert Binks, the first photographer to open a shop in Kenya and one of our oldest and best-loved citizens. Binks was in Nairobi processing film when Fritz was taken to the hospital there. "Poor chap, for a long time all he could say to me was, 'By God, Binks, what a blow, what a blow!'" Binks recalls. Fritz died three days later. So passed the most colorful of all the white hunters.

No mention of the white hunters would be complete without some reference to Binks himself, for, although not a hunter, he recorded on film many of the early safaris and was intimately concerned with this great era. Often a photographer was called upon to play a part hardly less perilous than that of the hunter. A quiet man but one possessing great nerve, Binks had many narrow escapes which he accepted as part of his work.

"I remember that I was with one safari that wanted pictures of a charging lion," Binks recalls. "There were two white hunters with us, Pearson and Postma. A lion was located in some heavy bush and I and another photographer put up our cameras in different positions so no matter how the animal came, one of us would get the picture. We were using the old-fashioned, hand-cranked motion picture cameras mounted on heavy tripods. Pearson stayed with me and Postma took up his stand with the other photographer. Then the lion was bolted by throwing stones into the bush.

"The lion did not charge. Instead, he rushed past us, headed for the open plains. Pearson fired to turn him. The lion spun around and charged. Pearson allowed him to come on while I ground away on the camera. When the lion was almost on top of us, Pearson took careful aim and squeezed the trigger. The cartridge misfired.

"Pearson was using a double-barreled rifle and could not fire again. He stepped between me and the lion, holding up his rifle crossways with both hands to break the lion's charge. The lion grabbed the rifle in his jaws but the force of the charge carried both the lion and Pearson on top of me.

"All I can remember is that great tail as long as my arm thrashing back and forth. Both Pearson and I were rolling around on the ground with the lion on top of us. Then Postma, the other white hunter, fired and hit the lion by a magnificent piece of good shooting as we were all mixed up together. The lion left us and charged Postma and the other camera. Postma fired again. The bullet went through the lion's mane, but the blast of the gun turned him. He bolted off into the bush. Later, we found him dead from Pearson's first shot."

I cannot leave Binks without recounting one of my favorite hunting stories in which he played a prominent part. He was with Rainey on one of the American's photographic safaris, and with the party was a certain Englishman whom I will call Lord X. This gentleman was very keen on pig-sticking—riding down wild boars on horseback with a lance. Binks took several hundred feet of this business and by

wished to get bulls carrying as much ivory as possible. The natives told us enthusiastic tales of a monster tusker not far from their village so we set out on the beast's spoor. The spoor showed that the bull was young and probably did not have good tusks but one can be mistaken in such matters so we kept on. After much hard work, we caught up with the bull. I remember that he was pushing over a tree at the time to get the leaves. His tusks weighed only about thirty pounds so he was useless for our purpose. He caught a bit of our scent and instantly became so aggressive we were hard put to it to get away without a charge. If he charged, we would have been forced to shoot him and then he would have counted on our license.

While we were still in the bush, Billy Judd went to see my wife Hilda. Billy was then an old man, although he was still very active, and possessed much of the amazing strength for which he was famous. Billy stood a little under six feet and weighed some two hundred pounds, about the same build as myself although I regret to say that I lack his great powers. He had a tremendous chest and shoulders and, according to rumor, was able to carry a mule on his back. But when he called on Hilda, he was white and shaking.

"Isn't your husband out after elephants?" he asked.

"He is," said Hilda, her heart sinking.

"Isn't he the only man out in the bush just now?"

"I believe he is," said Hilda. "What's happened, Billy? I must know."

Billy wiped his hand across his forehead. "I had a dream last night—a terribly clear dream. I saw a hunter charged by an elephant. His back was toward me but he was very like John. I saw the bull grab him with its trunk and then stamp on his face. The bull went away but the man was so mutilated that I could not recognize him. Hilda, if John is all right, for God's sake, ask him to come back at once."

Hilda is not superstitious, but she was so impressed by Billy's earnestness that she sent a messenger after me. As I was out in the blue, the man never found me.

Billy was so certain that I was the man he had seen in the vision that he set out after elephants the next day with his son without giving the matter a second thought. They also went to Mtito Andei and the natives told them the same story that we had heard. This bull was causing trouble among the shambas and the natives hoped to have him killed so they could get the meat. Billy and his son set out on the spoor and came up with the animal. Like us, they decided he wasn't worth shooting and tried to withdraw. The bull saw them and charged young Judd. The boy fired both barrels into the monster and then, while trying to reload and run at the same time, tripped over some creepers. Billy rushed up and fired at the bull to save the boy. The bull whirled and charged Billy. The animal grabbed the hunter in his trunk, threw him down, and stamped on his face. Billy died instantly.

For the most part, the white hunters were not sociable men. When I joined their ranks, I was no exception. We would meet briefly at the Norfolk Bar or in the bush, exchange a few words, and then go our separate ways. As a result, my memories of most of them were brief and fleeting. I recall hearing the Hon. Denys Finch-Hatton, the only white hunter who could boast a handle to his name, tell of guiding the Duke of Windsor who was then the Prince of Wales. The story made an impression on me because I have often been in a similar position with a notable client. The prince was a keen amateur photographer and most eager to get a picture of a charging rhino. The camera was set up and the rhino induced to charge. Finch-Hatton allowed the beast to get within a reasonably safe distance of the prince and then killed the rhino with a well-directed shot. The prince turned on him furiously.

"How dare you shoot without orders?" he snapped. "I wanted him to get right up to the camera."

"Your Highness," returned Finch-Hatton coolly. "Suppose you look at the matter from my point of view. If you, the heir to the throne, are killed, what is there left for me to do? I can only go behind a tree and blow my brains out."

Finch-Hatton said the prince considered the matter for a moment and then agreed that he was right. I have often wished that I had Finch-Hatton's calm assurance. A white hunter is responsible for his client's safety and if the client insists on taking unnecessary risks, the hunter is blamed. A difficult position for any man.

As time went on, clients began to pick their white hunters with great care—as was, indeed, their privilege—but the results were sometimes amusing. I recall that a noble idiot once arrived in Kenya with an extremely lovely lady friend of whom he was insanely jealous. This nobleman spoke to Captain Ritchie, then the head of the game department, about engaging the services of a white hunter. Captain Ritchie was having a drink with Phil Percival at the time. Phil has guided such clients as the Martin Johnsons and Ernest Hemingway and is often referred to as "the dean of white hunters."

After listening to the nobleman's needs, Captain Ritchie remarked, "I suggest you go out with either Phil Percival here or John Hunter."

The nobleman whipped out a little notebook and after hurriedly thumbing through the pages announced: "John Hunter is out of the question. He has the reputation of being a devil with women."

"Well, then, what about Phil?" suggested the captain.

The nobleman again consulted his little book. "Ah, that will be quite all right. I have Percival listed as 'perfectly safe.'"

In telling me the story, Phil added, "John, I assure you that I have never been so insulted in all my life."

Alas, I fear that was many years ago.

The old order changed and gave way to the new. Clients would fly out by plane, wish to go on a two-week safari, get their trophies, and fly back without loss of time. Many of the old white hunters were unable to accustom themselves to the change. One of them became a recluse, living by himself in the bush, and seldom seeing even his best friends. One of the few men who was able to adapt himself easily and efficiently to the change was Walter King. Wally King was an expert hunter but he also had a gift for organization and when Safariland, the biggest of the safari outfitting companies was organized, Wally was given the job of arranging for the safaris and seeing that the clients had everything that they desired.

This was often no easy task. One of Wally's first problems was to gratify a client who insisted that his wife and himself have riding mules to save them the trouble of walking. This was in the days of the old foot safaris when cars were unknown. The mules were available but in order to reach the district where the client wished to hunt, the safari would have to pass through several areas infested by tsetse fly of a type whose bite is fatal to livestock although harmless to humans. The problem was how to get the mules through the infected areas. To solve it, Wally had special flyproof carts made and when the safari reached these areas, the mules were put in the carts and pulled through by manpower.

When the motorcar came, the whole picture changed immediately. If a client had sufficient money, he could engage a fleet of lorries and travel in great luxury. The old-time white hunter, used to drinking out of mudholes and shooting what food he could, found it hard to think of a safari in such terms. Wally still remembers his paralyzed astonishment when a certain British millionaire required him to provide a complete refrigerator unit. Wally freely admits he was unable to rise to the occasion, so the client provided his own. It consisted of a lorry with a three-ton chassis lined with zinc. The client then installed in the chassis two of the largest refrigerators he could find in Nairobi and employed a special mechanic to look after the apparatus. The refrigerator was such a success that similar smaller units are a regular feature of large safaris today.

On another occasion, a rather plump oriental potentate told Safariland that he needed a vehicle to carry him along the narrow game trails in the bush as he could neither walk nor ride. Here was a puzzler. Finally Wally constructed a single-wheeled rickshaw affair, pulled by a man in front and pushed by another in the rear. This proved most successful.

To my mind, the great days of the luxury safari were in the 1920's. Money was no object and some of these safaris resembled small circuses. The tents covered an acre of ground, generators provided electric lights, a different wine was served with every course, and hot and cold water was laid on for the clients. When two of these great safaris met, the chefs competed to see who could arrange the most elaborate meal, and some of these banquets I have eaten in the heart of the African bush were better than any I have ever had in London.

With the world-wide depression, the safari business slumped and the great luxury safari became, to a large extent, a thing of the past. The modern safari is comfortable but not greatly luxurious, designed to meet the needs of well-to-do people who are not overly inclined to endure hardships but who do not require vintage wines with their meals.

The white hunters have also changed. They are generally quiet, capable men who have a job to do and who do it well. There is no place in the modern safari business for the eccentric, no matter how great his knowledge of bushcraft. A hint of scandal today would ruin a hunter and they all know it. It is, of course, a great improvement. Yet sometimes I wonder if the clients do not miss some of the romance of the old days. Indeed, not long ago I happened to hear a lady complaining bitterly about her white hunter. "I was three months alone in the bush with him," said the lady indignantly. "And all he did was show me animals. Did he think I came six thousand miles to look at a bunch of damn rhinos?" I wish I could have offered the lady some advice, but I fear that she was fifty years too late. The days of Fritz Schindelar are gone.

Daniel P. Mannix

XII

Major Robert Foran–British East African Police

As the colony began to grow, there came an increasing demand for an organization to enforce law and order. As with all young communities, Kenya had attracted not only some of the finest pioneer types but also some of the worst. Men who had made Great Britain, South Africa and Australia too hot to hold them flocked to this new frontier. The constant influx of East Indians also presented a problem, for, although many of these men were as good as the best, a large number of them came from the lowest strata of Indian culture and brought with them vices that revolted even the broad-minded natives. Hundreds of the natives themselves, their tribal life destroyed by the coming of the whites, were pouring into Nairobi and living by murder, robbery and prostitution. There were also constant minor uprisings among the wild tribes. To control this situation, an organization was formed called the British East African Police. These men combined the duties of· a frontier marshal in the early days of the American West with the responsibilities of a cavalry officer ordered to keep the Apache and Sioux on their reserves. As Great Britain could not spare white troops for this work, a few trained officers were told to organize native askaris for the job. One of the first of these officers was Major Foran.

Major Foran was typical of a class of Englishmen now virtually extinct. Kipling has immortalized this type in Stalky and Edgar Wallace in Saunders-of-the-River. Even physically they seemed to

230

run true to form. Major Foran was slightly above average height, lean and tough, with a close-clipped, military mustache and hard blue eyes. Like all such men, he hated "armchair" authority and his one idea was to get as far out in the blue as possible with his men and then drop the heliograph over the nearest cliff to make sure of cutting off all communications with the despised bureaucrats. He had a wry, arid sense of humor and absolute confidence in himself and his native troops. He was used to making instant decisions and, according to what he thought best, was prepared to use the kiboko, the rifle, or a genuinely sympathetic understanding in dealing with the natives. When given leave to return to England for a well-deserved rest, he stayed in Kenya and employed himself mountain-climbing or big game shooting. He was outspoken to the point of rudeness, contemptuous of polite formalities, and completely fearless.

Major Foran was an officer in the regular British army and as a young man served in the Boer War and later in the Waziri campaign against the hill tribes in northern India. After such a long tour of duty, the War Department decided that the regiment needed a rest and recalled them to England for two years. When Foran heard this, he stamped into his colonel's office and angrily resigned his commission. He had, he profanely explained, joined the army to see action, not to sit on his backside in an officers' club in Aldershot. His resignation was accepted and Foran looked about for something that promised excitement. He decided to go to Kenya and take up ranching.

He landed in Mombasa in 1904 and took the train to Nairobi. Nairobi was then a town of tents and corrugated-iron shacks. Church services were held in one of the local bars. In the newly founded cemetery, six of the stones bore the simple inscription, "Killed by a lion." The streets were mud and impassable after a rain. One humorist planted several banana trees in the main street where they flourished until knocked down by a passing oxcart. Crime was so prevalent that women stood guard with rifles to make sure that their washing wasn't stolen off the line.

Foran had several years' back pay in his pockets and spent his first few weeks in Kenya big game hunting. He went through the formality of buying a section of land for a farm but he never saw the place.

One day while Foran was buying supplies for a safari, R. M. Ewart, the assistant district superintendent, walked up to him. Ewart was an alert little man, very snappily dressed, and wore one of the huge sun helmets that were considered absolutely necessary for British officers in the tropics. "Aren't you getting a bit bored with this shooting nonsense?" he asked Foran abruptly.

"As a matter of fact, I am," admitted Foran. "Have you any other suggestions?"

"Happens I do," said Ewart. "We're starting a group known as the British East African Police and we need men with military experience as officers. Your duties will be to police the place, stop riots, arrest criminals, put down native uprisings—that sort of thing."

"When do I start?" asked Foran.

"At once. Report to the police barracks. We've just built 'em. They're under a Sikh inspector now named Besant Singh. He'll be your Number Two."

So Robert Foran became a policeman. He had no knowledge of law and as he was supposed to prosecute cases, he was afraid this might prove a handicap, but it soon turned out that nobody cared. A more serious matter was his inability to speak Urdu, the language of his Indian policemen. All the reports were kept in Urdu and the men spoke nothing else. Foran began to have an uneasy feeling that he had bitten off more than he could chew.

His suspicions were promptly confirmed, for within an hour after he accepted his new position, he received word that two drunken South Africans were shooting up one of the bars. An askari had asked them to stop and the men had fired at him. Foran felt that his dignity required that he handle this situation alone. Unwisely, he walked into the bar without first drawing his gun. He found the bar a wreck and himself looking down the barrels of two revolvers.

"Now see here, young'un," said one of the men, a big unshaven brute who handled the .45 with the ease of long practice, "You hop it, if you're smart. We had to leave the South for one killing, and we don't mind leaving here for another. And don't try any tricks with us.

We've been around. We learned to shoot in Texas. Look there." And he fired casually without seeming to take aim, shooting the cork out of a bottle behind the bar.

"That's the best shooting I ever saw with a handgun," exclaimed Foran, genuinely interested.

"That's nothing," said the gratified gunman. "I'll show you some real shooting." He stuck some matches up at the end of the bar and lit them with five quick shots.

"Let me show you what I can do," said his friend jealously. He also gave an impressive exhibition of trick shooting. Then they turned to Foran.

"Amazin'," said the young officer. "What about some more?"

"We'll show you plenty after we've reloaded," promised one of the men.

"Ah, so your guns are empty, are they?" remarked Foran, drawing his own revolver. "In that case, put up your hands and come with me."

Foran had scarcely gotten through putting the furious gunmen in Nairobi's one-cell jail, when a hysterical Indian rushed in to say that the bazaar was on fire. There was no fire department, so Foran organized a bucket brigade. His own men worked with a will but the crowd stood about watching idly and making no effort to help.

"Lend a hand with those buckets, won't you?" Foran shouted to the crowd.

One of the men stepped forward. "Sir, it is not our responsibility to put out fires. That is for you and your askaris. You're paid for it."

"By God, I'll make you help!" roared Foran.

"Sir, there is no law saying we have to help," said the man smugly.

"Probably there isn't," admitted Foran. "In that case, I arrest you all for blocking traffic. Sergeant, see that those criminals are put to work."

The big Sikh moved forward, fingering his kiboko. Within an hour, the fire was out.

Slowly the police force set about cleaning up the town. Foran devised his own system for dealing with drunks. He had them jailed overnight and the next morning, when the usual hangover set in, he made them eat a large bowl of dry porridge without sugar or cream. He also laid a heavy hand on his own askaris who he discovered had been blackmailing the local shopkeepers. Breaking up the red-light district of the town needed more careful handling. Before the coming of the whites, prostitution among the natives was unknown, but thousands of native men had left their reserves to work on the settlers' farms and many of these men had gradually drifted into Nairobi. They wanted women, and some of the shrewder and more sophisticated among them had seen that women were supplied. The obvious solution seemed to be to send these unhappy girls back to their villages but tests showed that virtually all of them had become riddled with venereal diseases. Not wanting to spread venereal infections throughout the whole colony, the police had to round up these women in small batches and see that they were cured before sending them home.

Nairobi was a hodgepodge of different races and creeds all with varying moral standards, and to do his job a policeman had to be an expert on comparative religions, customs and superstitions. Ritual murder followed by cannibalism often occurred among certain of the native tribes and was considered an intrinsic part of their religion. A Boer farmer came to complain that his wife had been unfaithful to him with his best friend. Under questioning, the Boer freely admitted that the friend had lived with them for several years and all three of them used the same bed, his wife sleeping in the middle. He couldn't understand why the British regarded this as an unusual arrangement. Certain of the settlers, isolated on their farms, considered that they were a law unto themselves and administered what they believed to be justice to their native boys in ways that did not always meet with the approval of the authorities. Each of these cases required careful handling, especially as the men involved almost invariably felt that they were following a course not only right but the only one possible under the circumstances.

When the Nairobi police force settled down into a smooth-running organization, Foran was promoted to assistant district supervisor and sent to Kisumu, the end of the railroad line on the shore of Lake Victoria. Kisumu was a small place, but a vitally that time Lord X's horse was so winded that his lordship ordered Binks to walk the animal back to camp and have him rubbed down. Binks was not Lord X's servant but in his usual quiet manner he took the horse and started off. "But the more I thought about the way he'd spoken to me, the less I liked it," Binks admits. "I decided that there was no reason why I should walk all the way back to camp leading that horse. So I mounted him and started off."

The path led up a steep hill, covered with great boulders higher than even a mounted man's head. Binks was halfway up the hill when he heard furious shouts from behind. He turned and saw Lord X on a second horse chasing him, with Rainey close behind. Lord X shouted, "Dammit, I told you to lead that horse, not to ride him," and followed this by a flow of profanity.

Just then Binks noticed an enormous regal python on a rock over the lord's head. The snake was sliding his great length over the stone toward the unconscious man. Ignoring his lordship's rage, Binks called down to Rainey, "Do you want a picture of a python? There's one just going to eat Lord X."

"For God's sake man, be careful!" Rainey shouted back, his voice shaking with apprehension. "Don't disturb that python. This will make a hell of a picture."

Unfortunately, Lord X got out of the way, thus ruining what would have been one of the greatest nature studies ever filmed. Binks and Rainey had to content themselves with photographing the capture of the snake by the native boys.

It is hardly surprising that these white hunters, constantly faced with the prospect of a terrible death and often isolated for months on end in the deep bush with no companion except their native boys, should on occasion be gifted with a strange insight not granted to other men. I remember especially the case of Billy Judd, one of the best. I will always believe that for a moment Billy was given the chance to see into the future although he was unable to interpret his vision correctly.

I had gone elephant hunting with a friend of mine near Mtito Andei, not far from Mount Kilimanjaro. We were after ivory and, as we were only allowed two elephants on our license, we naturally important one to the growing colony. It was the port of Lake Victoria and three steamers ferried the produce of Uganda across the lake to Kisumu where their cargoes could then be sent by rail to Mombasa. There had been an inexplicable outburst of crime in the town which was interfering with shipments and the local Indian police had been unable to deal with it.

Foran took two men with him who played an important part in his life. One of these men was Sergeant Ayenda, a topnotch soldier and drillmaster who could take a group of natives fresh from the bush and in a few weeks turn them into an effective, disciplined force. The other man was Sefu bin Mohammed, Foran's personal servant. In a country possessing none of the modern conveniences which we today take for granted, a good servant meant the difference between comparative comfort and being driven half mad by constant petty worries. Sefu knew more about Foran's moods, likes and dislikes, abilities and shortcomings, than Foran did himself. Sefu knew that his job was to keep the young officer well and happy so he could perform his duties, and Sefu worked at the task twenty-four hours a day.

There were only twenty white men at Kisumu and no white women. Foran met Dr. J. Haran, the medical officer, and Sergeant Milton, in command of the seventy-five askaris and twenty-five Indian troopers who patrolled the town. To the north of Kisumu were the Nandi, a warlike tribe much like the Masai. To the south, were the Kisii, a less warlike people but who occasionally cut up passing caravans and raided their neighbors for recreation. The tribe at Kisumu were the Kavirondo, a stark-naked people who were famous throughout Kenya for their high moral code. Unfortunately, the influx of foreigners had begun to have a demoralizing effect on the Kavirondo. They had begun to steal, an offense hitherto unknown among them, and some were even starting to wear clothes. Foran saw a beautiful young girl, completely innocent of any covering, look contemptuously at a young buck who had been to the mission school and was magnificent in shirt and trousers. "Are you deformed?" the girl asked him. "I suppose you must be, otherwise why should you want to cover your body with cloth."

There were a number of little Indian "dukas" (shops) in the town and every night two or three of these would be robbed. One night, Foran's own home was entered and some of his clothing taken. Sergeant Milton doubled the patrols, using his well-trained Indian police, but the robberies continued. Then one day, Foran came across two Kavirondo fighting over a pair of his shoes. They appealed to Foran to help them decide who owned the shoes. Under questioning, they frankly admitted that they'd stolen the shoes and took Foran to a hut jammed full of stolen clothing. "It's quite all right, Bwana," they assured him. "Your Indian policemen taught us how to do it. They collect part of everything we take."

Foran checked the records of his Indian police through Bombay and discovered that almost to a man they had criminal records. He had them deported and used African askaris to police the town. The crime wave promptly ceased.

One evening, Foran and Sergeant Milton were having a "sundowner" together and discussing the feasibility of laying out a rifle range for the askaris, who continued to cling to the belief that the lovely loud noise a gun makes was its important feature, not whether you could hit anything with it. The sun was sinking behind the waters of the lake, the evening breeze had sprung up, and there hadn't been a case of robbery for weeks. Both men were feeling very content and confident of the future. The soft-footed Sefu drifted in with a second drink at the correct moment and vanished again like a benevolent ghost. A native messenger came in with a note for Foran from Dr. Haran. Thinking it was probably an invitation to dinner, Foran opened it casually.

The note read:

Bubonic plague has just broken out in the Indian bazaar. Probably brought in across the lake from Uganda. Every effort must be made to keep it from spreading throughout the colony.

Foran knew this was something far more serious than a crime wave. His experiences in India had taught him how an epidemic can sweep through a country and how difficult it is to stop. He sent

Sergeant Milton to collect the askaris quietly and throw a cordon around the town. "No one is to be allowed in or out under any circumstances," he ordered. Then with Sergeant Ayenda and a small group he went from house to house, telling the whites what had happened and asking for their help.

When news of the plague spread through the town, there was a general panic. Terrified men and women tried to escape, but the askaris turned them back. There was a riot. Foran arrested and jailed the leaders. At first, only a few deaths were reported. Then people began to die at the rate of ten a day. Then twenty. Then thirty. The hospital was full and storehouses and private homes were requisitioned for the victims. The steamers were forbidden to land and the trains stopped.

Bubonic plague is spread by fleas carried by rats, so a gigantic rathunt was organized. Every shotgun, sporting rifle and trap in town was pressed into service. It was discovered that a mosque was the source of the epidemic. The old building was alive with rats, virtually all of them infected. Foran requested permission from the Indians to burn the building. The permission was refused. With the death toll mounting hourly, Foran did not spend much time arguing. He threw his askaris in a double rank about the building and burnt it with his own hand. This started a major riot. The disciplined askaris broke the mob and Foran had the leaders arrested. He promised that the government would rebuild the mosque and with this assurance, the trouble gradually quieted down. "Luckily for me, the government did agree to pay for having the mosque rebuilt," Foran remarked later. "Otherwise, I'd have had to pay for it out of my own pocket."

With the destruction of the mosque, the plague began to subside. However, the death rate was still high. A day or so later, Sergeant Ayenda brought Foran word that one of the managers of the railroad had been stopped by the askaris guarding the roads and was demanding to be allowed to enter the town.

Foran went to see the man. He found the manager cursing the askari and dancing with rage.

"How dare you have a man of my position stopped by natives?" the man roared. "I'm here to inspect the jetty. I demand that I be allowed to pass."

"If you come in, you won't be allowed to go out again," Foran warned him.

"We'll see about that, when the time comes," said the manager, striding past the askari guard.

The manager inspected the jetty and then, without bothering to speak to Foran, tried to leave. The askaris promptly hauled him back to town. "I can't run the risk of having you spread the plague," Foran told him briefly. "You'll have to stay here until the quarantine period is over."

"I'll have you broken for this!" screamed the furious manager. "I'll report you to the Commissioner of the Protectorate."

"If you cause me any more trouble, I'll have you thrown in jail with the rioters," Foran promised him.

The raging manager was forced to stay in Kisumu until Dr. Haran was able to give him a clean bill of health.

To prevent the spread of infection, the bodies of all who died of the plague were burned. Foran himself supervised this burning. One day he collapsed from a combination of sunstroke, exhaustion and the intense heat of the fire. For several days, he was laid up, delirious and totally blind. By the time he recovered, Dr. Haran was able to report that the epidemic was over.

During these periods of riots, crime waves and troubles with officials, a man in Foran's position had to trust absolutely to the loyalty of his askaris. A curious relationship and understanding sprang up between a white officer in command of native troops and his men. This relationship was partly expressed by an askari who was asked by a visiting British dignitary if his officer was a hard man. "He certainly is," said the askari. "But, you know, I'm a pretty hard man myself." * Although the askaris rarely questioned the

* I have included this story because it was told to me by an officer in the British East African Police and I think it is a good example of the reasoning of the average askari. However, I admit that I have heard the same story told of an American Marine and a Scottish Highlander. It may well have been told of Roman legionnaires.

authority of a white officer to command them, there was nothing servile in their attitude toward him. Foran once had an unexpected example of this fact.

In addition to his other duties, Foran was expected to come to the help of the Kenya African Rifles, a military force patrolling the country in case of an uprising. There was trouble with the Nandi in December of the year Foran went to Kisumu, so taking Sergeant Ayenda and fifty askaris, he went off to join the Rifle regiment. He made contact with the regiment out in the bush the day before Christmas. The regiment was under the command of a Captain Maples and he and Foran decided to celebrate Christmas Eve together. Both men had received hampers from home, containing such delicacies as plum pudding, turkeys, champagne, liquors, brandy and everything else suitable for a feast. They invited some near-by settlers and their families in for the party and prepared for a jolly evening.

At sunset, a runner appeared with a letter from a certain commissioner whom, I gather, neither Maples nor Foran held in very high regard. The letter said that the commissioner's fort was being surrounded by a force of Nandi spearmen, who were waving their weapons and uttering war cries. The commissioner demanded that help be sent him at once.

Foran and Maples talked the matter over. "I think the chap simply has the wind up," grumbled Maples. "Still, if the Nandi really do chop him, I suppose we'll have to fill out all kinds of beastly reports about it for the government. One of us had better run over there and see what's up. Let's flip a coin."

They flipped, and Foran lost. Cursing his luck, he left with Sergeant Ayenda and the askaris, while the grinning Maples ordered the two native cooks to prepare supper and put the champagne in a cool spot against the arrival of the guests. "Save you a drumstick and a glass of wine, old man," he called to Foran. The major's answer is unprintable.

Night had already fallen and as the party were entering Nandi country, they did not dare to show a light. A tropical storm burst, soaking them to the skin, turning the streams into rivers, and making the trails a mass of mud. By midnight, the storm passed and the moon came out. Foran and his men were now only a few miles from the fort.

Suddenly they heard the sound of owls calling in the bush around them. "Bwana, those aren't owls; those are Nandi," whispered Sergeant Ayenda. "Form company square!" shouted Foran. As the square formed the Nandi war cry burst out and black forms appeared leaping through the bush on all sides of them. "Front rank . . . kneel!" called Foran. "Front rank . . . fire!" One volley flashed out, lighting up the charging warriors in their grotesque war paint. Then the Nandi were on top of them.

Foran stood with his revolver in his hand. A spear leaped out of the darkness and buried itself by his foot. Almost at the same moment, he felt himself seized from behind and flung face downward into the mud. He knew the square must have broken and the Nandi were on top of him. He tried to use his revolver, but it was torn from his grasp. Strong hands were pinning him down. With his face in the mud, he couldn't even see what was going on. He could hear the battle raging around him, the yelling of the Nandi, the crash of the volleys and the orders of Sergeant Ayenda. Then the yelling faded away. The pressure on him relaxed and he was able to struggle to his feet. He found himself looking into the anxious face of Sergeant Ayenda.

"I hope you're not hurt, Bwana," said the sergeant. "I gave orders to six of my best men to throw you down and sit on you in case of trouble. We didn't want to run the risk of having you speared by some of the savages."

Foran expressed himself rather freely and ordered the march to proceed. They reached the fort at dawn. It turned out that the war party supposedly besieging the fort were a perfectly harmless group of Lumbwa tribesmen having a picnic on a near-by hill slope. Foran again expressed himself in his usual forceful manner and started back for camp, looking forward to the remains of the Christmas dinner.

When he and his party arrived in camp, exhausted and still

soaking wet, he found Maples lounging under a tree, patting his belly in a satisfied way.

"Gad, Foran, you should have been here!" he announced. "Best meal I've ever had. The turkeys were done to a turn, both o' them. The champagne was splendid. I've never tasted such brandy, and I wouldn't have believed that our cooks could have served up a pudding as they did that one. Too bad you missed it. I'm afraid we were all rather carried away and forgot to leave you anything."

"You mean that you didn't even save me a glass of wine or a slice of turkey?" roared Foran. "After all, one of those hampers was mine."

"I feel terribly about it, old boy," Maples assured him. "Look for yourself. Not a thing remaining."

Foran soon found that Maples was telling the truth. While he ranted and raved, Maples preserved a solemn and apologetic face. Then he began howling with mirth and rolling on the ground. Finally the story of the Christmas party came out.

There were two cooks, one a Swahili from the coast and the other a Goanese. While preparing the meal, the cooks had opened the bottles and systematically drank everything—champagne, dinner wines, brandies and liquors. Then they'd gotten into a fight over the right way to prepare the meal. The Goanese had grabbed a saucepan full of hot soup and slammed it over the Swahili's head. The Swahili had grabbed the saucepan and knocked the Goanese down with it. Then he had torn off the semiconscious man's trousers and, snatching the kettle of boiling water off the fire, given him a bath with it. This served to bring the Goanese to his feet and the two men fell on each other, using the turkeys as clubs. When the guests arrived, there was nothing left of the meal and they had had to spend the evening doctoring the two cooks who were in a critical condition from second-degree burns, cuts, bruises and internal injuries.

Foran's duties were not limited to putting down uprisings, police work and plagues. As there were only a handful of officials in the entire colony, these men were expected to know everything and be able to do anything. Once Foran received a hysterical message from a young settler to say that his wife was in labor and would Foran please help. Young bachelor Foran knew nothing about such matters and his army medical books didn't cover the subject of childbirth. However, he found a veterinarian pamphlet on how to deliver cows. Armed with this, he traveled out to the settler's farm where he found the young wife struggling in the agony of a breech delivery. While the young husband read him directions from the veterinarian pamphlet, Foran worked over the girl. The child, a little boy, was born and neither he nor the mother suffered any ill effects.

Learning to know the natives was not only part of Foran's job, he was also deeply interested in their beliefs and customs. Although one might think that a man in Foran's position would hardly have had an opportunity to eat and sleep, Foran found time to write several papers on such matters as native witchcraft, drum talk, secret societies and the history of the tribes. This, again, was typical of the British colonial officers of the time. They worked closely with the people and did their best to understand them. As a result, the people under their care, no matter of what race or creed, came to them for advice. If a native's wife died and he suspected witchcraft, he came to get Foran's opinion on the matter, knowing that Foran had a good practical knowledge of the subject. Foran went over the matter with him carefully, realizing that under certain conditions witchcraft can kill, as Dr. Cook discovered twenty years before in Uganda. If a settler came in with a complaint against the natives, Foran tried to find out why the natives were behaving as they did. Sometimes he counseled patience. Sometimes he used his askaris.

Many of the problems brought to him were minor ones, except to the individual concerned. The Indian stationmaster at one of the little stops on the Uganda-Mombasa railway once came to Foran with a letter he had written to the railroad authorities requesting leave to go to India. He asked Foran if he thought the letter was all right. Foran was so charmed by the letter that he copied it. Here it is:

Most Honoured and Respected Sir:

I have the honour to humbly and urgently require your Honour's permission to relieve me of my onerous duties at Londiani so as to enable me to visit the land of my nativity, to wit, India, foorsooth.

This in order that I may take unto wife a damsel of many charms who has long been cherished in the heart beats of my soul. She is of superflous beauty and enamoured of the thought of becoming my wife. Said beautious damsel has long been goal of my manly breast and now am fearful of other miscreant deposing me from her lofty affections. Delay in consummation may be ruination most dammable to romance of both damsel and your humble servant.

Therefore, I pray your Honour, allow me to hasten India and contract marriage forthwith with said beautious damsel. This being done happily I will return to Londiari to resume my fruitful official duties and perform also my maternal matrimonial functions. It is dead loneliness here without this charmer to solace my empty heart.

If your Honour will so far rejoice my soul to this extent and also as goes equally without saying that of said wife-to-be, I shall pray forever as in duty bound for your Honour's life-long prosperity, ever lasting happiness, promotion of most startling rapidity and withal the fatherhood of many Godlike children to gambal playfully about your Honour's paternal knees to heart's content.

If however for reasons of State or other extreme urgency, the Presence cannot suitably comply with terms of this humble petition, then I pray your most excellent Superiority to grant me this benign favour for Jesus Christ's sake, a gentleman whom your Honour very much resembles.

I have the honour to be, Sir, your Honour's most humble and dutiful, but terribly love-sick, mortal withal.

> (*signed*) Gokal Chand
> B.A. (failed by God's misfortune) Bombay
> University, and now Station Master, Londiani

"Don't change a word of it," Foran advised the anxious stationmaster. "I'm sure it will do the trick." I'm happy to report that it did and Mr. and Mrs. Chand lived many happy years in Londiani.

Like Gallio, Achaia's deputy to the Corinthians, Major Foran, "cared for none of these things" when it came to dealing with a religious group who were interfering with the good of the community. We have seen how he handled the Mohammedans who protested the burning of their mosque. In that case, Foran felt that although the Mohammedans were in the wrong, their error came about through an excess of religious zeal and they were sincere in their belief. Hence he guaranteed that the mosque would be rebuilt. In cases where he felt that a group was not sincere, Foran pulled no punches whatsoever. Some white missionaries belonging to a minor sect founded a mission in Foran's district and some months later Foran received word that they were engaged in ivory smuggling. Foran went with some of his askaris to search the mission. Foran insisted on examining the Inner Shrine which the missionaries kept carefully locked.

"You can't do that!" screamed the mission leader, throwing himself in front of the door with spread arms. "That is the Holy of Holies! I'll report you to the British Government!"

"Break down the bloody doors," said Foran briefly to his askaris. The doors splintered under the rifle butts. Inside was a great heap of ivory. Foran saw to it that the group were expelled from Kenya.

In administering justice, Foran was perfectly impartial. Once a case came up involving two white men who had beaten a native to death. These men were not settlers. They were South Africans passing through Kenya on their way north. They were probably either ivory hunters or prospectors. They had gotten so drunk in a small town that they were unable to find their way back to their camp and hired a native to guide them. On the way, the men began to suspect that the native was misleading them, although this was not the case. The drunks beat their innocent guide to death and then lay down to sleep. They were found the next morning beside the body of their victim.

Foran was at the trial. A jury of settlers sentenced both men to death, to Foran's great satisfaction. However, the men appealed the case and were later freed because there was a technical error in the manner in which the jury had been sworn in. Foran never got over this miscarriage of justice and still speaks of it bitterly.

On the other hand, Foran considered that allowing native tribunals to try cases was, at that stage of the development of the colony at least, a complete farce. The British tried this experiment but Foran was not impressed by the results. In one such case, there were three Kikuyu judges trying a fellow tribesman for a murder. The evidence was conclusive, but the judges voted for acquittal. Later, Foran asked for their reasons. One man explained, "According to our native laws, the killing was justified." The second judge said haughtily, "No Kikuyu ever commits murder." The third judge had an even simpler explanation. He merely said, "The prisoner was my brother."

According to his own accounts, Foran was never greatly beloved by officialdom. He was impatient of red tape and formalities, even in small matters. Once while he was stationed in Mombasa, Foran found that according to the customs of the time, he was supposed to leave cards on the wives of all the various officials. These ladies clung to social formalities with a tenacity all the greater because they were living in Africa. They might be forced into exile because of their husbands' official duties, but they took pride in never forgetting that they were English ladies and demanded that all the niceties of deportment be observed. Foran preferred playing polo to leaving cards but the ladies complained to their husbands and Foran received a crisp order to go through the ceremony.

Foran thought he could see a way to avoid the nuisance. He called in Sefu, his faithful servant, and gave him a bunch of cards and a list of the various homes where they were to be left. "Now this is very important, Sefu," he warned. "Be sure you see that the cards are left at the right houses. I'll give you fifty rupees if you do it right."

"On my life, Bwana," said the serious Sefu and left with the cards and list.

That evening, after a pleasant afternoon on the polo field, Foran dropped into the club for his sundowner. To his surprise, he noticed that people were avoiding him. When he tried to speak to his friends, they deliberately turned their backs. Finally a man came in whom Foran knew very well, but when Foran spoke to him, the man turned away without a word.

This was too much and Foran followed him and grabbed his arm. "What is this nonsense?" he demanded. "What have I done?"

His friend looked at him in astonishment. "Good Lord, man, do you mean to say you don't know?"

Then the story came out. Sefu had marched through the town, entering each place on the list and demanding that the lady of the house accept the cards and also initial the list to show that she'd received them. Some of the startled ladies were jerked off tennis courts but Sefu had been firm. He'd been told to see that those cards were delivered and he'd done his duty.

"You're in Coventry now," Foran's friend explained. "Nobody will have anything to do with you. What are you going to say to Sefu?"

"Congratulate him on doing a fine piece of work," retorted the undismayed Foran. "I promised him fifty rupees but I'll save at least a couple of hundred not having to stand people drinks at the club. It's only fair that I should split the profit with him, so Sefu gets a hundred rupees instead of the fifty."

When Foran returned to the region near Lake Victoria, he became involved in the Kisii Rebellion. At least partly as a result of the emotional problems caused by this rebellion, he later resigned from the British East African Police.

For some time, Kisii war parties had been attacking Indian trading caravans passing through or near their territory and also raiding neighboring tribes. As a result of these raids, the British had sent a series of protests to the Kisii and finally threatened punishment. While on a routine tour of inspection through the Kisii area, Foran saw the warriors were in paint and beginning to collect in groups on the hilltops, their usual rallying place. Foran reported the matter to Northcote, the district commissioner of the Kisii reserve. Northcote immediately set out with a few men to talk to the Kisii, hoping to stop the uprising before it got out of control.

That evening, Foran was called out of his tent by P. C. Ainsworth, the provincial commissioner and Northcote's immediate superior. Ainsworth was still in his pajamas. "A runner has just come in from Northcote," he told Foran. "He's been speared by a group of the Kisii warriors. His askaris carried him to a boma where they're holding out against the Kisii. You must go to his relief at once. When will you be ready to leave?"

"Within two hours," Foran promised.

The boma where Northcote and his men were making their stand was 130 miles from Foran's position. Foran had fifty-four askaris with him. Working fast, he collected provisions for a month in the bush, and a hundred rounds of ammunition. Grant, the district supervisor, gave him permission to impress 150 of the local natives as porters. With this force, Foran started out at ten o'clock that evening.

To reach Northcote in the shortest possible time, Foran decided to make a short cut across one of the inlets of Lake Victoria. This was a desperate decision. The short cut would save forty miles, but Foran had no boats and no way of crossing the inlet. He relied on reaching the inlet at dawn when, he knew, the native fishermen would pass through on their way to the fishing grounds. The inlet was some fifty miles away and to reach it by dawn, his party, including the loaded porters, would have to cover the distance virtually at a jog trot. Sergeant Ayenda kept the straggling ranks closed up and by an amazing feat of both endurance and bushcraft, the party reached the shores of the inlet in time to intercept the fishermen. Foran commandeered the canoes and started across the inlet. The canoes were heavily overladen and although the water was only about as deep as a man's shoulders, it was alive with crocodiles. One of the canoes did sink but the men, following Foran's orders, grabbed what supplies they could and held them above their heads until the other canoes could pick them up. In this way, the inlet was crossed.

The party was now in Kisii country. Before they had traveled far, they heard ahead of them the war drums signaling their approach and soon parties of armed warriors, in full fighting regalia, began to gather on the hills. Foran stopped, formed his men into a square, and moved on slowly, stopping to re-form at regular intervals.

At last, they saw the boma ahead of them with the British flag still flying over it. The force moved in. Northcote was still alive although in great pain. Foran promptly collapsed from an attack of malaria. He was out of his head for several hours and then too weak to move.

It is now necessary to explain the conditions among the Kisii which had led to the uprising.

The Kisii were under the dominance of a family—so large it might almost be called a clan—of hereditary witch doctors. This family was not of Kisii origin. It was apparently of Kikuyu stock, but it became so powerful and so ruthless that at last the Kikuyu expelled the entire group. The clan went to the Nandi who received them respectfully because of their great reputation. After a few years, the Nandi also had had enough of the group and threw them out. The clan then moved in with the Kisii.

Within an amazingly short space of time, this talented family achieved a position of great importance among the Kisii. At regular intervals, one of the witch doctors would order the Kisii warriors under his control to raid a certain village or attack a certain caravan within his area. If the raid was successful, the warriors would give their patron half of all loot.

When Foran was in the country, the witch doctors were all-powerful and the head of the clan was an old woman whose orders were unquestioningly obeyed by the rest of the family as well as the Kisii. This old lady had as the result of repeated successes gotten a little above herself and she was confident that the British did not dare to interfere with her activities.

While Foran was still lying on a heap of rushes in the boma, too weak to get up, Sergeant Ayenda went to him and said, "Bwana, you and I know that this old woman is the source of all the trouble. Now we are in a bad spot here and the Kisii are rising. They are in open rebellion and that means that sooner or later an army will be sent to put them down. That will cause a lot of trouble. Let me take six good men and slip out of the boma tonight. I know the village where this old woman lives. She has a guard but they have no guns. If we can capture her, we are safe, for these people won't dare attack us with their queen in our hands. I'll bring her here and you can force her to order the Kisii to stop the uprising."

Foran at first refused, considering the mission too dangerous. At last, he consented. Sergeant Ayenda picked his men and vanished into the night.

A short time after dawn the next morning, Sergeant Ayenda and his exhausted men returned to the boma, bringing the furious old woman with them. They had managed to overawe her guards with their guns and rushed her away without opposition. As neither the witch queen nor the Kisii had suspected such a move, they had been totally unprepared. Foran interviewed the woman. Although he told me nothing about the interview, I have not the slightest doubt that Foran gave her the choice of calling off the uprising or dying at the end of the rope. Be that as it may, the witch queen called in some of the Kisii warriors and told them to pass the word among the tribesmen that the rebellion was over and to go home. The warriors obeyed her implicitly.

The next morning, Foran, Northcote and the witch queen were sitting in the boma—as like as not enjoying a glass of native beer together, for the old woman apparently harbored no particular grudge—when a runner arrived with a note for Foran. The note was from a young army captain who had been sent out at the head of a punitive expedition to put down the Kisii Rebellion. He ordered Foran to report to him at once with his askaris. Foran tossed the note back to the runner and said, "Tell him the war is over," and continued talking to his friends.

The runner hesitated and then said, "But the army has arrived. See!" Foran rose and looked over the boma.

The boma was on top of a little rise. From the rise, Foran could look out across the valley. Far away, he could see the thin, pale fire that burning thatch makes and hear faintly the crackle of rifle fire.

"By God, they're burning the Kisii villages," exclaimed Northcote. "Get down there quickly, Foran, and stop them."

Foran hurried out to meet the expeditionary force. It was composed of seventy-two men from the Kenya African Rifles and a large number of Masai, used as irregular troops. Foran went directly to the young captain in command and explained the situation to him. The officer replied that the orders for the campaign had come from the highest authorities and he was unable to counteract them on his own responsibility. The war would have to proceed.

The Kisii warriors were not long in coming to the defense of their country. The war drums and war horns were already summoning the villages to arms and as the expeditionary force moved on, the painted warriors attacked with their shields and spears. But in addition to their rifles, the troops had a machine-gun that mowed the warriors down in windrows although they charged again and again with reckless courage. Finally, they broke. The yelling Masai charged in and completed the rout. For the next few weeks, the country was full of burning villages, herds of lowing cattle being driven off by the triumphant Masai, and groups of refugees fleeing for the hills. Several hundred Kisii died in this campaign. On the British side, there were two casualties. One was an askari who was shot in error by some friends while looting a Kisii hut. The other was a Masai who scratched himself on thorns trying to catch some of the Kisii cattle.

A short time after returning from this campaign, Foran suffered a nervous collapse. He was given a leave to recuperate. Foran spent the leave with a group of picked porters climbing Mount Elgon and shooting. While he was in the mountains, a runner reached him with a frantic message from his superior, saying that a serious emergency had occurred and he must return at once. Foran was then 159 miles from his base, but with his specially trained porters, he was able to cover the distance in record time, traveling day and night. He arrived at the base five o'clock one morning, half-dead with exhaustion. There he was informed that the inspector-general of the district was coming and had demanded a guard of honor, which Foran had to command. Foran got the guard together but the inspector-general changed his mind and never did show up.

Foran still had a couple of days of leave left him, but he decided not to bother with them and returned to his duties.

A few days later, Foran sat at his desk making out reports. Complaints from the home government had been piling up while he was away. Native taxes were paid in cattle, as the natives had no money, and this often meant that after a certain number of cows and bulls had been collected, the cows gave birth to calves, thus increasing the numbers of the herd. The home office insisted on regarding the cattle as cash and could not understand why Foran ended up with more animals than he had originally. Another point concerned the currency exchange from rupees to shillings. The rupee was worth 14.3 cents (Kenya currency). The shilling was worth an even 20 cents. When the rupees were changed into shillings, there was either a surplus or a deficit due to the fraction of a rupee left over. After balancing his books, due to this factor, Foran had been left with a surplus of three cents. The government demanded an explanation of where the three cents had come from. Foran had explained both these matters many times in letters but the foreign office still remained unconvinced.

After spending several days trying to make these matters and many similar problems clear to London, Foran suddenly collapsed across his desk and burst into hysterical tears. He was invalided back to England. He stayed there a few months and then returned to Kenya. He was one of the famous ivory poachers in Lado Enclave. After working as a journalist and free-lance writer for some years, he settled down on a farm. He is now retired and lives near Nanyuki, about a hundred miles north of Nairobi.

More than on any other one type, the British Empire was built on men like Foran. When, in an attempt to liberalize its policies, the government interfered with these men, they could no longer function. Whether this was good or bad, time alone will tell.

John A. Hunter

XIII

The Ivory Poachers
of the Lado Enclave

When King Leopold of Belgium died in 1909, a curious legal situation arose which resulted in one of the most colorful periods in Kenya history. This was the time of the ivory poachers of the Lado Enclave. The Enclave was a great area roughly a hundred miles square lying north of Lake Albert in the northwestern part of Uganda. One of the old poachers defined the area to me in this way: "It was bounded by Lake Albert to the south, the Sudan to the north, the Nile to the east and on the west you kept on going until the Belgians shot you." The Enclave was the home of the last of the great elephant herds, numbering four or five hundred in a herd, with the old bulls carrying two hundred pounds of ivory or better. This ivory was worth "a pound for a pound," that is, a pound sterling for a pound of ivory. All you were risking was a cartridge worth one and six and your life. A great bargain.

The legal considerations that suddenly threw the Enclave open to hunters are beyond me, but it would seem that King Leopold had held the country under a mandate as somewhat of his private property. On his death, it immediately became a no man's land until such time as the politicians could decide who was to have it. So for several months, there was no law in the Enclave. Anything you could get was yours. If you were killed by the remaining Belgian police, the natives, or by elephants or blackwater fever, no one asked after you. Once you crossed the Nile, you were outside of British

252

jurisdiction. Your blood was on your own head and your profits went into your own pocket.

A group of men, mostly from Kenya but some from Alaska, India and Europe, sped to the Enclave hoping to make a fortune in this "ivory rush." Many of them died there from elephants or the blackwater. A few made fortunes. A good shot could kill eight or ten elephants at a time and some men made $75,000 within six months. As the Belgians still claimed the Enclave, these men were technically poachers but as the British government did not acknowledge the Belgian claim, the hunters were not prosecuted once they managed to get back across the Nile with their ivory. That was good enough for the hunters and so the rush was on.

One of the first men to reach the Enclave was our old friend John Boyes. John had been living peacefully on his farm near Nairobi but as soon as he heard of King Leopold's death, he left the farm in the hands of his wife and raced for the Enclave. John had no idea where the elephant herds might be and in that vast area a man might well wander about for months until he came to the elephant country but John solved this problem in typical Boyes fashion. He went to the Belgian district commissioner and introduced himself as a trader. The two men had several drinks together and when John considered the time ripe, he confessed that he had a problem.

"I'm a timid man and mortally afraid of elephants," he admitted. "I certainly hope that there aren't any around in the districts where I intend to trade."

"Why, there are some herds there," said the commissioner.

"That's terrible!" said John. "I have a map here. If you'll please mark the places where the elephants are, it'll be a great favor to me."

The commissioner obligingly marked the areas and John departed with the map. Needless to say, it proved invaluable to him.

John collected a scratch group of porters and plunged into the jungle. Although not a professional hunter, John made up in determination what he lacked in bushcraft and within a month had collected thirteen thousand dollars' worth of ivory. Elephants are not sheep and he did not gain this sum without running risks. On one occasion, he fired both barrels of his rifle at a charging bull without doing apparent damage and then grabbed his second rifle from the hands of his gunbearer. Before he could raise the second rifle, the bull was on him. The elephant snatched the gun from his hands with its trunk and began to beat the rifle on the ground. John dived into cover while the rifle exploded and the furious bull charged on down the path, scattering the porters every which way. When John crawled out, he found the dead body of his gunbearer lying beside the shattered rifle. The bull had knelt on the man and driven one of his tusks through him. John stopped long enough to bury the gunbearer and then went on hunting.

Other hunters followed hard on John's heels. A few weeks later, John was spooring down an elephant early one morning and found the animal standing beside a tent. John shot him and there was a commotion inside the tent and two men rushed out. Their name was Craven and they were brothers. The elder brother had been a British naval officer but had left the service to take part in the ivory rush. The younger was the ex-champion boxer of the British army. He had left the service to go with his brother. "If we'd only known that 'phunt was there, we'd have gotten out of bed and shot him ourselves," said the elder, looking regretfully at the great tusks.

John later described these brothers as the two bravest men he had ever known. They were also two of the most successful hunters. They were inveterate gamblers and used to amuse themselves in the evenings rolling dice they'd made out of ivory chips to see who'd get the day's bag. The elder died a few months later of blackwater. The younger never recovered from the shock and left the country a broken man.

In the next few months, John met many other men who had come to the country hoping for quick riches. He met William Brittlebank, a graduate of Eton, who had traveled in Siberia, India, Australia and had taken part in the Klondike gold rush. In the Klondike, Brittlebank had fallen into a crevasse and broken both ankles. The bones had never mended properly and so he was forced to wear special metal boots to hold his ankles together. While after elephants, Brittlebank happened to hit oil near Lake Albert. While he was trying to obtain capital to exploit his find, the First World War came. Brittlebank instantly enlisted and died in battle.

John Boyes also met Banks, an old-time hunter, who while after elephants, was charged and tossed by a buffalo. Banks had a wound into which he could put both fists, but his craving for ivory was so great that he kept on hunting, washing out the wound in the evenings with permanganate of potash. A witch doctor warned Banks that if he stayed in the Enclave, he would have a run of bad luck. The next day, he was charged by an elephant and left for dead. The second day, his hut burned down. The third day, his gun exploded. The fourth day, Banks left the Enclave. "I'm not a superstitious man," he remarked, "but I think that witch doctor knew what he was talking about."

One of the great problems confronting the elephant hunters was the tall grass, often eight to ten feet high. A man couldn't see over the grass to get in his shots. Boyes tried to solve this difficulty by riding on his gunbearer's shoulders but the kick of the heavy elephant gun always knocked both men down and this was hardly pleasant. Finally Boyes managed to get a mule. This mule was a most docile and intelligent beast. At a word from Boyes, the animal would spread its legs and stand stock-still while John stood up on its back and got in his shots. John became deeply attached to this mule and insisted on taking the animal with him wherever he went. Once, while back in British territory, John was staying at a little inn with some of the other ivory hunters recuperating for another safari. John had the mule in the main room of the inn with him and the animal was sleeping peacefully in front of the fire. A visiting sportsman protested that he refused to stay in a room with a mule. The ivory hunters promptly threw the sportsman out, locked the door so he couldn't get in again, and then put the mule in the man's bed where the animal spent a very restful night.

After one of his trips, John had himself and his ivory ferried across Lake Albert on a sort of lake tramp steamer operated by a man named David Bennett. Bennett, who used to refer to himself as "Admiral of the Nile Flotilla," since his was the only boat in the area, was much impressed by John's stories. "My Lord, you've made more

in a month than I've made in three years on this old tub," he
exclaimed. "Lend me a gun." John contributed one of his heavy rifles
and Bennett promptly ran the ship ashore, impressed his native pas-
sengers at the point of the gun as porters, and set off after elephants.
John had to get his ivory across by canoe.

Bennett knew nothing about hunting and three months later staggered back to the lake with nothing to show for his safari but one
small tusk given him by a kindly native chief. Bennett was no wit
discouraged. He set off in his boat to Butiaba to outfit another safari.
But Bennett had overlooked the fact that he'd been carrying the
government mail on his ship and a furious official was awaiting
him. Bennett offered to take this official for a ride while discussing
the matter. He marooned him three days' walk from Butiaba, then
returned, got his supplies, and set off again.

Poor Bennett seemed destined to have hard luck. A few days out
with his new safari, he met with a tribe who showed great interest
in Bennett's repeating rifle. Bennett showed them how to load the
gun. The natives asked to see how it was unloaded. Bennett demon-
strated and then remarked, "Now the gun is useless." "That's all we
wanted to know," replied the native leader and jumped on Bennett.
The natives looted the camp, and carried Bennett off to their village
where he was kept a prisoner. "I didn't really begin to get worried
until they started feeding me well and insisting that I take a bath
every day," Bennett later remarked. "As they were all cannibals, I
thought that was a bit suspicious." Meeting some of the other ivory
hunters in the neighborhood, the natives became alarmed and let
Bennett go, first stripping him of everything he possessed.

Nothing could discourage Bennett. He was back again in a few
weeks with another outfit. This time, some natives, finding him in the
center of a field of tall, dead grass, fired the field on the sides just
as a joke. Bennett was nearly burned to death and saved his life
only by accidentally stumbling across a small bog. He buried himself in the mud until the fire had burnt out, but again he lost everything. I regret to say that Bennett, like so many others of the
poachers, finally died of blackwater fever.

The business of getting the poached ivory to market was always difficult and there was much discussion of the best way to cross the Nile under the fire of the Belgian patrols. Many a poacher, after enduring the hardships and dangers of months in the jungle, lost everything in that last perilous dash. The Nile was choked with masses of the floating sudd, but there were passages through it known only to the natives. The crossing was usually made at night. The canoes, laden to the gunnels with ivory and men, lay hidden in the high reeds until the scouts reported that all was clear. Then, at a given signal, every man bent to his paddle. Once in the open water, there was always danger of the canoes being attacked by night-feeding hippos, and the ever present crocodiles. If you fired at these submarine monsters, you brought the patrols down on you.

There were many different types of men among the poachers. There were graduates not only of Eton but also of the slums of Naples and the grim Scottish highlands. One of the poachers, a renegade Italian, had an ugly reputation for molesting native women. Although I am the last man to claim that the poachers were a group of plaster saints, I would like to say that this particular crime was absolutely unknown among them, with this unhappy exception. This man was pursued by a group of furious natives and one of them shot him with an old muzzle-loader while he was trying to cross a stream. Then they carried him back to their village, cut pieces off him until he died, and ended by devouring the corpse.

A very different type was an old Scotsman named McQueen, no kin of any kind to the pioneer McQueens of Nairobi. McQueen was not only a dead shot, but a fanatically religious man according to his own lights. If he heard a man swear, McQueen would turn on the transgressor and savagely denounce him—usually with such a flow of blasphemy that the victim was left open-mouthed and speechless. Whenever possible, McQueen made a point of attending church on Sunday morning. One day, on his way to a mission church, McQueen passed a native who was happily whistling a hymn as he walked along. The spectacle of a man whistling on the Sabbath was too much for the old poacher. He rushed on the astonished native and gave him such a beating that the man was left half-unconscious on

the road. McQueen then went on to the church and solemnly took
his place with the other worshipers, waiting for the service to begin.
The service was delayed and finally a man entered to say that there
would be no service that day as unfortunately the native minister
had been found in a serious condition on the road as the result of an
attack by a lunatic white man. This outraged McQueen who
promptly rose and explained to the amazed congregation the enor-
mity of whistling on the Sabbath. "But ye must na' be cheated oot o'
your chance to praise the Almighty," McQueen concluded. "I'll conduct the service mesel'." This he did, urging everyone to join in the
hymns and strolling up and down the aisles flourishing a kiboko
whip of rhino hide with a sharp eye out for anyone who wasn't
singing lustily. According to reports, the sound of those hymns could
be heard for miles.

James Manley, one of the old ivory hunters who has now retired,
tells me that some months after this event, McQueen was brought
into a station where Manley was, with his arm so badly mangled by
an elephant that the doctor decided to amputate. As there was no
anesthetic, Manley and the doctor filled the old man up on whisky
until he passed out (a process which depleted the station's stores for
months) and with Manley as assistant, the doctor set about amputat-
ing the arm. When it had been cut off, a village dog rushed in,
grabbed the arm, and ran off with it. Manley tried to catch the dog,
failed and remarked, "God damn that bloody dog," and then went
back to helping the doctor. When McQueen came out of his sleep
and was told that his arm was gone, he asked where it was. "Oh, we
buried it," Manley assured him. "I hope ye dinna omit to say a few
words o'er the arm first," said McQueen reprovingly. "There were
some words said over it, never fear," Manley assured him, so the old
Scotsman was well content.

"I remember that one of the native interns had to wash the old
man's teeth every morning while he was recovering," Manley recalls.
"There wasn't any toothpaste, so the man used soap. McQueen
always swore fluently through the whole process and before it was
over, his head was surrounded by a wreath of soap bubbles and
from the middle of the bubbles came a steady flow of the worst

profanity I've ever heard. It was quite a sight. Everyone in the station used to turn out to watch it."

McQueen went back to elephant hunting as soon as he was able to leave the hospital. He had a tripod built on which he could steady the gun while firing. I have been unable to find out what finally happened to him.

Inexperienced men who entered the Enclave were usually fortunate if they escaped with whole skins, to say nothing of finding a fortune in ivory. Yet there were exceptions. One young Englishman sauntered into the area, dressed as though prepared to take a stroll on Bond Street, without porters, without money, and even without a gun. When questioned, this youth would say airily, "Oh, I'm like Mr. Micawber—just waiting for something to turn up." The natives considered him insane and, as such, under the special protection of God. They fed him and passed him on from one village to another. Several months later, this man turned up at a Belgian outpost, his clothes in rags and in spite of the natives' help, half-starved. The Belgian official took pity on the man, fed him, gave him one of his old uniforms, and headed this strange individual back toward the Nile. Here he happened to walk in on an Indian poacher who had been in the Enclave for months and was preparing to smuggle his ivory across the river. Seeing the Belgian uniform, the Indian and his native boys leaped into their canoes and fled across the river, leaving their ivory behind. The Englishman went to the nearest village and demanded that the chief supply him with porters. The chief, never questioning the authority of a Belgian uniform, promptly produced the porters who ferried the ivory over the river where the man later sold it for a huge sum. He then left for England, having had a most profitable trip.

The determination of these men was truly astonishing. One man, with a huge horde of ivory, walked into the camp of a friend, only to find that a Belgian official had just arrested his friend and was in control of the camp. The official promptly arrested him also, confiscated not only his ivory but everything he possessed, had him flogged and then sent away with a warning. The man got back across the Nile, borrowed a gun, and coming back, continued his poaching. He killed eighteen elephants within a few days and having no ax, had to leave them until the tusks rotted out. He managed to impress some porters, returned with his ivory, sold it, and went back to the Enclave where he was killed by an elephant the next day.

The Belgians waged a constant war against the poachers and many are the stories that the old-timers love to tell of outwitting the patrols sent against them. When possible, they tried to ingratiate themselves with the Belgians. John Boyes tells of a group of the poachers who, while waiting for a chance to cross the river from the British side, asked the visiting Belgian official to join them for dinner and to discuss the situation. The Belgian complied and Boyes poured him a drink, telling him to say "When." The Belgian said nothing and when his glass was filled, drained the whole thing at a draft. This impressed even the hardened poachers who poured him a second. The Belgian drank that also, apparently thinking the whisky was some sort of wine. Having finished, the official said briskly, "Now, gentlemen, let's get down to business," and promptly toppled over in a dead faint. The poachers naturally considered this a heaven-sent opportunity and hurriedly crossed the river with their outfits, pausing on the way to deliver the still unconscious Belgian to his native askaris.

My old friend Billy Judd must receive credit for one of the most elaborate hoaxes on the part of the poachers. Billy was in a village when the natives brought him word that a Belgian patrol was on a hill overlooking a swamp which he must cross to reach the Nile. The natives were usually on the side of the poachers as, after an elephant was shot, they received the meat as their share. Billy had a number of poles cut and whitewashed with the clay the natives used to waterproof the mud walls of their huts. He sent the main part of his safari with the ivory to the rear of the hill while he started openly across the swamp with a few porters carrying the white poles. The patrol hurried down from the hill to arrest him and the ivory reached the river in safety.

The game did not always go to the poachers. Bennett's ship on the lake once sighted a man, stark naked except for his sun helmet, wildly signaling. The man turned out to be a poacher who had been caught for the third time by a Belgian officer. The Belgian, who was becoming tired of the game by that time, had the man stripped, flogged and sent back naked. He had left him the helmet to protect him from sunstroke.

The poachers seldom came to actual blows with the Belgians but at times they had no choice. "Karamojo" Bell was once forced to use his rifle. Bell was quite possibly the greatest elephant hunter that ever lived. He won his nickname by his remarkable feats in the Karamojo area in the northwestern part of Kenya. Bell was an astonishing shot. Manley once saw him shooting fish with a rifle as they jumped from the surface of a lake after flies. He was famous for using a very light-caliber rifle, knowing the anatomy of elephants so perfectly that he needed no other weapon. Bell had crossed the river to the Belgian side and, as the canoe leaked, had removed his boots to keep them dry. While he was putting them back on, he was arrested by a group of Belgian askaris. There was no law against crossing the river so Bell had a clear conscience. He told the boys he would go with them as soon as he put on his boots. One of the men grabbed him and a fight started. Bell, knowing the character of the Belgian askaris who were simply armed savages and not above killing and eating their prisoners, grabbed up his gun and fired into them, killing one man. Then he jumped into his canoe and pushed off. The furious askaris fired after him but, luckily for Bell, they were poor shots. The askaris then rounded up Bell's native porters, selected one, and shot him in retaliation. In such manner was justice performed in the Enclave.

There are only a few of the old ivory poachers still with us. One of these men is F. H. Clarke, who is now seventy and has a farm near Nakuru in Kenya. I will tell Clarke's story at some length as I believe it will give the reader a fair idea of the type of man who engaged in this hazardous business.

Clarke came out from England in 1904 as a young man, and took a job as a clerk in a store for the then fabulously high wages of twenty pounds a month (about a hundred dollars). "There was no future for a man without family or backing in England, so I decided to try my luck in Africa," Clarke explains. Clerking was not for him, and soon afterward he met a prospector named MacAlister who believed that there was gold along the western shores of Lake Albert. Clarke went out with MacAlister but they found no gold, only blackwater fever and MacAlister died of it. Clarke was now on his own. Then he heard of the ivory rush. He invested his scant capital in an old 10.75 mm. Mauser and joined the hunters.

"The great secret—if there was any one secret—of success in ivory-poaching was to get the co-operation of the natives," Clarke explained. "The best way to do that was to kill a rogue elephant that had been destroying their villages. I remember going after one rogue that almost did for me. I'd spoored him down with my gunbearer. We couldn't see him but we could hear his belly rumbling while he fed. We started to crawl up on him. Suddenly the belly noises stopped. That's a bad sign. I knew it meant that he'd seen us. While I was looking around, my gunbearer touched me on the shoulder and pointed up. I looked where he pointed and saw the bull's ivory gleaming right over my head. Then I saw something like a snake wriggling through the brush toward my chest. It was the bull's trunk. I didn't even have time to bring the gun to my shoulder. I fired from my side. It was the luckiest shot I ever made, for the bull went down. When we came to cut out the tusks, we found a gallon of pus at the root of each of them. The creature must have been half-mad with pain, which is why he became a rogue. After that, I didn't have any trouble with that tribe. They scouted up elephants for me, warned me if patrols were near, and fell all over themselves getting food for my porters."

Clarke was not always so fortunate in his relations with the natives. "Once, while we were in pygmy country, I sent two of my boys back with mail to the lake. Next morning, one of them staggered into camp. He said they'd been attacked by pygmies and his friend was killed. You can't let the natives cut up your boys like that, so I started out to see what could be done. We came to the place where the runner had been killed. The pygmies had built a fire there and were eating him. All that was left of him was one of his arms. I fired at the little blighters and got a few before they dived into the jungle.

When I came to examine them, I found that one was still alive. The bullet had just grazed his skull. He was an old chap, shriveled and toothless, but otherwise quite sound. We took him along, partly as a hostage and partly as a kind of pet. Gave him a suit of clothes, as he was completely naked, and fed him well. The old chap had the time of his life, although we kept him tied up so he couldn't bolt, and I learned to talk to him a bit. Those pygmies are remarkable bushcraftsmen. They know the jungle better than I know this house, and even had a special name for each of the big trees in an area. We took him around with us for six months and then, as we were leaving the district, turned him loose. Funny thing, he gravely took off all his clothes, laid them in a neat pile, bowed to us, and then trotted off stark naked into the jungle. We never saw him again."

Many of Clarke's memories concern such practical matters as transporting and selling the ivory. "When you saw a herd, your natural tendency was to shoot the bulls with the heaviest ivory," he remarked. "I always considered that a mistake. Seventy-five pounds was the ideal weight for a tusk. Once you got over that, it meant that one porter couldn't carry it. The tusk had to be slung from a pole and two men carried it. The porters hated that. It made an awkward load on the narrow trails and the men couldn't shift the load around as they could with a single tusk. Also, many of the hunters would stay in the jungle until they had several hundred tusks. I don't believe that was practical. I'd get fifty or sixty tusks and then head for the river."

Selling the ivory also presented problems. The British levied a 25 per cent tax on all ivory brought into the country from the Belgian side and this tax cut heavily into the poachers' profit. Only one of the poachers ever hit on a device to avoid this tax. Robert Foran smuggled his ivory across the river one dark night and then kept his canoes hidden in the reeds on the British side. When morning came, he and his men raced back across the river to the Belgian side, all working madly at the paddles as though pursued. The amazed Belgian official came out to meet them and Foran explained that he had been poaching ivory on the British side of the river and wanted to sell it to the Belgians. The Belgians greatly resented the fact that the British made no attempt to arrest the poachers once they had crossed the river and were even buying their poached ivory, so he was delighted to turn the tables on them. He bought Foran's ivory for a good price and, as there was no import tax on ivory in the Belgian territories, Foran realized a 100 per cent profit. He then crossed to the British side of the river and converted his francs into pounds without trouble.

"Foran was a smart man and as far as I'm concerned, anyone who got any ivory in the Belgian area deserved to make every penny he could on it," remarked Clarke after I'd told him this story. "Hunting elephants isn't child's play even at best, especially with the guns we had at the time. I remember many close shaves that I had. Once I was paddling along the shore of Lake Albert with a canoeful of boys looking for elephant. We used to go out early in the morning and watch for the white egrets. They hang around the elephant herds, you know. We sighted some egrets and paddled toward them, keeping close into the bank. There was an elephant all right, but it was a cow. We'd run across that cow for three successive mornings and it always meant a long, hard paddle after we'd seen the birds to check and make sure it wasn't a bull. I decided to scare her away from the lake and fired into the air. Instead of running, the cow charged. I'll never forget that sight. The water was splashing up around her as she came, nearly swamping the canoe. The canoe was pitching about so I could not get her in my sights. The boys backed water like mad but there was a long, shelving shore there and she came right on. I don't believe she was more than twelve feet from us when we finally got into water over her depth. Last time I ever tried to frighten a cow elephant."

Clarke speaks most frankly about the basic stock-in-trade of all ivory hunters—courage. To these men, courage was not an abstract virtue. It was a commodity which they all possessed to a greater or less degree but which they perfectly realized was subject to fluctuations. "If a hunter had a narrow escape with an elephant, he always made it a point to go on hunting immediately," Clarke remarked. "Otherwise, he might lose his nerve. Like taking a bad fall in the hunting field, the best thing to do is mount again and keep on. But with most of us the breaking point came eventually. A man was lucky if he could foresee it and stop in time, but many of us couldn't —like poor Billy Pickering."

Billy Pickering was a well-known member of the poaching fraternity and a man of great courage. One day, Clarke received word that Billy had been killed by an elephant. The bull had torn the man's head off with its trunk and then trampled the body. The head was found later, completely intact, lying some distance off in the bushes.

"I talked to some of Billy's native boys," Clarke explained. "One of them told me a curious thing. He said, 'The elephant charged our bwana just as had happened many times before. The bwana raised his rifle and looked along the sights but he didn't pull the trigger. He stood there as though he couldn't move. The bull came on and killed him as you know.'

"I'd never known a braver man than Billy, but I could guess what had happened. Billy had simply come to the end of his rope. His nerves had had such a strain put on them in the months he'd spent elephant hunting that suddenly they couldn't take any more. They just froze. That was the end of Billy.

"I kept on hunting for several months after Billy's death. Nearly all of the hunters died sooner or later, either blackwater or elephants, so you got to expect it. Then one morning I was going down the Semliki River in a canoe with my boys and we unexpectedly came on a big bull with fine ivory drinking from the river. The canoe was about six yards from him. The boys sank their paddles deep in the water to hold the canoe steady and I raised my gun. I wasn't nervous in the slightest. After all, I'd been doing this kind of thing for months. Do you know I couldn't pull the trigger? My whole arm seemed to be paralyzed. The canoe kept floating on downstream with the boys trying to hold it in place and me still trying to pull that bloody trigger. I couldn't move a muscle. Finally the bull turned and swung away. I laid my gun down and said, 'Well, boys, that's that. We'll take what ivory we have and head back for British territory. I'm through.' I didn't want to go the way of poor Billy and so many of the others. I stopped right there."

When Clarke retired as an ivory poacher, he became a game warden in Kenya and, like many another old hunter including myself, devoted himself to protecting the game that he had once specialized in killing. Later, he retired to his farm near Nakuru, about a hundred miles north of Nairobi, where he still lives.

When a treaty was finally drawn up between the British and the Belgians concerning the administration of the Enclave, the poaching died a natural death. Only one or two of the poachers continued their hunting in defiance of both sides. One of these was a man named Rogers, who came from California. He continued to raid the Enclave from the Sudan, retiring across the border when closely pressed. The manner of his death was as follows:

A young British officer was chasing Rogers with a small group of askaris. One of these askaris, an expert tracker, and a few followers outdistanced the main party. Rogers had in the meanwhile crossed the border into the Sudan with his safari and, knowing that he was now legally safe from pursuit, slowed down his march. But borders meant nothing to the askaris and when they overtook Rogers' party, the tracker fired at the poacher, mortally wounding him.

When the white officer arrived, Rogers was lying in his tent covered by a blanket. He looked up at the white man and asked bluntly, "Did that man shoot me on your orders after I'd crossed the border?"

The officer explained the circumstances. Rogers listened to him intently. Then he drew a cocked revolver from the blanket and handed it to the officer.

"I'm satisfied that you're telling the truth," he said. "And it's lucky for you that I am. I'm dying and I swore that I was going to kill you before I died. Now stay with me until the end comes."

It came a few hours later.

I know that many of my readers will have little sympathy for men who were not only violating international law but also killing in large numbers the last of the great elephant herds, much as famous American hunters slaughtered thousands of American bison. Yet others may perhaps excuse an old hunter if he regards these men with a certain respect. To my mind, the most fitting tribute to the ivory poachers was paid by the late Theodore Roosevelt during his trip to Uganda. The ex-President insisted on meeting the poachers and had dinner with a group of them. During the meal, Mr. Roosevelt raised his glass and announced, "To the ivory poachers of the Lado Enclave!" The hunters protested good-naturedly, and pointed out that from the British point of view they were not poaching. "Then I'll change the toast," said Mr. Roosevelt. "To the company of gentleman adventurers—for such you would be called in Elizabethan times."

The people of Kenya have never forgotten this toast, and as virtually every hunter of the time who was worth his salt was up poaching in the Enclave, they have cherished the phrase. The memory of the Company of Gentleman Adventurers is still beloved by us all.

Daniel P. Mannix

XIV

Sir Vincent Glenday
of the Northern Frontier

It was 1913. A group of eager young men were sitting in the anteroom of the Colonial Office, awaiting the orders that would scatter them to the four corners of the world. This was their first assignment and no one knew what his fate might be: South America, India, Australia or Europe. One of the group was a twenty-one-year-old youngster named Vincent Glenday. Glenday was not apprehensive about his orders. He had just graduated from Oxford with honors, had an outstanding record at games, and was a graduate geologist. He felt confident that he would be given a post commensurable with his record.

The secretary appeared with a sheaf of orders. He looked at the young men and then asked commiseratingly, "Which of you is that poor devil Glenday?"

"I am," said the astonished young man.

"Well, you've drawn the prize," said the secretary. "You're being sent to the N.F.D."

N.F.D is the Northern Frontier District of Kenya. Glenday had never heard of it. During the next twenty-five years he learned more about it than any other man in the world.

North of the pleasant White Highlands the land drops away sharply into a great desert nearly one hundred thousand miles in extent. This area, larger than the British Isles, reaches from the Indian Ocean on the east to Uganda on the west. North of it, the land begins to rise again until it forms the fertile plateau of Abyssinia.

Several nomadic tribes wander over these wastes with their camel herds, following the grass and water. The principal group are the Somali, a wild, fierce people who have been called "parasites of the camel" for they live almost entirely on the milk from their camel herds and carry all their belongings on the backs of these curious beasts. At the end of the last century, the area was divided between the British and the great Emperor Menelik of Abyssinia by simply drawing a line across it. This arrangement was not a happy one. As Glenday put it, "They got the water and we got the grazing." The nomadic tribes paid no attention to the boundary and wandered back and forth as they had always done. This led to constant quarrels between the Abyssinians and the British. To keep the peace, the British built a few small forts along the border in the heart of the desert. It was to one of these forts that Glenday was being sent.

Glenday was a powerfully built young man, about average height, and inclined to be thickset. He has always been a keen sportsman and told me that the hours he spent with a shotgun after sand grouse, or with a rifle after big game, were the happiest of his life. Although I do not believe that he ever exhibited the daredevil recklessness that was characteristic of a certain type of young British officer of that time, he obviously enjoyed pitting his wits against danger, whether his adversary was an enraged bull elephant or an Abyssinian raider. I cannot imagine Glenday hitting a lion with a beer bottle as did Fritz Schindelar, nor can I imagine him failing to place his shots expertly and methodically in the face of a charge.

When Glenday arrived in Mombasa, he took the train to Nairobi and from there went north by ox wagon with a small detail of askaris. When the road gave out, the party abandoned the wagons and took porters. When the desert was reached, the porters were sent back and camels hired. With the camels mincing over the hard, sandy soil, bare except for a few skeleton thorn trees, the caravan moved north toward Moyale Fort, on the border between Kenya and Abyssinia. It was to Moyale that Glenday had been assigned.

From Nairobi to Moyale is 380 miles. The caravan took three months to cover the distance.

Moyale Fort was built on a slight rise of ground within a stone's throw of the Abyssinian frontier. It was a rectangle three hundred by one hundred yards. The outer wall was ten feet high, loopholed for firing. Inside was a guardhouse with a curtained wall along the top. There was a storeroom, and the foundations of a three-storied tower. There were also two long parallel buildings used as barracks, office and hospital. Outside the fort was a cluster of mud and wattle huts, inhabited by traders and natives. Water came from two wells: the "government well" (three-quarters of a mile from the fort) and Nimau Well (a mile away). When these wells dried up, water had to be carried from a third well five miles away. The fort was not erected around one of these wells because they were in depressions and riflemen on the hills could have then fired into the fort.

The garrison of Moyale consisted of Captain Dickinson in command of the troops, Dr. Chell, the medical officer, and fifty native askaris. Glenday was the assistant district commissioner for the area. This group was supposed to police a hundred miles of border.

One of the main purposes of the forts was to prevent raiding parties from Abyssinia carrying off camels and women. As there were only half a dozen forts scattered along eight hundred miles of border the Abyssinian raiders could cross the border, strike and be back in their own territory before an expedition could be organized to catch them. "The pattern was roughly like this," Glenday explained. "Some young Abyssinian leader would have the word passed through the villages that he was planning a raid. Anyone could join, with a prospect of getting enough loot to make him rich for life. When the 'oll' (war party) was assembled, they'd move south across the border, traveling very light and fast. They'd attack a Somali or Boran village, first trying to surround it so no one could get away. Generally, they'd attack at dawn. They'd kill everyone in the community, except the young girls who could be sold as slaves. They'd castrate the dead males, even children, and carry the genitals back with them as souvenirs to show that they'd killed a man. Then they'd start back for the border, taking the camels and girls with them.

"If they did a clean job of it, we'd never know until they were safe across the border. But usually some tribesmen would escape in the raid. I remember one case in particular. A Somali was shot through the stomach, speared five times and left for dead. Under a blazing sun, the man crawled from noon until evening with his guts hanging out until he reached a government boma. We had little bomas (small encampments surrounded by thorn bushes) scattered about the country, each with a white officer and a few askaris. If a fugitive could reach one of these bomas, the officer would send word to the nearest fort by runner. As soon as we received the message, we'd send out a force to cut off the raiders."

The arrival of one of these runners must have been a dramatic moment. A hasty conference, the bugler sounding "Assembly," the men pouring out of their barracks and racing down the camel lines, the long-legged beasts swaying to their feet, and the hurried departure from the fort across the desert.

"The camels were amazingly intelligent," Glenday remarked. "They quickly learned the different bugle calls for water, food, and so on and would respond to them. The Somalis were quite impressed with our beasts—in fact, it was the first time I ever saw a Somali take an interest in anything we did. I remember once hearing an old Somali remark to a friend when he saw our camels taking their places in response to the bugle, 'If they can make camels do that, they can't be as big fools as they seem.'"

It was impossible to press even camels too hard in the murderous desert heat. By long practice, a sort of formula was worked out. Start in the evening if possible. Halt from nine A.M. until two P.M. Then go on from two P.M. until six P.M. Rest until three A.M. Then march from three A.M. until nine A.M. The camels could go for two weeks without water if they were allowed to graze for five hours a day. If there wasn't time for that, they had to be given water every forty-eight hours.

"Catching raiders who had a long start was a difficult job," said Glenday, smiling reminiscently. "It called for very nice calculations. You see, we had one great advantage. We knew that they'd have to go from well to well across the desert as they couldn't take enough water with them to cut across country. These wells are remarkable things, some of them fifty feet deep and cut straight down through solid rock. No one knows who made them or what tools they used. The trick was to guess at what well the oll would probably be and head for it. I remember once trying to cut off some Mar raiders and racing for a group of wells several days' march from any other water. We reached the wells only a day after the raiders had left. They'd played a very clever trick on us. After watering, they'd taken some old men and women that they'd picked up on the raid, cut their throats and stuffed their bodies into the wells. In the hot desert, the bodies had begun to putrefy almost at once and by the time we got there, the water was undrinkable even for the camels. We started back at once, but before we reached the next water, most of our camels had died. We only barely made it ourselves. I sent the raiders a very insulting message, through one of the roaming tribes, casting aspersions on their ancestry. They sent me a message back saying, 'If you hope to catch us, you'll have to be quicker on your feet, White Horse.' "

Glenday was known as the White Horse along the frontier because he rode a white stallion. Because of their greater speed, horses were used whenever possible. Only on long treks over waterless wastes were camels or mules employed.

Chasing Abyssinian raiders was only one of Glenday's duties. He spent most of his time traveling from tribe to tribe, holding "barazas" (meetings), and listening to the complaints by the various local sheiks. British officials have bitterly referred to the Somalis as the "Irish of Africa" because they are on principle "agin the government" and refuse to be controlled. Physically, they are one of the finest of the African tribes. The men are tall, lean and dark-skinned, with features more delicately cut than most Europeans. The women are famous for their beauty and have always brought top prices as slave concubines. To see a Somali girl at a well with her giraffe-skin bucket on her shoulder, naked to the waist, and her great mane of ebony hair over her shoulders, is a sight to remember. "The Somali are generally admitted to be the most difficult of all Kenya tribes to handle," Glenday told me. "They are temperamental, treacherous, cruel and as fighting men are marks above any other tribe. I never allowed myself to grow sentimental about them, but I became deeply attached to the Somali."

At these barazas, young Glenday was called upon to give instant decisions on matters crucially affecting the fate of several hundred people and, to a certain extent, the destiny of the British Empire. A sheik would stand up and remind Glenday that the government had assigned certain wells and certain grazing areas to the Gelible clan. This sheik's people belonged to a different clan, but the sheik would argue, with many genealogical details, that his group was actually a subclan of the Gelible and so were entitled to water rights, especially as their wells had dried up. The Gelible sheik would then protest that there was scarcely enough water for his tribe. Glenday would pass judgment to the best of his ability and then another sheik would rise to say that lions were killing his camels and he wanted a few guns so the herdsmen could protect the animals. Glenday would remind him that the last time guns were issued to his people, they had used the weapons to stage a raid on the Boran tribe. That, the sheik indignantly explained, was only because the Boran had raided them the year before. When this point was decided, still another sheik would protest that Abyssinian raiders had carried off several young women from his clan. If it happened again, he was going to pursue the raiders across the border, treaty or no treaty. As this might lead to war with Abyssinia, Glenday would try to calm the angry man. "Very well then," the furious sheik would retort, "if you don't want us to retaliate, give us the protection the British government promised. Otherwise, let us handle it in our own manner."

Unavoidably, there were times when the British closed their eyes to retaliatory raids. A young officer named Captain Aylmer was shot by raiders and the avenging patrol followed the raiders into Abyssinia and killed nine of them in a running fight. "However, this sort of thing always caused endless trouble and we did everything possible to prevent it," Glenday assured me.

Although Glenday spoke Somali fluently and lived intimately with the tribesmen, he took care never to lose his identity as a

British officer. "Personally, I think it's foolish for a European to pretend that he's a native," he told me. "I remember one man stationed along the frontier who became so impressed with the Somalis that he dressed like one, tried to observe all their customs, and spoke nothing but Somali, which he did very badly. I once saw this chap walking through the streets of a village in his robe with the natives giggling at him. Even from the rear, you could tell at once he wasn't a Somali—didn't walk like one. He was later killed by the natives. They had lost all respect for the chap and considered him an idiot."

Glenday never made any secret of his own limitations while he was dealing with the natives. "The Somalis can do with an amazingly small amount of water," he told me. "Half a cupful a day can keep them going. I've seen young officers, hoping to win the respect of their men, try to do the same. I never did. Often when we were out in the desert, the tribesmen would come to me and say, 'Not being a Somali, you haven't our endurance. We'll give you part of our water ration.' I always answered, 'What you say is true. I cannot endure thirst as you do. Thank you very much for the water.' When you're living constantly with the natives, it's impossible to keep up any sort of pretense or try to deceive them. They'll see through at once. No matter how big a fool you are, it's better to admit it at once rather than put on a show."

Small parties from the forts were constantly being attacked, either by Abyssinian raiders or hostile tribesmen. Once Dr. Chell was taking a government caravan of camels loaded with twenty thousand dollars as payment for the troops when he was attacked by Abyssinians. The caravan was in the bottom of a gorge and the raiders opened fire from both sides. Dr. Chell led a charge up the side of one hill and cleared it. Then his askaris opened fire on the raiders on the opposite hill and forced them to retreat. Dr. Chell lost one man in this action. He did not stay to see how many the raiders lost.

Even large expeditionary forces were not immune from attack. At Gumburu, a force of 9 British officers and 187 askaris was wiped out. Occasionally, even one of the forts would fall. A young officer named Lieutenant Elliott was in command of a fort named Serenli, several hundred miles to the east of Moyale. A clan called the Aulihan raided another clan called the Marehan, killed eight men and captured nearly a thousand camels. Lieutenant Elliott told Sheik Abdurrahamn Mursaal, the chief of the Aulihan, that the camels must be returned and blood money paid for the dead men. Mursaal called a meeting of his headmen. "Am I a dog that the British should tell me what to do?" he demanded. He had his headmen take an oath on the Koran to follow him. At the head of five hundred men he moved on Serenli, timing his march so he arrived at night. A few of the attackers were sent ahead while the rest waited under cover of darkness. The askari guard at the gate hailed the men. They answered that they were lost in the desert and managed to get close enough to rush the gate. The guard gave the alarm before he was cut down. There was a machine gun mounted on the wall that swept the area around the gate, but two of the askaris in the fort were connected to the Aulihan by marriage and had agreed to betray the fort to the attackers. These men tried to seize the gun. The native sergeant of the guard killed one of them and was shot by the other. Meanwhile, the raiders had gotten over the wall and opened the gate to their friends. Lieutenant Elliott, just awakened, rushed out of his quarters with a lamp in one hand and his revolver in the other. He was instantly shot down and then finished with knives. Only one man, dressed in woman's clothes, managed to escape. The victorious Mursaal sacked the fort and escaped with thirty camel loads of loot. Later, he was tracked down by a patrol and hanged.

The accusation has often been made that some British officers regarded campaigning in the N.F.D. more as a form of sport than as a solemn duty for king and country. I suppose this accusation is true, at least in part, and it is probably the only way a certain type of officer kept from cracking under the strain. Glenday spoke of both the Somalis and the Abyssinian raiders with the same tolerant, good-humor I have heard white hunters use in referring to dangerous big game. Of course a lion will try to eat you if he gets a chance. It's his nature. But a lion is a good chap all the same and don't forget that a lion has his side of the question too. The only criticism I heard Glenday make of the natives was the Abyssinians' habit of poisoning people. "They were really amazing poisoners," he claimed. "If you asked what had happened to somebody, the usual answer was, 'Oh, he took a cup of coffee.' The poison was usually given in this manner because their coffee is so strong that it conceals the taste. Whenever we ate with them, we took along our own food and cooks. Before giving you a drink—they often used buffalo horns set in silver for goblets—it was courtesy on the part of the host to have a slave take a sip first. A nice custom, but as slaves were fairly cheap I never depended on it. I recall that once we were entertaining an Abyssinian chief and by mistake gave him some chili sherry used for seasoning instead of wine. He took one drink and then spat it out in a rage. 'Ah, so you'd try to poison me!' he roared. I tried to explain that a mistake had been made but the old fellow wasn't having any of it. 'I know poison when I taste it,' he shouted and stamped out. Very embarrassing."

Those days now seem to belong to another era. The young officers, only a few months away from the playing fields of England, leading their Mohammedan Somali levies with the cry of "Allah Akbar! (Allah conquers!)," while the Christian Abyssinian raiders charged yelling "Mirian! Mirian!"—Mirian being their word for the Virgin Mary. The evening meals far in the desert with askaris keeping guard around the thorn boma while the senior officer stood up with an enameled mug holding a spoonful of wine and saying, "Gentlemen, the King!" There was the story of an officer, determined to exhibit his British imperturbability, who insisted on dressing immaculately when roused by a night attack on his isolated boma. As a result, he came out to find most of his askaris dead and the raiders looting the post. There was also the story of a young captain fighting his way back to a captured Maxim gun, determined to take the bolt so the gun could not be used by the raiders. His body was later found together with those of his Somali warriors who had died trying to save his corpse from mutilation. There were parties when Glenday's servant was happily able to report next morning, "Bwana, everyone had a fine time. Only the old men were able to sit on their horses." Summing it up, Glenday said, "The only way to hold the frontier was to sit on it. We didn't have motorcars, we didn't have wireless, and we didn't have planes. But the only people who know the frontier are those who lived there in the days gone by."

The frontier forts were so isolated that the First World War had been in progress for several months before Glenday heard about it. One would have thought that a conflict in Europe could have little effect on the N.F.D. But the world was growing smaller, as the British scattered along the border soon discovered.

Some years before, a remarkable leader had appeared among the Somalis. This man was known as the "Mad Mullah." As a young man he had been deeply religious, denouncing such worldly practices as drinking tea made from the leaves of desert plants and chewing the fat meat on a roasted sheep's tail. As a result, he had become regarded as a holy man, or mullah, and gathered a large following. The Mullah had then set out to convert other groups to his beliefs, and had announced that everyone not joining his followers (called dervishes, the oriental term for a crusader) were infidels. As the women and camels of infidels became the rightful property of his dervishes, the Mullah converted a number of able young warriors to his creed. As he grew in power, the Mullah became increasingly fanatical. On one occasion, he had a dream that three hundred women of a certain clan had not said their prayers properly. He had the women staked out on the desert and their ovaries cut out. Incidents like this won him the name of the "Mad Mullah" but as far as desert strategy went, he was a brilliant leader. His dervishes showed a fanatical courage in battle, being inspired by a strong religious faith and also by the fact that the Mullah was in the habit of castrating any man who ran away from a fight.

The British had sent several expeditions against the Mullah, one of which was wiped out at Gumburu when the wild tribesmen broke the British square. At last, however, the Mullah had been defeated and forced to retire into an inaccessible part of the desert where he still continued to exert an enormous influence over the tribesmen. "According to one's point of view, the Mullah was a devout man trying to purify his religion, a power-hungry fanatic attempting to establish himself as a dictator, the leader of a bandit gang, or, as one sincere member of Parliament described him, 'a brave man striving to free his country from foreign domination,' " Glenday explained.

When the First World War broke out, the Mad Mullah, who in many respects was crazy like a fox, realized that the British were in no position to send support to their garrisons in the N.F.D. With his horde of wild dervishes, he began to plunder the country. The British government was in a quandary. In spite of the war in Europe, it would have been possible to send an expeditionary force against the Mullah, but wars against nomadic desert tribesmen were notoriously long, costly affairs often ending in a stalemate. Also, the Mullah had sent letters to the British commissioners which were published in the British papers. A typical one read: "I seek only to rule my own country and protect my religion from foreigners." Many members of Parliament believed him. Many more felt that the N.F.D. simply wasn't worth a war. The usual argument ran, "These tribes have been fighting among themselves for centuries. Let's get out and allow them to settle their own differences."

As Glenday pointed out, "Even granting that we had no moral obligation to protect the tribes who had trusted us, times had changed. The old-time native wars, fought with spears and arrows, were a thing of the past. The Mullah's dervishes were armed with modern rifles. In order to placate him, the government had given the Mullah a seaport which, the Mullah claimed, he needed in order to export goods to make his country self-supporting. He used the port to import guns and ammunition in exchange for ivory and hides. The Mullah was no longer a raider in the old sense of the term. He was at the head of a well-equipped army and was setting out on a career of conquest."

However, the British decided to evacuate the forts. As the troops were withdrawn, the Mullah's men moved in. In some cases, the retreating troops could hear the screams of the native victims in the forts as they were stabbed and mutilated by the dervishes. The effect this had on the British officers, who had lived with the tribes for years and fought side by side with them against the Abyssinian raiders, was indescribable.

The officers of the N.F.D. may have been short on social consciousness but they possessed a well-developed sense of responsibility. They had given their personal assurance to the tribesmen that the British government would help them. "A Somali doesn't understand politics and has no use for a man who doesn't keep his word," remarked Glenday. When the troops were withdrawn, several officers obtained permission from the government to stay behind with the tribesmen and help them resist the Mullah's dervishes. One of these officers was Glenday.

The tribe with which Glenday lived was the Gurre. For three years, he wandered about with this tribe, cut off from communication with Nairobi, living on camel's milk and whatever supplies he could get from his former enemies in Abyssinia, who were also suffering from the Mullah's raiders. He had a half company, composed of men from the King's Rifles and the Armed Constabulary. To a certain extent, he could also count on native levies from the tribesmen. "They were first-class fighting men, but it was impossible to hold them together for more than a few days," Glenday explained. "Then they'd want to get back to their women and camels. You could hardly blame them. When they were out in the bush with me, their families and herds were at the mercy of any roaming dervish bands."

Most of the fighting was done in bush country. Glenday made up his own rules as he went along. "In dense bush, it's absurd to form a square," he told me. "The Somali are excellent shots and they simply lie out in cover and systematically fire into a square. You can't see them and they can see you. The best plan is to fight as they do—scatter out through the bush and shoot anyone you see. However, some knowledge of military tactics is a great help."

Glenday remembers one affair when bush-fighting techniques were nicely combined with more standard methods of warfare. "We had camped for the night in some dense bush," he told me. "It's always best to camp in bush, never in a clearing. Otherwise, the attacking force is in cover and you're exposed. I had my askaris and a Gurre levy. The attack came at dawn, as most such attacks do. I was in my tent at the time and my men were watering the camels at a waterhole. Of course, we had flank guards thrown out through the bush, all lying down. In bush, a sentry never stands. He lies down so he can see through the stems of the bushes. But the attack was so well delivered that the enemy was able to slip past our sentries and was on top of us before we knew what was happening."

Two of the spearmen rushed into Glenday's tent, hoping to catch him asleep. "They nearly did too," Glenday recalls. "I bolted out the back as they came in the front." The enemy riflemen fired at the group watering the camels. "The camels didn't pay any attention to the shots," Glenday explained. "They were kneeling at the time so the copper water tanks could be put on their backs. But when the bullets started to hit the tanks, the noise made the camels bolt. We were caught completely off guard and the camp was a madhouse—shots, screams, panic-stricken camels and the war cries of the attackers. My men scattered through the bush in all directions. If the enemy had followed us, we might well have been finished. But luckily they stopped to loot the camp and round up the camels."

After the first shock of the surprise was over, Glenday and his men rallied in the bush. "Before making camp at night, we always fixed on some spot as a rallying point in case of an attack," he explained. "It might be a big tree or a rock or some other place we could easily find. If we were scattered, it was agreed that we'd all meet at that spot. I had the bugler call in the flank guards. A bugle is invaluable in the bush. The sound carries a great distance and your principal difficulty in bush country is keeping in touch with your men. When the flank guards came in, I divided my force into two groups. Then we attacked the camp from both sides. The raiders hadn't expected that. They were surprised to find themselves between two fires. They fought very bravely for a few minutes and then broke. We lost fifteen Gurres and three askaris. They lost between fifty and sixty men."

When the European war was over, the British were able to send troops to the N.F.D. again. Glenday's men were used as scouts for the main body.

"Our part was mostly bush fighting—short, sharp encounters," Glenday recalls. "The attacking force always had an enormous advantage, so each side always tried to attack. It was a game of hide and seek on a large scale. After four years in the country, I'd begun to fancy myself as a bushcraftsman, but compared to the Somalis I was nowhere. Some of their feats seemed like magic."

Glenday recalls one occasion when he and his Somalis were going along the edge of a great patch of bush, several miles across. Suddenly, one of the Somalis stopped and said, "There're dervishes in there." Glenday asked him how he knew. "I can smell their camels," answered the man. Glenday spread out his men as skirmishers and entered the cover. They found the body of dervishes fifteen miles deep in the bush. "Camels are fairly odorous, but I don't understand how a man can scent them fifteen miles away," Glenday remarked. "At all events, he was right."

Much of the fighting was done with native levies, many of them drawn from Kenya tribes who had no experience in desert fighting. As the Somali despised these weaklings from the south and the more advanced southern natives regarded the Somalis as savages, there was constant friction between them. Glenday's knowledge of the Somali temperament was often invaluable in keeping peace among the different groups.

"Toward the end of the European war, a young K.A.R. officer was sent up to help with some Kavirondo askaris," he once told me. "The Kavirondo, coming from the shores of Lake Victoria, were completely unaccustomed to desert conditions and needed a great deal of water. On one of the marches, their officer came to me and said, 'My men must have at least two cups of water a day.' 'We haven't enough water to give every man even one cup,' I told him. 'I know it, but the Somalis can do with less,' he explained. 'You must order them to turn over half of their water ration to my men.' I knew that if I ever ordered the Somalis to do such a thing, we'd have the devil of a row on our hands, but the officer was quite right; my Somalis could do with less water and his Kavirondo couldn't. After thinking the matter over, I went to my Somalis with a very long face and said, 'We are in a bad way. Those poor, weak

Kavirondo can't live on their water rations. I don't know what to do.'
The Somalis admitted it was very sad but made no suggestions.
However, during the next two days, I noticed that they were
watching the Kavirondo closely. The K.A.R. officer kept insisting
that I order the Somalis to divide their water with his men, but I
could only say, 'Wait.' I remember he became annoyed and suggested I didn't have my men under proper military discipline, which
was quite true. At the end of the two days, my Somalis came to me
and said, 'We must keep these miserable Kavirondo alive somehow.
Now we have a good idea. Being Somalis, we can endure what
these sissies can't. We'll turn over part of our water ration to them,'
I said. 'Thank you very much,' and so it was settled."

The Mullah had become so powerful that he might have been
able to defy the British if the expeditionary force had not been able
to use a new weapon against him. This weapon was the airplane.
When the Mullah first saw the planes, he cried joyfully, "These are
great birds, sent down by Allah to carry me to heaven." Donning his
finest robes, he went out to greet the planes, leaning on the arm of
one of his sheiks. The first bomb dropped by the planes killed the
sheik and burned off the Mullah's robe. But the dervishes did not
panic. They took open order, lay down and started firing at the
planes with their rifles. But their day was over. The dervishes could
hold their own against any ground force, relying on their speed and
the difficulties of transporting men and supplies across the desert.
But they could not fight against the planes.

"Naturally, the planes didn't have the whole show to themselves,"
Glenday points out. "Someone had to bolt the dervishes out of the
bush, chivy them about and run them down. The Mullah was holding out in a stone fortress called Tale with his wives and the pick
of his dervishes. Tale was really an amazing place. It was surrounded by a high wall, tremendously thick, and had nine circular
towers with a system of inner rooms and passages. Of course, the
Mullah had had four years to build it and was able to impress the
entire countryside as labor. When the planes bombed it, the Mullah
fled with his wives and a few followers. He left a garrison behind
with orders to hold Tale to the last man."

The Mullah fled for the Abyssinian border. A specially formed camel corps set out in pursuit, mounted on swift-racing camels which had been saved for this purpose. At intervals, the Mullah left behind him groups of women and children, knowing the pursuing force would not abandon them in the desert and so would be hampered in their movements. Much of the country was cut up by rocky ridges and the Mullah stationed picked bands of dervishes at the passes through these hills with orders to fight to the death. These bands died fighting, but die they did and the Camel Corps kept up the pursuit. At last, the Mullah had only a handful of followers left. Leaving these men to guard a waterhole, the Mullah went on alone. What happened to him is not known, but it is thought that he perished in the desert.*

After the collapse of the Mullah, the N.F.D. returned to a condition vaguely resembling peace. As Glenday put it, "A caravan could start out with a reasonable certainty of reaching its destination." Today, the N.F.D. is still a closed section and anyone entering the area must have a special pass. However, although there are still occasional raids, the wholesale massacres of the past are unknown. The principal problem today is a large hospital which the Russians have founded in Abyssinia with a medical staff who, the British suspect, are more interested in training Communist guerrillas than in healing the sick.

Glenday received the African General Service medal for his work along the frontier. Later, he was given posts in Zanzibar and Saudi Arabia. In Arabia, he saw some Somali slaves who had been captured by the Abyssinians during raids and sold across the Red Sea. The slaves were astonished when he spoke to them in their own language. Later, Glenday was knighted for his services and he is now Sir Vincent Glenday. He married late in life, never having had time for matrimony during his wild career along the border. His wife was the widow of one of Glenday's young officers who was poisoned by the Abyssinians. Sir Vincent is now retired and he and Lady Glenday live in a very pleasant home in the suburbs of Nairobi,

* I have also heard that the Mullah reached Abyssinia where, after trying vainly to raise a new army, he finally died.

commanding one of the most magnificent views in the colony. They
have a little boy, a cheerful, lively youngster, whom Sir Vincent
frankly adores. Sir Vincent is now engaged in writing his memoirs.
It should be one of the most interesting and important books ever
to come out of Africa.

Daniel P. Mannix

XV

Dr. L. S. B. Leakey—
White Kikuyu

When John Hunter and I began this book, we had intended to confine ourselves to the early days in Kenya. Above everything, we resolved to make no mention of the Mau Mau and Kenya's present problem because we both felt the subject has been already adequately covered by newspapers and magazines. However, as the book continued to grow, we both felt that some reference would have to be made to the emergency. The present "native problem" has its roots deep in the past—back to the time when the British first entered East Africa to break the Arab slavers and Joseph Thomson opened the northern route to Uganda. I am convinced that the British did not enter East Africa originally from imperialistic motives. First, the British government, urged on by the altruistic Anti-Slavery Society, established stations along the coast to prevent the slave trade. Then explorers went inland, seeking adventure. Then the missionaries followed. These men encouraged the natives to want a better way of life and the railroad was put through so that goods could be transported in and out of the country. The settlers arrived to help support the railroad. These settlers took land which the expanding native population later came to need and this led to the present trouble.

The so-called "native problem" is enormously complex, but to my mind the man best able to understand it is Dr. L. S. B. Leakey of Nairobi's Coryndon Museum.

In scientific circles, Dr. Leakey is undoubtedly the best-known citizen of East Africa. A world-famous anthropologist, his discovery of the Kanam jaw, possibly the oldest human remains, ranks with the finding of Java man and Pekin man. Born in Kenya, he grew up among the Kikuyu and today is an elder of the tribe. He is the recognized authority on this remarkable people and his great work on the Kikuyu, many years in the making, will be published this year. Although Dr. Leakey is basically a scientist, from a political point of view his knowledge of the Kikuyu has become of vital importance to the colony.

Since the doctor openly boasts that he is as much a Kikuyu as a European, he is regarded with considerable suspicion by the settlers. Because he has condemned the present uprising and knows so much about the inner workings of the tribe, the Mau Mau has announced that he is the Number One man on their death list. As a result, the doctor always goes armed and is followed by an askari with a rifle even when he walks from one room to another in his offices at the Nairobi Coryndon Museum.

Before meeting Dr. Leakey, I had been warned by several people that the doctor, although a nice chap, was a hopeless sentimentalist about the Kikuyu. I can only say that if Dr. Leakey is a sentimentalist, he certainly has me fooled. A slender, quick-moving, quick-talking man, he has the heaven-sent gift granted to few scientists of being able to state his views clearly and succinctly. As the only man who can claim to be a bridge between the natives and the whites, I believe that any solution of the present struggle will have to be based largely on Dr. Leakey's knowledge of the Kikuyu.

Dr. Leakey's parents were missionaries. His mother came to Kenya in 1891. Her health gave way under a combination of overwork and tropical diseases. The doctors sent her back to England with the warning never to return to Africa. However, the girl had seen how desperately the natives needed help and fretted herself to pieces in her enforced inactivity. In 1901, she married a young curate named Harry Leakey and together they returned to Kenya. They moved into a mud and wattle hut in the heart of the Kikuyu country. As the thatched roof leaked, they covered it with tarpaulins and an old tent. As there was no glass in the windows, Mr. Leakey constructed crude wooden shutters. There was no fireplace, but they kept themselves warm with a brazier full of hot coals in the middle of the floor.

In this house, Dr. Leakey was born in 1903.

He was the first white child most of the natives had ever seen and they came for miles to admire this strange phenomenon and solemnly spit on him, a gesture of deep respect. "Fortunately, my parents understood the significance of this ceremony," Dr. Leakey explained. "You see, if an enemy can get possession of your spittle, he can use it to put a death curse on you. So by spitting on someone, you put yourself completely in his power. Father and mother realized the tribute that was being paid us, but after the visitors had left, mother would give me a bath. As we had a large number of guests, I was probably the best-washed baby in Kenya history."

Young Leakey grew up among the Kikuyu children. He learned to speak Kikuyu as a child and he told me that even today he speaks it more readily than English. As he grew older he automatically went through the same training as his Kikuyu friends. When he reached puberty, Leakey, together with his friends of the same age, were made members of the tribe and assigned to a certain "age-group." These "age-groups," somewhat similar to fraternities, are groups of young men sworn to help and defend each other in all emergencies. Leakey's group is called the "Mukanda" and he is still a member.

In the midst of today's troubles, Dr. Leakey looks back nostalgically on the friendship that existed between him and his young Kikuyu playmates. He organized a football team and was elected captain. He was also a member of a Kikuyu team which played a game called "spearing the hoop," which involved throwing a spear through a rolling hoop. Here a Kikuyu boy was captain and Leakey merely one of the players. When the boys grew older, it was tribal custom for each boy to build a small hut of his own with the help of his age-group where the boy could go when he wished to be alone. Leakey's friends helped him build his hut and he helped them build theirs. "I remember I was away so much that my parents were worried because I kept missing my meals," Dr. Leakey told me, smiling.

As a boy, Leakey had several hobbies. He was a first-rate field naturalist and, with the help of an old native hunter, he learned to catch small animals and birds which he sold to the wild animal dealers who were beginning to enter the country. He was also deeply interested in archeology and made a collection of prehistoric obsidian arrow and spear heads, which were occasionally turned up by plows or washed out of banks after a heavy rain. Later, two archeologists passed through Kenya, and the boy was heartbroken when these men claimed that all prehistoric weapons were made of flint and his precious collection was probably nothing but pieces of old beer bottles. Of course, the men were wrong and young Leakey had actually stumbled on an important find.

Leakey also seriously considered becoming a missionary like his parents. He never had a great religious call, but he was fascinated by the Kikuyu and becoming a missionary seemed to be the only way he could work with them. Knowing the tribe so intimately, he felt that they were unfairly criticized by the white settlers and their customs misunderstood.

"For example, Europeans often said that the Kikuyu men were lazy because they refused to carry loads," Dr. Leakey explained. "The Kikuyu consider that carrying a load is a woman's job. But there's a reason for this. The man had to walk ahead with his spear and shield to guard against a sudden attack. He couldn't be hampered by a load. Another wide misconception concerned the 'bride price.' When a man wanted a wife, he had to give the girl's parents a certain number of sheep and goats. The settlers believed that Kikuyu women were simply chattels, to be bought and sold. Actually, the 'bride price' was considered a show of good faith. No man is going to put up several dozen valuable sheep or goats if he isn't serious. Then, too, it acted as a stabilizing influence on the girl. She regarded herself as a valuable investment. If the marriage broke up, the bride's parents had to return the marriage portion and as a result they naturally did everything in their power to see that the marriage went smoothly."

Young Leakey became convinced that the natives were mentally equal to the whites. "People forget that the natives were deprived of reading, had no schooling, and that a European child, even in a semiliterate family, has many chances for observation which were denied them," he claims. "But the natives were not stupid. They played a game called 'giuthi' which consists of moving combinations of small objects back and forth among a series of holes. Later, I tried to introduce this game into England and was told that it was so complicated and required such elaborate computation that no one but a mathematical genius could play it. Among the Kikuyu, even children play it."

When he was sixteen, Leakey was sent "home" to an English public school. At that time, it was considered a rule as immutable as the laws of the Medes and Persians that all young colonials should be given the civilizing effects of a public school. Leakey had never seen more than three or four English boys before in his life, and the discipline, restraint and bullying inherent in the English public school system produced a marked effect on him. English parents living in the colonies, who often made great sacrifices to send their children "home," seldom seemed to realize what their offspring suffered. For children, life in the colonies was free and pleasant. Exiled to English schools, the boys were shut up in ill-heated barracks full of critical and often brutal youngsters, forced to memorize such useful subjects as the conjugation of irregular Latin and Greek verbs, and made to take part in sports under the constant threat of a flogging. This system produced many magnificent men, but it also had its drawbacks.

In Kenya, Leakey had helped his father teach in the mission school, earned a small but substantial income as a wild animal trapper, built a house that was actually better than his parents' home, and as a "young warrior" had been treated with respect among the Kikuyu. The other members of the "age-group" were mostly married and raising families, and Leakey tended to identify himself with them. In an English school, he found himself a fag (boy servant) to a stupid lout who was mentally far younger than he was. If he refused to obey any order the older boy gave him, he was thrashed with a cane. Once when he fought back, he was promptly flogged by a group of the upper classmen and locked in a coal hole. Every boy in the school knew more about sports, schoolboy customs and how to get along in a large group than he did. He was not a particularly good athlete. Even football, at which he'd excelled in Kenya, was a completely different game as played in England. He could not swim, as in Africa there are too many crocodiles in the rivers to permit swimming. He was behind in his studies, never having had Greek which the other boys had been taught since they were little children. Even in other subjects, Leakey was an indifferent student. This may seem incongruous, since today Dr. Leakey is regarded as one of the most brilliant men Kenya has produced, but men who later show great ability in some special field are often poor students in school.

In school, Leakey gave up all idea of becoming a missionary. He found himself unable to experience the simple, sincere religious faith that his parents had possessed. Instead, he became more and more devoted to the study of primitive peoples. He had been very happy among the Kikuyu and he felt that in many respects they were no more superstitious and custom-bound than his schoolmates. "At least the Kikuyu customs were based on common sense," he said. "But why were English schoolboys compelled to wear a straw hat and a dark suit? Why did we have to go to bed at a certain hour, even if there was work still to be done? I remember that I once tried to play tennis in shorts and a 'bush' shirt. The shocked masters ordered me off the courts and said I was indecent. A few years later, they were wearing such dress themselves. One doesn't have to be a native to have fetishes."

Leakey decided to become an anthropologist. To do this, he would have to have a university degree. His parents didn't have enough money to send him through college, but Leakey decided that by working during the vacations he could put himself through. A more serious difficulty was that in order to fulfill the entrance requirements he must have two modern languages. He had a shaky background of French but he needed another language. The requirements merely stated that the language must be one "spoken by a significant number of people." Leakey had a brilliant idea. He applied for entrance to Cambridge, naming French and Kikuyu as his two languages.

The college authorities were stumped. Partly because they could see no way to refuse and partly, I suspect, because they admired the young man's cheek, they admitted him. However, as there was no one who could examine him in Kikuyu, the dons insisted that he present a certificate showing that he could speak the language. Leakey got the certificate from a Kikuyu chief who, as he could neither read nor write, had to dictate the certificate to a missionary.

Leakey worked his way through Cambridge by taking tutoring jobs and selling wood carving sent to him by his native friends in Kenya. In 1924, he had a stroke of great good luck. The British Museum sent an expedition to Kenya to collect fossil remains and Leakey got a minor position with the group. In addition to the fossils, the expedition also found some Stone Age artifacts and Leakey, already keen on archeology, decided to specialize in the study of ancient man, although he still kept up his great interest in the whole development of primitive society.

In the next four years, Leakey went on several other expeditions to East Africa and wrote a treatise on comparative types of bows and arrows among African tribes. Archeologists began to take an interest in the young man's work. In his research, Leakey was a great believer in practical experience rather than theory and occasionally carried his beliefs to extremes that must have astonished his professors. In order to better understand how early man used his tools, Leakey skinned antelopes and scraped their hides with Stone Age knives he found in an ancient burial mound. He also chipped out duplicates of the old arrow and spear heads himself to study the problems involved in making the weapons.

Once his enthusiasm for practical demonstrations nearly got him expelled from Cambridge. In his room at the college, Leakey had a large collection of ancient and modern native artifacts, including a big signal drum. One evening, some friends dropped in and during the course of the conversation, Leakey remarked that the drum could be heard for three miles. His friends doubted it. A bet was made and the other undergraduates took off in their cars and scattered around the outskirts of the town to listen while Leakey set up the drum by an open window. When he decided that his friends were in position, Leakey proceeded to beat a long roll on the drum. The demonstration was an unexpected success. The window opened on a close and Leakey hadn't taken into consideration how the surrounding buildings would magnify the sound. That drum had been made to signal across mountain ranges and through jungles. The noise it made in the confined area sounded like a jet bomber taking off in a tunnel. Leakey hurriedly stopped his drum practice but already windows were flying up and students and professors were pouring out of the buildings to find out what had happened. A few minutes later Leakey saw the proctors, who act as college police, going from one dormitory to another, trying to locate the source of the disturbance. Leakey moved quickly. The drum was far too big to hide, so he put it in the middle of the floor, covered it with a tablecloth, and laid out his tea set on top of it. When the proctors arrived, Leakey was drinking tea. "Someone's been making a terrible row around here," he indignantly told the proctors. "I certainly hope you can find the idiot." The proctors assured him that they'd do their best and continued their search in other quarters.

According to requirements, Leakey was supposed to be continuing his study of the Kikuyu language while at Cambridge. When the time came for him to graduate, he had to be examined in the subject. The college authorities wrote to the School of Oriental Languages to discover if there was an expert in Kikuyu available to give the examination. The school replied that they did know of a man who was a recognized authority on the Kikuyu and their language. Satisfied, the college sent Leakey to be examined by this expert. When Leakey arrived at the school, he found that he was the man who had been listed as the expert. Needless to say, Leakey passed the examination with flying colors.

After graduation, Leakey received a grant to conduct archeological researches in Kenya. Working on a small budget and often under extremely primitive conditions (at one time, Leakey and his staff lived in a disused pigpen on a settler's farm) Leakey made a number of important finds. The sites of two of his best-known discoveries, at Olorgesailie and Kariandusi, are now under the supervision of the Royal National Parks of Kenya. Archeologists consider these spots the finest known examples of the living sites of hand-ax man.

In 1932, Dr. Leakey discovered the now world-famous Kanam jaw. Several years of careful archeological detective work preceded this find. Using his knowledge of the habits of modern native tribes as a guide, Dr. Leakey reasoned that primitive man probably constructed his villages near a lake, near good grazing land, and in an area that was exposed to neither the heat of the lowlands nor the extreme cold of the mountain districts. In the course of a million years, both the climate and the nature of the country have changed considerably so the problem was to find from geological data where such sites had been. After many months of painstaking research, the most likely spots were finally selected. One of them was Kanam. On March 29, 1932, one of Leakey's native assistants turned up a jaw with two teeth still in place. This was *"Homo Kanamensis,"* one of our earliest ancestors. The find established Dr. Leakey as an internationally known archeologist.

Dr. Leakey continued to keep in close touch with his old friends among the Kikuyu, and when any problem arose concerning the tribe, he was often called in as consultant. One afternoon while the doctor was on an archeological "dig," he received an emergency call from the governor of Kenya. Dr. Leakey left at once and arrived in Nairobi late that evening, still wearing his mud-stained field clothes. In the governor's home, he found the governor, the chief native commissioner, and the provincial commissioner of the Kikuyu awaiting him.

For several years, there had been growing unrest among several of the native tribes, particularly among the Kikuyu. The trouble was mainly based on a desire for more land, although many other factors—political, economic and social—were also involved. As the most rapidly increasing tribe and also as the most politically conscious, the Kikyuyus spearheaded the unrest.

Since the time of John Boyes, the Kikuyu had more than tripled in numbers. The area assigned to them as a reserve which had seemed more than ample at the time was now so crowded that in some sections there were five hundred people to the square mile. The Kikuyus claimed that vast sections of land had been stolen from them by the early settlers and were demanding that it be returned. Secret societies were formed under leaders whose cry was: "Before the whites came, everything was fine. They have taken our land. Throw them out, seize their farms, and let us return to the ways of our fathers."

"We want to find out if the Kikuyu have a legitimate grievance," the governor told the group around the table. "Was land taken from them unfairly and if so, how much? Other commissions have investigated the matter, but the consensus of their reports has been that the Kikuyu accounts are so confused and so obviously untruthful that they have been unable to discover the facts. What is that truth? With unrest steadily growing in the colony, we must find out as quickly as possible. I would like to appoint a commission, composed of you gentlemen, to investigate the situation."

The three men accepted the assignment. This was the beginning of an investigation that lasted for months and took the investigators to all parts of the vast Kikuyu reserve.

There was no doubt that the Kikuyu were very cheerful and completely unscrupulous liars. The commission found that forty thousand Kikuyus solemnly claimed to have owned one white settler's farm. Elders of the tribe swore that their people had been living in areas which the early explorers like Joseph Thomson described as wastelands, roamed over by great herds of game. Finally, while talking to one old chief, Leakey burst out laughing.

"Why do you tell such lies?" he asked.

The chief assumed an expression of injured innocence. Then he smiled also. "We have a saying, 'Always lie to a stranger. Later, if you find he can be trusted, you can tell him the truth. And besides, you never know. Maybe he'll believe you.'"

Leakey explains this by saying, "The Masai settled any arguments with spear and knife. The Kikuyu have always depended on their wits. According to them, there is nothing dishonorable in trying to outwit your opponent. This is not a particularly noble attitude but today the Masai are a dying people and the Kikuyu are the most influential tribe in Kenya."

Leakey frankly admits that often a Kikuyu will lie under conditions which both puzzle and infuriate a white man. He gives this example: "Suppose you're driving along a road and give a Kikuyu a lift. You ask him where he's going. To you, this seems a perfectly natural question, but the Kikuyu has been reared to regard any stranger with suspicion. He reasons, 'Why is this man asking me that? Perhaps he wants to find out where I'm going for some evil purpose of his own.' He will probably lie. That shouldn't disturb you. You expect him to lie. You simply say, 'Ah, I happen to be going to so-and-so. What a pity you aren't headed in the same direction.' Then he will say, 'Oh I was lying to you before. Let me off at such-and-such a place.' The fact that he lied doesn't bother him in the slightest and shouldn't bother you."

The commission made a number of interesting discoveries. Probably the most important one was that although a number of Kikuyu had sold land to settlers, the Kikuyu had considered that they were merely renting the land since, according to their tribal law, no one could sell land without the consent of the clan. This had been an honest misunderstanding on both sides, but now the settlers had fenced the land, built homes on it, and spent large sums clearing the fields, putting in irrigation ditches and so on. A second and a third generation was growing up on these farms and trying to dispossess the farmers would be utterly impractical—roughly equivalent to telling an American farmer that his land belonged to the Indians.

A previous commission had already given the Kikuyu 245,120 acres to recompense them for such errors. This was considered to be far more land than the Kikuyu had any historic claim to. However, with the tribe increasing so rapidly, the commission of which Dr. Leakey was a member felt that still more land should be given the Kikuyu. The question was, where was it to come from?

The population of Kenya has grown so swiftly that no new areas suitable for native farming are readily available. There are large forest reserves on the mountain slopes but these forests are absolutely vital for holding back the torrential rains which can wash away the top soil over a vast area within a few days. Already so many of these forests have been cut down that erosion is a major problem. There are hundreds of miles of bush country, but this is semidesert. Some of it, by great expense, can be reclaimed by digging boreholes and building dams to catch the flash floods during the rainy seasons, but neither the colonists nor Great Britain has the money to finance such a gigantic undertaking. Also, already so many boreholes have been sunk that the water table is dropping at an alarming rate and much of the underground water has been found to be full of chemicals that can only be removed by extremely costly filtering plants.

In spite of these problems, which frankly seem to be almost insurmountable, the commission still believed that some attempt must be made to give the Kikuyu more land, even though the cost would be tremendous.

However, after talking to the various Kikuyu clans with Dr. Leakey acting as interpreter, the commission felt that the land question was only one of a series of problems confronting the natives. "We came to the conclusion that the whole native tribal structure had disintegrated," Dr. Leakey explained. "The natives were not accepted by the whites and they were no longer members of a tribe in the old sense of the term. They had become irresponsible drifters."

Dr. Leakey gave a number of examples. One of the important issues was religion. Under the old tribal system, the witch doctor was a very important man. The witch doctor often misused his powers— as in the case of the hereditary clan of witch doctors among the Kisii. But he was also the source of law and order in the tribe. The natives had no police force. They didn't need one. If a crime was committed, the witch doctor was called in to find the culprit. The natives believed implicitly that the witch doctor had at his command spirits who could hunt down a malefactor no matter where he was. As the offender also believed this, crime was very rare. No one wanted to run the risk of having evil spirits put on his trail.

By destroying the authority of the witch doctors, the European left the natives without any restraining force. In fact, today the witch doctors are being subsidized by the government in hopes that their

influence will counteract the power of the Mau Mau. It was supposed that Christianity would take the place of the old tribal religion
and act as a purifying influence. Many of the natives have become
sincere Christians but even more found the teachings of the missionaries difficult to understand. Dr. Leakey recorded a conversation
between some Kikuyu and a missionary.

The Kikuyu: "You say a man should have only one wife. Why?
Didn't Abraham and David have many wives and didn't God love
them?"

The Missionary: "That was a long time ago. Christ changed all
that."

The Kikuyu: "But God and Christ are one. Did God then change
his mind?"

The Missionary: "Conditions were different in the time of Abraham
and David. There are many laws in the Old Testament that we no
longer observe."

The Kikuyu: "Aren't the Ten Commandments in the Old Testament?"

The Missionary: "Yes, we have preserved some of the laws."

The Kikuyu: "But by what authority did you select the ones you
intended to observe?"

No other religious question aroused so much ill-feeling as the
question of circumcision. Among the Kikuyu, both young men and
girls were circumcised. Until this ceremony was performed, the
youngsters could not become members of the tribe. The girls were
circumcised by an old woman who cut away the lips of the labia to
expose the clitoris. When correctly performed, this operation was
harmless but occasionally infection would set in or scar tissue form
that prevented the girl from performing her natural functions. So
many of these unfortunate children came to mission hospitals that
the missionaries were loud in their opposition to the practice. But the
Kikuyu considered that an uncircumcised girl was an outcast and
insisted on the ceremony. Antagonism over this issue reached such a
point that a woman missionary was seized by a group of Kikuyu men
and circumcised so savagely that she later died. Young native girls
who refused to submit to the operation were not infrequently beaten

and even tortured by their parents. Dr. Leakey recalls one case of some young girls being hung up by their feet over a fire. The girls later fled to the mission where several attempts were made by the tribe to kidnap them.

In spite of such conflicts, Dr. Leakey believes that the Kikuyu trusted the missionaries as they did no other foreigners. "The Kikuyu knew that the missionaries were there to help them, not to make money," he told me. "And the missionaries were the only group in Kenya of which that was true."

There were many other confusing issues. The demands of the settlers for labor caused thousands of young Kikuyu men to leave their homes and take jobs on farms or in Nairobi. These men, cut off from their traditional tribal life and paid only the low wages that most settlers could afford, became a serious menace. A large number of them turned to crime. A man like Major Foran, dispensing justice on the spot, could in a rough and ready way, handle them. But when more orthodox courtroom methods were introduced, the highly intelligent Kikuyu discovered what they considered to be a delightful new game.

"A native regards a courtroom trial quite differently than we do," Dr. Leakey explained. "He often considers it simply a battle of wits. I remember once listening to a group of elders in a native village trying cases. The cases concerned theft, murder, adultery, and so on—all of great importance—and the elders listened carefully to the evidence before giving their verdict. Then one man stood up and quite casually announced that he was bringing charges against a neighbor's rooster for raping one of his hens. Now this charge was quite as absurd to a native as it would be to us, but the elders, without changing their expressions, listened to all the evidence and finally gravely sentenced the rooster to lose two tail feathers. Natives enjoy this kind of mental gymnastics and think that it's good for young men to learn how to speak in public and how to present their ideas, regardless of how ridiculous the case may be. In a European courtroom, they use the same techniques. The results are often entertaining, but seldom helpful."

Before the coming of the whites, the Kikuyus had developed a system of tribal culture that worked fairly well. Now the old customs were growing increasingly more difficult to follow. Originally, the Kikuyu had a remarkably effective manner of rotating their crops and preserving the soil. The method is too complicated to describe in detail, but it depended on planting a number of different crops together, the growing period of each crop being so timed that one crop would protect another. In an attempt to help the natives, agricultural experts from England explained that by separating the crops in different fields, the yield could be greatly increased. The natives tried it. The yield was indeed increased but the heavy tropical rains, which the English experts knew nothing about, quickly washed away the top soil. Then the experts realized their mistake and tried to induce the natives to return to their old system. The natives refused. They liked the high yield and also they had begun to abandon their traditional crops in favor of new ones that were commercially more profitable but were also ruinous to the soil. When the soil was exhausted, the natives would simply burn out a section of forest and start over again. As a result, the reserve was gradually being destroyed.

Attempts were made to teach the natives farming methods that would preserve the soil. These attempts were generally met with sullen and, then later, open defiance. The natives argued, "Your experts were wrong once before. Why not again?" They also felt that these methods would involve a tremendous amount of extra work and in the long run do no particular good as the reserve was already so overcrowded that no amount of terracing and contour-plowing could ever make the land support its greatly increased population.

An almost equally serious problem was the enormous increase in the native herds which were overgrazing the reserve and gradually turning it into a dust bowl. As Lord Delamere had learned, livestock in Kenya had been subject to a fantastic number of diseases. When the whites brought these diseases under control, the natives' livestock multiplied like rabbits. The natives regarded livestock as currency and refused to kill off their surplus beasts, much as a white man would refuse to solve the problem of inflation by burning half of his dollar bills.

The commission came to the conclusion that the Kikuyu could not continue as a completely agricultural community. There was simply not enough suitable land to make it possible. "Even if all Europeans left Kenya and their farms were turned over to the natives, that would provide a solution for only a short time," Dr. Leakey argued. "The Europeans own only about one-fifth of the land in Kenya and much of that is not suitable for the Kikuyu type of farming. At the rate the natives are increasing, the European farms would be little more than a drop in a bucket—or say a glass of water in a bucket."

The commission felt that some attempt to find jobs for the Kikuyu —as artisans, tradesmen or in factories—must be made. Unfortunately, the enormous influx of East Indians into the colony, many of whom are highly skilled artisans and excellent tradesmen, makes it difficult for the Kikuyu to compete in these fields. There are very few factories in Kenya and so far the lack of sources of natural power and the cost of exporting machine-made goods to the coast and then hundreds of miles by ship have discouraged industry. However, in spite of these drawbacks, the commission believed that some type of employment for the natives must be found.

The astronomical rate of native increase is probably the most serious matter of all. Dr. Leakey points out that in the old days, the Kikuyu had a simple but effective method of limiting their families. "A Kikuyu woman did not have relations with her husband for two and a half years after the birth of a child," he told me. "This was because she was nursing the child and, according to tribal law, could not become pregnant again until the child was weaned. Now, no such custom is observed."

The commission believed that the Kikuyu should be encouraged to adopt some method of limiting their families. The use of contraceptives is condemned by powerful religious groups and the Kikuyu themselves love children and like having a big family. It is also true that as the "bride price" is now paid in money, Kikuyu parents regard girl children as a sort of annuity for their old age. However, if the native population continues to increase at its present rate, it is difficult to see how the country can be made to support them.

When the commission's report was submitted, the government

did what it could to act on the various suggestions. Given time and a sufficient amount of capital, something might have been done. However, neither time nor money was available. In 1948, that terrible native organization known as the Mau Mau made its appearance.

It is thought that the Mau Mau originated in the mind of a highly intelligent, European-educated Kikuyu named Jomo Kenyatta whose native name means "The Burning Spear." Kenyatta was a mission boy who showed such great talent that he was sent to England to complete his education. In England, Kenyatta wrote a book about his people, glorifying their past history and pointing out how superior their ancient life was to their present degenerate state. He became a friend of Paul Robeson, the American singer who has made no secret of his left-wing affiliations. Later, Kenyatta spent two years in Moscow. He returned to Kenya and immediately plunged into politics.

Within the next few years, Kenyatta became the unquestioned champion of the Kikuyus against the whites. The tribe literally worshiped him. He created his own school system with money contributed by the Kikuyu, and in these schools, Kikuyu children were taught to sing Christian hymns with the name "Jomo" substituted for that for "God." He was a man of tremendous personal magnetism. An Englishwoman who attended one of his meetings told me, "When Kenyatta held out his hands to the crowd and ordered, 'Bow down!' I felt an almost irresistible desire to obey."

Dr. Leakey was not impressed by Kenyatta. "His book on the Kikuyu is a very inferior work," he remarked. "Actually, Kenyatta knew comparatively little about the history, religion and customs of the Kikuyu. He was a mission boy who spent most of his time abroad. In his book, he frequently makes misstatements in order to exaggerate Kikuyu cultural achievements and often when describing ceremonials he invents details that never existed."

To a large extent, Mau Mau followed the ancient format of native secret societies. Magic has always played a large part in the life of African tribes. Secret societies practicing weird rites are common. These societies, however, combine magic with some more practical motive. If a group of young natives decided to form a gang to rob and murder travelers, they call themselves "Lion Men," dress in the skins of lions, and kill their victims according to certain rites. When Kenyatta began his operations, there was already a political-magical-robbery-*cum*-murder secret society among the Kikuyu called "The Forty." The name came from the fact that it had been formed in 1940. There is evidence that Kenyatta worked with the leaders of this group, hoping to use them for his own ends. Out of this combination arose Mau Mau.

Quite possibly, the tough, gangster-like leaders of The Forty began to take matters into their own hands and Kenyatta found himself virtually a figurehead. This new group set out to recruit members wholesale and gain a complete ascendancy over the entire Kikuyu tribe. Organizers were sent out to various native villages. Anyone joining the Mau Mau paid an initiation fee of sixty-two shillings and fifty cents—about nine dollars or six weeks' wages for a native. The organizer kept half this sum and sent the rest back to headquarters. Anyone initiated could also become an oath-taker and start getting new members on his own.

Apparently the Mau Mau intended, once they had complete control of the Kikuyu people, to stage a sudden uprising, murder all the whites in the colony, and present the British government with a *fait accompli*. As virtually all the houseboys and farmhands on the white estates were Kikuyus, and as the Kikuyu outnumbered the white colonists fifty to one, this plan seemed perfectly feasible. During his seventeen years in England, Kenyatta had met a number of liberal members of Parliament who expressed great sympathy with the Kikuyus' plight and he probably reasoned that these men would not allow the government to send troops to put down a successful insurrection but would let Kenya go.

The great majority of the Kikuyu, although they supported Kenyatta in principle, were not willing to take part in a wholesale massacre of the British and a general uprising. The Mau Mau realized that this majority would have to be forced into the society by intimidation. Naturally, anyone forced into the Mau Mau against his will would go at once to the British authorities. To prevent this, the Mau Mau invented a very terrible and elaborate oath which members of the tribe were forced to take. Once having taken this oath, even against his will, a native was afraid to violate it. If he did violate it, the Mau Mau hatchetmen saw to it that both he and his family were murdered.

The details of the oath-taking ceremony are unprintable. I can only say that they combined sodomy, sadism, cannibalism and sexual relations with animals. Anyone going through this performance felt that he was permanently cut off from all hope of redemption. He had not only violated all Christian ethics but also all his tribal beliefs. He had nothing left to him but the support of the society.

The plot would have succeeded if it had not been for two factors. Many of the Kikuyu were sincere Christians. They no longer believed in the evil spirits that were supposed to punish a violator of the enforced oath and they were willing to die rather than come under the dominance of the Mau Mau, which forbade the practice of Christianity as a foreign religion. There were also elderly members of the tribe who were as deeply shocked by the nature of the oath as were the Kikuyu Christians. Both these groups betrayed the Mau Mau to the British authorities.

At first, the authorities were inclined to consider the Mau Mau as merely another of the freak, native secret societies that were always springing up. However, it rapidly assumed a more serious aspect. White settlers were murdered. Armed bands of Mau Mau began to attack isolated police posts. Then they turned on native villages whose inhabitants had refused to take the oath. In the little community of Lari, some forty miles north of Nairobi, the Mau Mau raiders killed some two hundred men, women and children. Some of the children were skinned alive and then thrown in the flames of their burning homes. One of the survivors reported seeing a Mau Mau cut off a woman's breasts and then drink her blood. The Mau Mau openly adopted a policy of terrorism. A few weeks later, I am told, they killed a white settler, disemboweled his pregnant wife and then forced her to eat bits of her unborn child.

Many of the hard, old-time settlers had a simple solution for the problem. "Just turn the Masai, Nandi and the Somali loose," they

suggested. "They'll fix the Kikuyu." The British government refused
to do this and actually it is very doubtful whether it would have
done any good. The Kikuyu were armed, many of them with remarkably effective homemade guns the clever native smiths had made
themselves in forges hidden deep in the mountains. Unless the other
tribes were also armed, they wouldn't stand much chance against the
Kikuyu and the last thing the government wanted to do was to arm
these wild, irresponsible tribesmen.

Troops were brought in from England and a campaign started
against the terrorists. Kenyatta was arrested, and accused of manag-
ing an unlawful society. To defend him, a noted British lawyer
named D. N. Pritt volunteered his services and flew to Nairobi. Mr.
Pritt is known for his liberal views and had obtained the release of
Gerhardt Eisler when Eisler jumped ship in England. Dr. Leakey
was court interpreter during the Kenyatta trial.

Dr. Leakey dislikes discussing the trial, but I talked to a young
army officer who was present. He told me, "Pritt was obviously fighting for time and doing everything he could to delay proceedings.
Whenever Leakey translated some witness's statement, Pritt would
interrupt and claim the translation was incorrect. Finally, on some
minor point, Pritt said, 'Dr. Leakey, are you sure that's precisely
what the witness said?' Leakey replied, 'There is no exact word in
English that corresponds to the Kikuyu term he used, but the
expression implies . . .' Here Pritt flung his papers on the desk and
shouted, 'How does the court expect me to conduct this case when
the court interpreter admits he can't translate the witness's state-
ments? I demand that he resign.'

"As there are very few men in the colony who can speak fluent
Kikuyu, finding another interpreter would take weeks, as Pritt knew.
However, something happened which he didn't expect. Leakey
promptly resigned and then asked to be sworn as a witness for the
Crown. Leakey then gave a careful, destructive analysis of Mau
Mau, showing that although it claimed to be a tribal movement it
was in direct violation of all tribal customs and traditions, and
quoted a number of prominent Kikuyu elders who violently condemned it. His testimony had a tremendous effect."

As a result, Dr. Leakey was publicly condemned by the Mau Mau and put at the head of their death list.

Throughout the trial, Kenyatta remained calm and fenced expertly with the prosecutor, Mr. Somerhough. Only once did he break down. Suddenly, during the cross examination, Kenyatta broke out, "The wages given our people are so low that we live in serfdom. Once a man could feel like a man. That was changed and we were subjected to the color bar and all kinds of humiliations. When you've taken somebody's whole ancestral culture and left him nothing in exchange . . ." He began to weep.

"Please go on," said Mr. Somerhough bitterly. "I assure you that we're hanging on your words."

Kenyatta recovered himself. "I hope you continue to hang and do not fall off," he said fiercely. "If you had to change places with an African and live like him for a week—or even two days—you'd know what it is like."

Kenyatta was convicted and given seven years' hard labor. The British have now some twenty thousand troops in Kenya trying to track down the terrorist groups hiding out in the Abardare Mountains. Lincoln bombers and rocket-firing planes have been brought in. I find it hard to believe that the Mau Mau can hold out indefinitely against such odds but it is even harder to believe that after the uprising has been put down, it will not appear again under some new name.

Dr. Leakey, as director of Nairobi's Coryndon Museum, is still continuing his archeological researches. Dr. Leakey has no formula which he thinks is guaranteed to bring peace to Kenya. "Simply trying to restore the Kikuyu to their original pattern of tribal life is impractical," he told me. "Conditions have changed so much that even if it were possible, the Kikuyu themselves would refuse to do it, in spite of the Mau Mau claims."

As a general program, Dr. Leakey believes that every possible attempt should be made to find the Kikuyu more land, industries should be encouraged that would give the young native men and women employment at reasonable wages, and some method of "planned parenthood" should be made available to the tribe.

Of course, it is impossible for an American writer who has spent a total of only ten months in Kenya to make any sort of practical or moral judgment of the people, white or dark, and their present problems. Both John Hunter and I have been primarily interested, not in social or political questions, but rather in a frontier narrative made out of the lives and adventures of many and various people. Some were cruel, some prideful; probably a number of these pioneers were unwise, as all humans are. Many were heroes in the best sense of the word. But they all shared in a quality of courage which is the essential ingredient—at any frontier, on any continent, and at any time.

Bibliography

Baker, Sir Samuel, *Ismailia*
Barrie, James M., *An Edinburgh Eleven*
Boyes, John, *Company of Adventurers*
——, *John Boyes, King of the Wa-Kikuyu*
Brode, Heinrich, *Tippoo Tib*
Burton, Richard F., *Zanzibar*
Colville, Colonel Sir Henry, *Land of the Nile Spring*
Cook, Dr. Sir Albert, *Uganda Memories*
Coupland, Sir Reginald, *East Africa and Its Invaders*
——, *The Exploitation of East Africa*
Dutton, E. A. T., *Lillibullero*
Felkin, J., *Uganda*
Fisher, Ruth, *Twilight Tales of the Black Baganda*
——, *On the Borders of Pigmy-Land*
Foran, Major W. Robert, *A Cookoo in Kenya*
Grogan, Colonel E. S., *From the Cape to Cairo*
Harford-Battersly, C. F., *Pilkington of Uganda*
Hill, M. F., *Permanent Way*
Hinde, S. L., *The Fall of the Congo Arabs*
Huxley, Elspeth, *White Man's Country*
Jackson, Sir Frederick, *Early Days in East Africa*
Jardine, Douglas, *Mad Mullah of Somaliland*
Leakey, L. S. B., *Adam's Ancestors*
——, *Kenya Contrasts and Problems*
——, *White African*
——, *Mau Mau and the Kikuyu*
Livingstone, David, *Travels and Researches*
——, *Letters*
Lugard, Captain F. D., *Rise of Our East Africa Empire*
Moore, E. D., *Ivory, the Scourge of Africa*

307

Portal, Sir Gerald H., *Mission to Uganda*
Preston, R. O., *Early Days in East Africa*
——, *Genesis of a Colony*
——, *Construction of the Uganda Railroad*
Rayne, Major H., *The Ivory Raiders*
Stanley, H. M., *Through the Dark Continent*
——, *Through Darkest Africa*
Swann, Alfred J., *Fighting the Slave-Hunters in Central Africa*
Thomson, Joseph, *Through Masailand*
Thomson, Reverend J. B., *Joseph Thomson*
Tucker, Bishop, *Eighteen Years in Uganda*

Additional information about the following may be found from these sources: Kabarega—see references in works by Major J. R. Macdonald, Casati, Emin and R. P. Ashe. Dr. Sir Albert Cook—see records at Kampala Hospital and Church Mission Society, London. Joseph Thomson—see records and letters in the Macmillan Library at Nairobi and the Peace Memorial Museum, Zanzibar.